My Brother's Keeper

WHAT THE SOCIAL SCIENCES DO (AND DON'T)
TELL US ABOUT MASCULINITY

MARY STEWART VAN LEEUWEN

author of *Gender & Grace*

InterVarsity Press

Downers Grove, Illinois

InterVarsity Press
P.O. Box 1400, Downers Grove, IL 60515-1426
World Wide Web: www.ivpress.com
E-mail: mail@ivpress.com

InterVarsity Press® is the book-publishing division of InterVarsity Christian Fellowship/USA®, a student movement active on campus at hundreds of universities, colleges and schools of nursing in the United States of America, and a member movement of the International Fellowship of Evangelical Students. For information about local and regional activities, write Public Relations Dept., InterVarsity Christian Fellowship/USA, 6400 Schroeder Rd., P.O. Box 7895, Madison, WI 53707-7895, or visit the IVCF website at <www.ivcf.org>.

Scripture is taken from the New Revised Standard Version of the Bible, *copyright 1989 by the Division of Christian Education of the National Council of the Churches of Christ in the USA. Used by permission.*

Cover photograph: Galleria dell' Academia, Florence, Italy/Bridgeman Art Library

ISBN 0-8308-2690-4

Printed in the United States of America ∞

Library of Congress Cataloging-in-Publication Data
Van Leeuwen, Mary Stewart, 1943-
  My brother's keeper: what the social sciences do (and don't)
tell us about masculinity / Mary Stewart Van Leeuwen.
    p. cm.
  Includes bibliographical references.
  ISBN 0-8308-2690-4 (pbk.: alk. paper)
    1. Masculinity—Religious aspects—Christianity. 2. Men (Chris-
tian theology) 3. Religion and the social sciences. I. Title.
  BT703.5.V36 2002
  261.8'3431—dc21

                                                                    2002009248

P	17	16	15	14	13	12	11	10	9	8	7	6	5	4	3	2	1
Y	15	14	13	12	11	10	09	08	07	06	05	04	03	02			

To my students
past, present and future

Contents

Introduction

T HE IDEA FOR THIS BOOK TOOK ROOT IN THE LATE 1990S, almost a decade after InterVarsity Press had published my earlier volume *Gender and Grace*. At that time Rodney Clapp, who had done much of the editing for *Gender and Grace,* asked if I was willing to have that book go into a second, updated edition. After thinking about this possibility for a while, I made an alternative suggestion. *Gender and Grace* addressed a critical conversation, rooted in my identity as a Christian social psychologist, between the ethical claims about gender emerging from late-twentieth-century feminism and those of the evangelical and Reformed traditions. In it I made the case, as a social scientist and lay theologian, for mutuality rather than hierarchy in gender relations and for flexibility rather than rigidity in gender roles.

Much of the research included in that book came from the rapidly expanding interdisciplinary literature that has come to be known as women's studies. But the last two decades of the twentieth century also saw the emergence of a smaller yet equally important literature in men's studies. I proposed to delve into this literature in order to write a companion volume to *Gender and Grace*. My idea was to revisit that book's themes of "love, work and parenting in a changing world," but this time in the context of some significant work on men and masculinity being done by historical and practical theologians, social historians, cultural anthropologists, biologists, psychologists and other social scientists. In 1999 InterVarsity Press, which had done an admirable job of producing and marketing *Gender and Grace*—as well as facilitating its translation into three other languages—endorsed this proposal.

In one sense, any attempt to separate men's from women's studies is an artificial exercise, because gender is to a large extent a relational phenomenon. In every time and place, men construct and express masculinity in response to women's construction and expression of femininity (and vice versa) in the context of cultural values that are often subject to change. Nevertheless, certain enduring asymmetries in men's and women's experience make it worthwhile— and perhaps for a woman psychologist especially worthwhile—to examine processes such as socialization, work, religious participation and parenting with particular reference to the lives of boys and men. Males differ from females more than just biologically. In most cultures their first caretaker is not a same-sex adult whom they can unreflectively emulate but a woman from whom they must at some point begin to differentiate themselves. In Western society it is easier for women than for men to be pious, dependent and self-disclosing without violating the culture's longstanding ideals about gender stereotypes. Despite three decades of feminist influence, it is still more difficult for men than women to separate their sense of gender identity from the societal mandate to be economically successful, to be sexually aggressive, to acquire power over women and to compete constantly with other men.

How are we to judge such gender-associated asymmetries? I believe that a well-crafted Christian worldview can and should take account of the implications of creation, sin and redemption for gender relations, as for everything else. Moreover, such a worldview offers men, no less than women, their best hope for finding a "third way" of living that can transcend the opposing rigidities of gender stereotyping and unreflective androgyny, respecting yet also challenging the cultural matrix in which they find themselves. It is the goal of this book to help readers to understand some of the cultural, historical, developmental and biological forces within which men as well as women are called to make responsible and just decisions about gender relations as God's stewards and regents on earth.

I have already noted that this book differs from *Gender and Grace* in taking the examination of masculinity as its main angle of vision. But there is a second difference as well. Whereas *Gender and Grace* argued that the trajectory of the biblical drama is toward mutuality rather than hierarchy in gender relations, this book assumes that conclusion and goes on to show how various configurations of masculinity—past and present, intra- and crosscultural—can either support or inhibit such mutuality. Thus it is likely to be of most interest to readers who are in agreement with an egalitarian ethic to begin with. However, those whose reading of Scripture leads them to embrace some form of male headship in marriage and/or church and society almost always frame this view in terms of an ideal of servant leadership and self-giving that gets scant support in Western culture when embraced by people of either sex. To the extent that this book supports such generic Christian virtues and helps readers of both sexes understand the challenges men face in practicing them, I trust that it will be helpful to readers on both sides of the gender-roles debate.

Many people helped to bring this book to fruition. I am grateful to Eastern University and to the Louisville Institute's Christian Faith and Life Sabbatical Program for funding that enabled me to complete much of the manuscript. During the

1990s the members of the Religion, Culture and Family Project, directed by theologian Don Browning at the University of Chicago, provided me with tremendous collegiality and interdisciplinary conversation on many matters related to gender. I also wish to thank the people on the "Brothers" e-mail list (which included a lot of sisters as well) who read chapters as they were written, and several of whom regularly gave me helpful feedback and criticism. The latter included my colleagues Phillip Cary, David Copelin, Nelson Hayashida, Charles Lippy, Diane Marshall, Eloise Meneses and Betsy Morgan, all of whom scrutinized my writing from disciplinary or professional viewpoints other than my own.

Once these colleagues' suggestions had been incorporated, the students in my Philosophy of Gender class at Eastern University reviewed the entire manuscript just before its publication. Kay Busillo, Nancy Hazle, Vangie Jaggard, Faith Martin and Dudley Morrison made sure that my style remained accessible to the nonacademic readership, as did various lecture and workshop audiences that listened to chapters in progress in places as disparate as the United Kingdom, the Canadian prairies, and the Eastern and Midwestern United States. Jonathan Beasley, reader services librarian at Eastern University, was a constant help in tracking down elusive references and sources.

My sons Dirk and Neil Van Leeuwen, who appeared intermittently in *Gender and Grace* as two preadolescent scamps with rather definite views on gender, gave me feedback on some chapters of this volume from their more nuanced perspectives as recent university graduates. Last but certainly not least, their father and my husband, Raymond Van Leeuwen, was a constant dialogue partner and frequent biblical and theological resource as I wrote. I have often commented—only half in jest—that I married an Old Testament scholar because it saved me so many trips to the library. However true that may be, I value him much more for the quarter of a century of marriage, parenting, mutual aid and admonition that we have shared. Much of what I endorse in *My Brother's Keeper* has been not only dug out of libraries and research archives but field-tested in our life together.

The book is richer and better because of the gracious help I have received from all of these people. Its remaining limitations are, of course, my own responsibility, and they are many. I have written this volume as a woman trying to understand men, as an educated Westerner trying to do justice to cultures and subcultures other than my own, and as an academic psychologist trying by turns to be an amateur theologian, historian, biologist and therapist. Consequently, in the course of my writing I have frequently felt like a fool rushing in where angels fear to tread. Nevertheless, it is my hope that the result will prove helpful in the ongoing challenge of gender reconciliation, which remains a vital part of Christians' redemptive calling before God.

BACKGROUND

ISSUES

Masculinity Under Siege

M Y YOUNGER SON, A UNIVERSITY SENIOR, recently celebrated his twenty-first birthday just as I was coming home from a trip to the province of Saskatchewan, Canada. To mark the occasion I bought him a humorous card showing an Archie Bunker-type character draped across an inner tube, floating on an otherwise empty expanse of water. "SAVE THE MALES," the outside of the card proclaimed—and inside, along with the birthday greeting, "because every so often one like you comes along."

A card like this speaks volumes about the ambiguous state of gender relations at the dawn of the third millennium. And indirectly, so did the gift accompanying it. My hosts in the city of Regina, Saskatchewan, had taken me to visit the national training barracks and museum of the Royal Canadian Mounted Police. There, as I had hoped, I was able to choose from an array of shirts, hats and jackets embroidered with the R.C.M.P. crest. I apparently chose well, because my Canadian-born son was pleased with his crested T-shirt the same color as the Mounties' famous scarlet jackets. Yet demographically he is in the category of persons now least likely to become R.C.M.P. trainees. The museum contained, among other things, a collection of posters from old movies about Mounties, all featuring Anglo-Saxon males with names like "Sergeant Preston of the Yukon" and "King of the Royal Mounted." But today, I was told, the incoming classes of cadets are by design made up almost entirely of female, aboriginal and Francophone Canadians. It seems that masculinity—or its white Anglo-Saxon version at any rate—is not what it was when my brother and I absorbed those Mountie tales as children back in the 1950s. Is this really the case, and if so, does it represent good news, bad news or some of both?

Just Who Needs
Rescuing?

My son's birthday card was obviously designed for women buyers with feminist sensibilities, or at least for those who see some humor in the perennial battle between the sexes. After more than three decades of second-wave feminism, some might argue that a card like this one conveys good news, pointing toward the possibility of a cease-fire between men and women, if not quite a permanent peace.

Some men, its message implies, are very much worth rescuing, either because they are just naturally good guys or because they have happily learned better ways to behave than most of their peers. And if some are worth relating to, perhaps there's hope for the rest. That's quite a different message from Gloria Steinem's famous statement in the 1970s to the effect that "a woman without a man is like a fish without a bicycle."

Others might draw quite the opposite conclusion: that individual men may indeed merit praise and assistance but that men as a group are still too privileged and powerful in comparison to women for anyone to start feeling sorry for them. Susan Faludi, in her 1991 book *Backlash,* claimed that women's progress in the 1980s was largely a case of three steps forward, two steps back: whenever they advanced toward the elusive goal of social and economic equality, ways were found to halt or even reverse those gains.[1] And it is not just women who make such assertions. "Few men," wrote sociologist Allan Johnson several years after Faludi, "realize how much they deaden themselves in order to support (if only by their silence) a system that privileges them at women's expense, that values maleness by devaluing femaleness, that makes women invisible in order to make men appear larger than life."[2]

Backlash was criticized for its misuse of statistics and underrepresentation of American women's progress since the 1960s, but neither Faludi's nor Johnson's concerns are entirely dated. In the late 1990s, women's median salaries in the United States were 74 percent of men's, with a wage gap of varying size persisting in all ethnic groups.[3] Worldwide, almost twice as many women as men are illiterate, and around most of the globe women put in longer hours than men in both

---

[1]Susan Faludi, *Backlash: The Undeclared War Against American Women* (New York: Crown, 1991).

[2]Allan G. Johnson, *The Gender Knot: Unraveling Our Patriarchal Legacy* (Philadelphia: Temple University Press, 1997), p. 232.

[3]*Statistical Abstract of the United States*, 117th ed. (Washington, D.C.: U.S. Bureau of the Census, 1997).

domestic and waged work.[4] International health experts estimate that around 100 million women and girls have experienced genital mutilation, and rape as a tool of war has been tragically common in places such as the former Yugoslavia.[5] In both Canada and the United States, approximately 25 percent of married or formerly married women have suffered severe physical abuse at the hands of a male partner; in Asia, Africa and Latin America, the figure is more than 50 percent.[6]

Religion and Gender

Do Christian women fare any better? In some ways it seems they do not. For example, the few well-designed surveys of physical, sexual and emotional abuse among Christian groups (including one I helped conduct for my own denomination in the early 1990s) yield prevalence rates very similar to those found in the North American population at large, with women more likely than men to have experienced some or all three types of abuse at some point in their life.[7] Some critics take this as evidence that religious orthodoxy of any sort is detrimental to women, and suspect that a species of "hard patriarchy" is reemerging, especially in conservative Christian circles. And in international perspective, there is reason to worry about the connection between religious conservatism and injustice toward women. For example, from the late 1990s until late 2001 much of Afghanistan came under the control of the fundamentalist Muslim Taliban forces, who reimposed a rigid system of male headship extending across all spheres of life. Under its sway, women were caught in an assortment of no-win dilemmas. They were banned from working in the public arena, even if they were war widows and the sole support of their children. They could not be treated by male doctors, yet only a few women doctors from pre-Taliban days were permitted to continue practicing. They could not attend school or university and had to be heavily veiled and accompanied by

---

[4]United Nations, *The World's Women: Trends and Statistics, 1970-1990* (New York: United Nations Publications, 1991).

[5]Ibid., p. 401.

[6]United Nations, *The World's Women, 1995: Trends and Statistics* (New York: United Nations Publications, 1995). Although research shows that women may also abuse males, women are more likely than men to be injured and hospitalized and to require medical care. In the United States wives are more likely to be killed by their husbands than by all other categories of perpetrators combined. See Neil S. Jacobson and John M. Gottman, *When Men Batter Women* (New York: Simon & Schuster, 1998).

[7]Committee to Study Physical, Emotional and Sexual Abuse, Report 30, *The Agenda for Synod of the Christian Reformed Church in North America* (Grand Rapids, Mich.: C.R.C. Publications, 1992). See also Nancy Nason-Clark, *The Battered Wife: How Christians Confront Family Violence* (Louisville, Ky.: Westminster John Knox, 1997).

a male relative in public or risk suffering physical violence.

In Western nations, and particularly in the United States, some worry about a form of muted or "soft" patriarchy that persists in Christian circles, despite (or perhaps in reaction to) three decades of gains for women. Thus in 1989 the conservative evangelical Danvers Statement declared that "Adam's headship in marriage was established by God before the fall, and was not a result of sin. . . . In the church, redemption in Christ gives men and women an equal share in the blessings of salvation; nevertheless, some governing and teaching roles within the church are restricted to men."[8] Likewise, almost a decade later, in 1998, American Southern Baptists amended their Faith and Message statement to require wives to "submit graciously to the servant leadership of their husbands, even as the church willingly submits to the leadership of Christ."[9]

Even in churches that ordain women the rhetoric of gender partnership is better than actual practice. In a 1994 survey of fifteen Protestant denominations, researchers found that female M.Div. (master's of divinity) degree holders took on average more than twice as long as their male peers to get their first post in a church. Moreover, women working in full-time clergy jobs earned significantly less than men, even when other factors such as education, work experience, congregational size and type of position were controlled for.[10] It is not clear how much this difference reflects continued discrimination against women clergy and how much reflects women's choices to slow their careers to devote time to their families. But other studies showing a higher dropout rate of women clergy because of self-reported demoralization and discouragement suggest that continued discrimination plays at least a partial role.[11]

Man Overboard!

So there is plenty of data to support the argument that, on the whole, it is women rather than men who still have the greater hurdles to surmount. But while acknowledging the importance of such data, many observers, including myself,

---

[8]The Danvers Statement (Wheaton, Ill.: Council on Biblical Manhood and Womanhood, 1989). For a further discussion of this document, see Mary Stewart Van Leeuwen, *Gender and Grace: Love, Work and Parenting in a Changing World* (Downers Grove, Ill.: InterVarsity Press, 1990), chap. 12.

[9]Baptist Faith and Message, article 18 (Louisville, Ky.: Southern Baptist Publications, 1998).

[10]Barbara Brown Zinkmund, Adair T. Lummis and Patricia M. Y. Chang, *An Uphill Calling: Ordained Women in Contemporary Protestantism* (Louisville, Ky.: Westminster John Knox, 1997).

[11]See Mark Chaves, *Ordaining Women: Culture and Conflict in Religious Organizations* (Cambridge, Mass.: Harvard University Press, 1997), chap. 1.

see the man on the inner tube as a symbol that men too are struggling. Back in 1947, journalist Ferdinand Lundberg and psychiatrist Marynia Farnham wrote a book titled *Modern Woman: The Lost Sex.* In it they admonished post-World War II females never to compete with men in the public sphere but to devote themselves entirely to their homes and children.[12] Fifteen years later, writing *The Feminine Mystique,* Betty Friedan helped launch the second wave of feminism by insisting that women's resulting domestic isolation and economic dependency had produced a "problem that has no name."[13] Now, some three decades later, it seems that men are the ones with problems needing to be named, for we have books appearing with titles such as *Refusing to Be a Man,*[14] *The Man Who Never Was,*[15] *The Men We Long to Be,*[16] *The Trouble with Testosterone,*[17] *In a Time of Fallen Heroes,*[18] *Lost Fathers,*[19] *Lost Boys*[20] and *Silent Sons.*[21]

Significantly, just as profeminist writings come not only from women, neither are books proclaiming a "masculine crisis" written only by men. The same Susan Faludi who described a backlash against women in the early 1990s ended the decade with a book twice as long that she titled *Stiffed: The Betrayal of the American Man.*[22] "Blaming a cabal of men has taken feminism about as far as it can go," she concluded after six years of delving into men's psyches. "If my travels taught me anything about the two sexes, it is that each of our struggles ← depends on the success of the other's."[23] Using detailed case studies, Faludi claimed that American males since World War II had been cheated, or "stiffed," out of the kind of mentoring needed to help boys become men with the skills and motivation to serve their communities in useful ways. Her book shows how the aerospace industry has replaced loyalty to its employees with unapologetic worship of the bottom line. The American space program of the 1960s and 1970s turned skilled fighter-jet pilots into passive glamour boys orbiting the

---

[12]Ferdinand Lundberg and Marynia F. Farnham, *Modern Woman: The Lost Sex* (New York: Harper, 1947).

[13]Betty Friedan, *The Feminine Mystique* (New York: W. W. Norton, 1963).

[14]John Stoltenberg, *Refusing to Be a Man* (New York: Penguin Meridian, 1989).

[15]Janet Sayers, *The Man Who Never Was* (New York: BasicBooks, 1995).

[16]Stephen B. Boyd, *The Men We Long to Be* (New York: HarperSanFrancisco, 1995).

[17]Robert M. Sapolsky, *The Trouble with Testosterone, and Other Essays on the Biology of the Human Predicament* (New York: Touchstone, 1997).

[18]R. William Betcher and William S. Pollack, *In a Time of Fallen Heroes: The Re-Creation of Masculinity* (New York: Guildford, 1993).

[19]Cynthia R. Daniels, ed., *Lost Fathers* (New York: St. Martin's, 1998).

[20]James Garbarino, *Lost Boys: Why Our Sons Turn Violent and How We Can Save Them* (New York: Free Press, 1999).

[21]Robert J. Ackerman, *Silent Sons: A Book for and About Men* (New York: Simon & Schuster, 1993).

[22]Susan Faludi, *Stiffed: The Betrayal of the American Male* (New York: Wm. Morrow, 1999).

[23]Ibid., pp. 605, 595.

earth. Unionized manufacturing work has given way to service jobs with low pay and few benefits, while much more money has gone into the pockets of elite, high-tech information workers.

What's left for many men, Faludi concluded, is only "ornamental masculinity." As men's opportunity to be useful providers and protectors has eroded, some have begun to pursue the precarious routes to self-esteem and financial security long required of women: dressing glamorously, cultivating sexual attractiveness, and looking for ways to get media attention, whether as goofily dressed football fans, inner-city gang leaders or iron-pumping gym rats, all of whom were among Faludi's subjects. Along with this have come some intriguing gender reversals. For example, between 1989 and 1996, men's clothing sales in America rose 21 percent to record highs; meanwhile women, perhaps taught by thirty years of feminism to look for less superficial routes to a secure identity, spent 10 percent less on clothing in the same period.[24]

At the same time, the success of the British comedy *The Full Monty* suggests that the emergence of ornamental masculinity is not just an American phenomenon. In that film, laid-off male workers from Britain's formerly proud Sheffield steel mills eventually scrape together a living and a dubious sense of self-esteem by becoming dancers and strippers in a men's burlesque show.

Some Sobering Statistics

Do such case studies reflect overall negative trends in men's lives? There is demographic evidence to confirm that they do. Since the 1950s, suicide rates for young white males in America have nearly tripled, and just between 1986 and 1998, the rate for African American boys almost doubled. In 1997, 15 percent of American boys seriously considered suicide, and 5 percent actually attempted it. (Although females actually make more suicide attempts, two to four times as many males—depending on age category—succeed, since they are apt to use guns rather than pills as their method.)[25] In the United States more women than men now complete high school and obtain bachelor's and master's degrees, and analogous performance differences by sex have been found in the United Kingdom, Western Europe and Australia.[26] Between 1970 and 1993 in the United States, the homicide rate among fifteen- to nineteen-

---

[24]Ibid., p. 517.
[25]Garbarino, *Lost Boys,* p. 9.
[26]William Pollack, *Real Boys: Rescuing Our Sons from the Myths of Boyhood* (New York: Random House, 1998), chap. 10.

year-old males more than doubled before beginning to level off. In 1995 a third of all American males in that same age bracket reported carrying a weapon (gun, knife or razor) in the previous month, compared to only 8 percent of their female peers.[27]

When we look beyond boys and young men to the lives of adult males in general, other warning signs appear. In all age groups in the United States, men's death rates from both internal and external causes exceed women's, peaking at almost three times women's rate among fifteen- to twenty-four-year-olds.[28] In addition, men commit suicide at about three times the rate women do between the ages of twenty-five and sixty-five, and at rates four to six times higher thereafter.[29] Men are three times more likely than women to abuse alcohol and three times more likely to be diagnosed with antisocial personality disorder, which is characterized by an absence of moral sensitivity and guilt about harming others.[30]

In America men seem to be less vocationally flexible than women. In 1995 an average of 58 percent more women were in traditional men's jobs (e.g., doctor, police officer, clergy, accountant, mail carrier) than in 1983. Only 20 percent more men were in traditional women's jobs (e.g., nurse, elementary teacher, physiotherapist, social worker), even though men are courted for such jobs—at generally better pay than women used to earn in them—and even though traditional male factory jobs are now scarce.[31] Finally, men, along with women, seem less concerned to establish stable families than before. In the mid-1990s America's divorce and nonmarital pregnancy rates were the highest in the industrialized world (although they rose everywhere throughout the twentieth century).[32]

Such demographic data confirm that men do have problems, many of which have grown more serious over the past couple of decades. It seems time to take a closer look at the nature and causes of these problems, and at possible remedies.

---

[27]Freya Lund Sonenstein, "Teenage American Males: Growing Up with Risks," *Scientific American,* special quarterly issue, "Men: The Scientific Truth About Their Work, Play, Health and Passions," August 1999, pp. 86-91.

[28]Martin Daly and Margo Wilson, "Darwinism and the Roots of Machismo," in *Scientific American,* "Men," pp. 10-14.

[29]U.S. Bureau of the Census, 1996. At all ages, American women's suicide rates were 10 per 100,000 people or less. Men's rates varied from 20 to 70 per 100,000, rising especially after age sixty-five.

[30]Hilary Lips, *Sex and Gender: An Introduction,* 3rd ed. (Mountain View, Calif.: Mayfield, 1997), chap. 9.

[31]U.S. Bureau of Labor Statistics, 1997, quoted in *Philadelphia Inquirer,* February 2, 1997, p. D1.

[32]David Popenoe, *Life Without Father* (New York: Free Press, 1996), pp. 43, 63.

Can Men Be Studied as Men?

Yet a fair number of people have given me odd looks when I've told them I'm working on a book about masculinity. Some doubted that an entire volume could be written on the subject. Others questioned whether a woman could or should write it. Still others wondered why I would not want to focus just on women—as if masculinity and femininity were like parallel railroad tracks, traveling quite independently of each other. Where does such skepticism come from? To answer that question we need to look at the way men and women were studied in the recent past by psychologists and other social scientists, and then to consider an alternative approach.

My own desire to become a psychologist began when I was a sixth-grader back in the 1950s. My older sister, who was herself studying psychology in university, would arrive home for the summer and let me read her textbooks from the previous year. At that time, and for many years thereafter (indeed until well after the second wave of feminism began in the 1960s), I noticed a curious thing about these textbooks: their indexes often had entries for "women" but never any for "men." This always struck me as puzzling, especially in a discipline that defined itself as the study of *human* behavior and mental processes. Moreover, discussions about women were generally limited to what the writers assumed were their unique problems: What made some women suffer from penis envy, and how could this unfortunate affliction be cured? Why didn't little girls engage in rule-governed games as much as boys, and how did this limit their cognitive and moral development? Why did they not generally do as well as men on certain tests of mathematical or spatial ability?

As I look back, one thing now seems obvious about those textbooks: the standard for optimal human behavior was simply assumed to be male. Women were different or "other," and so needed special mention because they fell short of that standard in ways that were presumed to cause problems. They were, as the title of a 1947 essay by Dorothy Sayers put it, "The Human-Not-Quite-Human."[33] Textbook writers thus tended to think of gender as something extra that women had to cope with in a way men did not. This was not unlike Western-world Caucasians' habit (also common at the time) of assuming that race or ethnicity was something only groups other than themselves possessed, or Midwestern Americans' assumption that they alone spoke English without an accent. It

---

[33]In Dorothy L. Sayers, *Unpopular Opinions* (1947); reprinted in Sayers, *Are Women Human?* (Grand Rapids, Mich.: Eerdmans, 1971), pp. 37-47.

is very difficult for members of any group that is socially dominant in a given time or place to look reflectively at themselves, to welcome such scrutiny from anyone else or indeed to see any need for it at all. As the old proverb puts it, a fish in water does not usually know that it is wet.

It is important to stress that this is a human problem, not a uniquely male problem. We learn from the book of Acts and Paul's epistles that during the early days of the church it took much prayer, diplomacy and even the occasional confrontation for ethnic Jewish Christians to conclude that Gentile Christians did not have to become exactly like them in order to have God's approval.[34] And in what is now a famous paper among students of gender and ethnicity, educator Peggy McIntosh wrote about how difficult it was to realize that, even as she chafed at how men took for granted their privileges as males, she herself was carrying "an invisible knapsack of privilege" as a white person living in America. In that knapsack were "special, assurances, tools, maps, guides . . . emergency gear and blank checks" that allowed her to assume all kinds of things that her African American neighbors usually couldn't. For example, "I can go shopping alone most of the time, fairly well assured that I will not be followed or harassed by store detectives. . . . I can talk with my mouth full and not have people put this down to my color. . . . If a traffic cop pulls me over, I can be fairly sure I haven't been singled out because of my race. . . . When I am told about our national heritage or about 'civilization,' I am shown that people of my color made it what it is."[35]

That it took McIntosh (by her own admission) so much effort to think of these and other examples of her "white privilege" underscores the fact that it is easier for all of us to notice those who are imposing limits on us than to reflect on our own roles as people who may limit others. And although this is a generic human weakness, it has throughout history been a particular temptation for Christian men, some of whom still practice a variation on the mistake of the old textbook writers by assuming that "manliness" and "godliness" are the same thing. For example, Promise Keepers, a Christian parachurch organization for men begun in the early 1990s, teaches its men-only gatherings about seven promises essential for the practice of godly masculinity. These are excellent ideals to focus on, and it is true that in terms of actual practice male evangelical conservatives—as well as the women they are married to—are much more gender egalitarian than their

---

[34]For an excellent study of how the early church overcame this ethnocentrism, see Spencer Perkins and Chris Rice, *More Than Equals: Racial Reconciliation for the Sake of the Gospel*, rev. ed. (Downers Grove, Ill.: InterVarsity Press, 2000).

[35]Peggy McIntosh, "White Privilege and Male Privilege: A Personal Account of Coming to See Correspondences Through Work in Women's Studies," in *Race, Class and Gender: An Anthology*, ed. Margaret L. Anderson and Patricia Hill Collins, 2nd ed. (Belmont, Calif.: Wadsworth, 1995), pp. 76-87 (quotations from pp. 77-80).

rhetoric often suggests.[36] But as Rebecca and Douglas Groothuis have pointed out, there is nothing in such promises—which include concerns for evangelism, mutual accountability, support of the church, racial reconciliation and sexual purity—that does not apply equally to *all* Christian believers.

To the extent that these seven promises are held up as a description of godly masculinity, they imply that "there is something distinctively masculine about godliness [and this] . . . can lead to a devaluation of femininity. If Christian men are like Christ not simply because they are Christians, but also because they are men, then men are simply more Christlike than women."[37] The confusion is reinforced, they add, "by the [Promise Keepers'] habit of equivocating between the generic and gender-specific meaning of terms such as man, men, and sons."[38] For example, even a conservative Bible translation such as the New International Version renders Ephesians 4:24 as "Put on the new *self,* created to be like God in true righteousness and holiness." However, editors of the Promise Keepers magazine, *New Man,* cited the older King James translation ("that ye put on the new *man*") as their inspiration for the magazine's name, ignoring the generic intent of the original Greek and thereby conflating manliness with godliness.[39]

▌*Gender as a Cultural Activity*

But if a fish in water does not normally know it is wet, that is all the more reason for finding ways to study the water. This is especially so at a time when the fish themselves *are* beginning to think twice about their previously taken-for-granted environment and roles, as some men are doing today. How then should we approach the study of gender, if we are no longer to treat it as an extra appendage that produces special limitations for women that are not shared by men?

---

[36]On egalitarian tendencies among evangelical women, see for example Brenda E. Brasher, *Godly Women: Fundamentalism and Female Power* (New Brunswick, N.J.: Rutgers University Press, 1998); R. Marie Griffith, *God's Daughters: Evangelical Women and the Power of Submission* (Berkeley: University of California Press, 1997); and Christel Manning, *God Gave Us the Right: Conservative Catholic, Evangelical Protestant and Orthodox Jewish Women Grapple with Feminism* (New Brunswick, N.J.: Rutgers University Press, 1999). On the mixture of hierarchical and egalitarian themes in the Promise Keepers' and other evangelical family-oriented literature, see William H. Lockhart, "'We Are One Life,' but Not of One Gender Ideology: Unity, Ambiguity and the Promise Keepers," *Sociology of Religion* 61, no. 1 (2000): 73-92.

[37]Rebecca Merrill Groothuis and Douglas Groothuis, "Women Keep Promises Too: Or, The Christian Life Is for Both Men and Women," *Perspectives: A Journal of Reformed Thought* 10, no. 7 (1995): 19-23, quotation from pp. 19-20.

[38]Ibid., p. 20.

[39]See also Mary Stewart Van Leeuwen, "Servanthood or Soft Patriarchy? A Christian Feminist Looks at the Promise Keepers Movement," *Journal of Men's Studies* 5, no. 3 (1997): 233-61.

Unlike the writers of my sister's textbooks, scholars today are beginning to realize that masculinity, like ethnicity, is an ongoing cultural production. By definition, gender encompasses the attitudes, behaviors and meanings that we attach to biological sex in various times and places. It is a dynamic, negotiated cultural and social activity—as much a verb as a noun—that involves men every bit as much as women. And rather than thinking of gender *roles* as two fixed, separate railroad tracks moving in parallel, we might better picture gender *relations* with a metaphor of a canoe on a lake.

Two people in a canoe may go for some time implicitly agreeing about who will paddle in which position, on which side and so on. But if one person eventually decides to paddle on the other side, to shift weight or even to stop paddling altogether, the other person must somehow adapt if the boat is to keep upright and moving. Much like canoeing, gender involves habitual practices— deemed "feminine" and "masculine"—that go on for some time, punctuated with shifts initiated by persons of one or both sexes. Thus gender is not something that just happens to us by reason of biology or socialization, though as we will see in chapters to come, these too are important.[40] "Doing gender" is a responsible cultural activity whose mixed blessings need to be critically examined, not least from the standpoint of a Christian worldview.

To embark on such a venture we have a growing set of resources to help us. Since the late twentieth century an interdisciplinary literature in men's studies has been emerging to join the more established field of women's studies. It includes periodicals with titles like *The Journal of Men's Studies* and *Masculinities*. It also includes professional organizations, social action groups, and a growing stream of books drawing from disciplines as diverse as biology, cultural history, psychology and religious studies. The result is a rich body of research, both academic and applied, affirming that men can indeed be studied in their ongoing, complex relationships with others. I will draw on this expanding literature generously—though not always uncritically—in chapters to come.

Why Would a Woman Write About Men?

I noted earlier that some people have questioned not so much whether men can be written about as men but whether such writing can be adequately done by

---

[40]For a further discussion of this "critical theory" approach to gender, see Mary Stewart Van Leeuwen, Annelies Knoppers, Margaret L. Koch, Douglas J. Schuurman and Helen L. Sterk, *After Eden: Facing the Challenge of Gender Reconciliation* (Grand Rapids, Mich.: Eerdmans, 1993), especially chaps. 8, 15 and 16.

women. This seems like an odd assumption, akin to believing that only native Russians can become Russian language teachers or that only people who have had children can do research in developmental psychology. But if we change the question slightly, from "*Can* a woman write about men?" to "Why would a woman *want* to write about men?" then I think it is a question well worth answering. In my own case, there are two reasons for taking on the challenge of being a female Christian social scientist writing about masculinity.

To begin with, the study of any group of people benefits from both insider and outsider perspectives. So, for example, it was important for middle-class white women in America to tell the story of their frustration with gender arrangements in the 1950s, including the isolation and economic vulnerability many of them felt as full-time housewives. But it was equally important for women of color to speak up and remind middle-class white women of things they had failed to notice because they were too immersed in their own subculture. For example, most married black women (and not a few working-class white women) never even had the choice to be bored in suburbia, because their earning power was always needed to help keep their families financially afloat.[41] Likewise, it is important for cancer patients to share their firsthand experiences with others and to have a voice in the management of their illness. They, after all, are the ones who have been living most intimately with it. But it is equally important to have cancer specialists who see the bigger picture in terms of available treatments, possible complications and prognosis, even though most will never have had cancer themselves.

It is not that one perspective is "better" than the other but rather that a richer picture is obtained when we combine the close-up, subjective experience of the insider with the more panoramic and detached view of the outsider. For this exercise to work, of course, members of both groups must feel equally able to speak freely without fear of reprisal. One cannot, for example, imagine many black slaves giving an unvarnished "outsiders' account" of their masters a century and a half ago, even if they were invited to do so. They had too much to lose by taking such a risk. Today some people of both sexes still claim that women cannot speak freely about men, and that men cannot listen honestly to women, because of an enduring power imbalance between the sexes. But I number myself among those who believe that we are entering a new and more promising era.[42]

---

[41]See, for example, Patricia Hill Collins, *Black Feminist Thought: Knowledge, Consciousness and the Politics of Empowerment* (Boston: Unwin Hyman, 1990).

[42]See, for example, Faludi, *Stiffed;* Young, *Cease Fire!* and also Don S. Browning, Bonnie J. Miller-McLemore, Pamela D. Couture, K. Brynolf Lyon and Robert M. Franklin, *From Culture Wars to Common Ground: Religion and the American Family Debate* (Louisville, Ky.: Westminster John Knox, 1997); Lisa Sowle Cahill, *Sex, Gender and Christian Ethics* (Cambridge University Press, 1996); and Elaine Storkey, *The Search for Intimacy* (Grand Rapids, Mich.: Eerdmans, 1995).

For instance, in the summer of 1999, as I began writing this book, the U.S. women's soccer team won the women's World Cup before enthusiastic audiences totaling almost 700,000 people. Carly Fiorina was appointed CEO of Hewlett Packard electronics, one of the U.S. top thirty corporations, and Colonel Eileen Collins became the first woman commander of a space shuttle mission. In 1999, 12 percent of elected representatives in the U.S. Congress were women, compared to 4 percent in 1977. In state legislatures, women held 22 percent of seats, compared to under 3 percent in 1969, and women were mayors in twelve of the one hundred largest U.S. cities.[43] In the public sphere women are making impressive gains, not just in North America but in many nations around the world.[44]

On the domestic level there is also reason for guarded optimism. In a 1998 random-sample survey of American attitudes about gender, almost half of all male and female respondents (and much more than half among eighteen- to forty-year-olds) rejected gender-traditionalist statements such as "A husband's job is more important than a wife's," "For a woman, taking care of children is the main thing, but for a man his job is," and "It is generally better for a marriage if the husband earns more than his wife."[45] Such attitude shifts are mirrored even in some evangelical churches. For example, only a year after the Southern Baptist announcement that wives were to "submit graciously to the servant leadership of their husbands," the denomination's largest state convention voted to reject that particular clause of the Baptist Faith and Message statement. "The Bible doesn't teach that the husband is the general and the wife is a private," concluded the Reverend Charles Wade, executive director of the dissenting Texas convention.[46]

There is, to be sure, still a gap between attitudes and behavior. For example, women working full time in the waged workforce still do about twice as much housework as their husbands, and this is a source of ongoing contention. Nevertheless, "after nearly a generation of sharing the workplace and renegotiating domestic duties, most men and women agree that increased gender equity has enriched both sexes. Most men in the polls said they were happy to share child care and domestic work, [and] the world of [waged] work is increasingly a man's

---

[43]Dick Polman, "A Woman in the White House: Did Dole Help or Hurt Cause?" *Philadelphia Inquirer,* October 24, 1999, pp. D1, D4.

[44]See in particular the *Human Development Report of the United Nations Development Program* (New York: Oxford University Press, 1995).

[45]Richard Morgan and Megan Rosenfeld, "With More Equity, More Sweat," *Washington Post,* March 22, 1998, pp. A1, A17.

[46]"Baptists in Texas Reject a Call for Wives to 'Submit' to Husbands," *New York Times,* November 10, 1999, p. A21.

and a woman's world."[47] So although there are still distortions in relations between the sexes, we have come far enough for some women scholars, including me, to want to examine the architecture of gender more specifically as it concerns men. If gender, like canoeing, is a relational phenomenon, it is important to explore how men are responding to recent shifts made by women in the cultural canoe.

Opposite Sexes or
Neighboring Sexes?

My second reason for taking on this project is really the reverse of the first, for although in one sense women and men are "outsiders" to one another, in a deeper sense they are not. Decades ago lay theologian Dorothy Sayers wondered why women and men were referred to as "opposite sexes" rather than "neighboring sexes."[48] The question is still a good one today, especially given the popularity of books such as John Gray's *Men Are from Mars, Women Are from Venus*. Gray treats the sexes as if they were distinct species raised on different planets who, having stumbled into each other's territory as adults and experienced sexual attraction, must now spend vast amounts of energy learning to decode each other's values, habits and emotional sensibilities. His working assumption is that all behavioral sex differences are biological or metaphysical givens, subject to little individual variation and largely immune to environmental influence.[49]

Gray has done no systematic research to support his claims, but there is a large social science literature that calls his assumptions into question. Over the last thirty years of the twentieth century, modest average sex differences in spatial and verbal skills became even smaller as educational opportunities were equalized for boys and girls. And even where somewhat larger differences exist—for example, in communication and conflict-management styles between spouses—the amount of variability *within* each sex still exceeds the small average difference *between* the sexes.[50]

One way to understand this is to think of the very ordinary example of height. It is obviously not the case that all men are taller than all women: height distributions for the sexes give us largely overlapping "bell curves," with the range of

---

[47]Ibid., pp. A1, A17.

[48]Sayers, "Human-Not-Quite-Human."

[49]John Gray, *Men Are from Mars, Women Are from Venus* (New York: HarperCollins, 1992). For a more flexible approach that attempts to lodge the debate within biblical parameters, see Norman Wakefield and Jody Brolsma, *Men Are from Israel, Women Are from Moab* (Downers Grove, Ill.: InterVarsity Press, 2000).

[50]See Lips, *Sex and Gender,* and Van Leeuwen, *Gender and Grace,* for further discussion of these issues.

heights among men *and* women being much greater than the average difference between them. This, of course, has not stopped our culture from pretending that the differences are more absolute than they really are. Thus when Prince Charles became engaged to Princess Diana in 1980, many of their photos were taken with the princess standing a step lower than the prince, to give the illusion that he was much taller than she, rather than the same height. Men, we have been told, must ideally be taller (as well as richer, smarter and older) than the women they marry—which has meant in the past that extraordinary women, as well as rather undistinguished men, have found it hard to get married at all. Cultures can become quite irrationally attached to certain convictions about gender![51]

The truth of the matter is that women and men are both from planet earth. Far from being suddenly thrown together at the point of sexual maturity, in virtually all cultures they are raised in families together, educated through much of their childhood together, and taught the stories and visions of their people side by side. It is also true that masculine and feminine "subcultural" activities emerge, or are imposed, in varying degrees and at various stages of the life cycle in all cultures, as we will see in later chapters. But as Sayers discerned, this hardly justifies the rhetoric of different planetary origins. At most it makes men and women neighboring—not opposite—sexes.

Even C. S. Lewis, Sayers's more gender-traditionalist contemporary, recognized this truth. In his science fiction story *Out of the Silent Planet,* a linguist is abducted to Mars and there attempts to learn the language of its inhabitants, the *hrossa.* There is, of course, no guarantee that sentient creatures on other planets (should we ever find any) will share the same deep language structure as humans on earth—any more than cats or dogs do.[52] But in this imaginary case they do, and Lewis's hero Elwin Ransom, fascinated by his chance to write the first *Concise Martian-English Dictionary,* makes a great effort to win the trust of the first shy *hross* that he meets:

> Neither dared let the other approach, yet each repeatedly felt the impulse to do so.
> . . . It was more than curiosity. It was like a courtship—like the meeting of the first
> man and the first woman in the world. It was like something beyond that; so natural is the contact of sexes, so limited the strangeness, so shallow the reticence, so
> mild the repugnance to be overcome, compared with the first tingling intercourse
> of two different, but rational species.[53]

---

[51]Jessie Bernard, *The Future of Marriage* (New York: World, 1972).

[52]As psychologist David Myers rightly observes, "Other worlds may have languages that, for us humans, are unlearnable, but our world does not" (Myers, *Psychology*, 5th ed. [New York: Worth, 1998], p. 323).

[53]C. S. Lewis, *Out of the Silent Planet* (New York: Macmillan, 1965), p. 56.

When we turn to the biblical account of that first man and woman, we find that indeed they do not come from separate planets but both are "dust of the earth." And we also learn that they share something even more significant:

> In the image of God he created them;
>   male and female he created them.

> God blessed them, and God said to them, "Be fruitful and multiply, and fill the earth and subdue it; and have dominion over the fish of the sea and over the birds of the air and over every living thing that moves upon the earth." (Gen 1:26-28)

Among Reformed theologians this passage is known as the "cultural mandate," and we will have reason to return to it often in chapters to come. For now we need mainly to note this: God does not say to the woman "Be fruitful and multiply" and to the man "Subdue the earth." *Both* mandates—to exercise accountable dominion and accountable generativity—are given to both members of the primal pair.

The passage need not be taken as a blanket endorsement of androgyny, for reasons that we will explore in later chapters. But it does suggest that any construction of gender relations involving an exaggerated separation of activities by sex—as happened, for example, in Western society after the Industrial Revolution—is eventually going to run into trouble because it is creationally distorted and therefore potentially unjust toward *both* sexes.

Looking Ahead

This first section of the book takes a look at general issues concerning masculinity. I have begun with a brief survey of the general state of males in the Western world some thirty years after the advent of second-wave feminism. To complement that, we need to take a look at the past and see how it interacts with the present. In chapter two I will suggest how a study of masculinity can be undertaken within the parameters of a Christian worldview. And in chapter three I will look closely at the social and cultural setting of the early Mediterranean church in order to see what impact it had on gender relations and, in particular, assumptions about masculinity.

In the second section of the book (chapters four to six) I will be examining masculinity through the lens of three different academic disciplines: biology, developmental psychology and cultural anthropology. In the third section (chapters seven to nine) I will focus on some specific challenges in the study of masculinity. These include a look at the claims of evolutionary psychology, the

changing place of religion in Western-world men's lives over the past two centuries, and the impact on men's lives of two successive waves of feminism during the same period.

Finally, in the last three chapters I will concentrate on some practical issues,
such as marriage and parenting, sexuality, and the organization of work, in pursuit of what I believe can be a more hopeful future for relations between the
sexes and between men and their children. But we cannot fully understand the
present or plan for the future without seriously considering the past. And we
cannot study history or anything else without honestly acknowledging our
deeper worldview—that which supplies answers to basic human questions such
as *Who are we? Where are we? What's the fundamental human problem? What's
the solution?* So let's turn to worldview commitments and their interaction with
the history of Christianity and masculinity.

The Biblical Drama and
the Gendered Powers

NOT TOO MANY YEARS AGO a colleague invited me to talk about gender issues to an introductory sociology class in the Christian college where we both taught. My chief memory, however, is not of my own interaction with his students but of my colleague's summary of some data he had collected the week before. He had asked the students to do a word-association exercise: they were to indicate, for a lengthy list of adjectives, whether they associated each word with being feminine, masculine or neither. The list looked a lot like ones developed by social psychologists interested in gender stereotypes; it included words like *strong, submissive, patient, emotional, kind, self-reliant, self-controlled, nurturant, aggressive, gentle, ambitious, joyful, modest, faithful, tough* and *loving.* How had the students, as a group, rated each adjective in terms of its perceived gender valence? This was the data analysis he was sharing the day of my visit.

But unmentioned to his students before their responses were collected (and perhaps unnoticed by you, dear reader) was the fact that my colleague had randomly distributed through his list the adjectival forms of most of the fruits of the Holy Spirit: love, joy, patience, kindness, faithfulness, gentleness and self-control. These character ideals are listed by Paul in his letter to the Galatian church (Gal 5:22-23) and are the basis of many sermons and Sunday school lessons. They are presented as generic virtues to which all Christians should aspire, not assigned according to sex. There is even a pious Christian saying to the effect that the fruits of the Spirit do not come in pink or blue.

Did the Christian students' ratings affirm the sex-neutrality of these particular personality traits? Well, yes and no. On average, they were somewhat more likely to rate the "fruit" adjectives as gender-neutral than the others in the list (such as *strong, emotional, self-reliant, nurturant*). But there was still a definite tendency to see those qualities as more feminine than masculine, especially the adjectives *patient* and *gentle*. And when the data pool was divided according to the sex of the respondents, it was evident that the men were more likely than the women to associate *all* of the "fruit" adjectives with femininity.

Real Men
Don't Pray?

Christians have appealed to the Bible as an authoritative guide to gender roles and virtues since the time the canon was closed in the fourth century. The goal of this chapter is to clarify my own position as to how the Bible should be used in this regard and to show why accepting its authority is an asset, not an impediment, to doing social science as a gender studies scholar. In the process I will outline what it means to hold a Christian worldview and will show the relevance of that worldview to questions about gender. The next chapter will consider various biblical accounts of relations between women and men, and among men themselves.

We need to be aware that unconscious cultural assumptions are often at work alongside people's surface rhetoric about the Bible, as my classroom example pointedly demonstrates. The results of that exercise parallel studies using more representative samples of the population. *Gender stereotypes* can be defined as beliefs about the psychological characteristics and activities typical of males or females. They are relatively stable attitudes about masculinity and femininity, though their strength varies from group to group. For example, men typically have more strongly stereotyped beliefs about both sexes than women do, but African Americans of both sexes endorse gender stereotypes less strongly than Caucasian Americans. Moreover, most individuals hold less stereotyped views of themselves than of their own sex as a whole.

Yet in spite of these differences, and despite the great changes wrought by feminism in recent years, gender stereotypes have remained remarkably consistent over the several decades they have been studied, not just in North America but in many nations both north and south of the equator.[1] In general, the traits attributed to men cluster around a factor variously termed *agency, power* or *achievement:* among other things, men are rated as more aggressive, ambitious, direct, logical and independent than women. By contrast, women's ascribed

---

[1]John E. Williams and Deborah L. Best, *Measuring Sex Stereotypes: A Multination Study,* rev. ed. (Newbury Park, Calif.: Sage, 1990).

traits focus on a core of features often labeled *receptivity, niceness* or *warmth-expressiveness:* for example, they are rated as more tactful, nurturing, coopera-tive and emotional than men.[2] But these differences, while they continue to be statistically significant, are far from absolute. Thus, on a ten-point scale ranging from "passive" (1) to "active" (10), females on average might be rated at 6.2 and males at 7.4. In fact, according to one reviewer of the literature, "the mean rat-ings of males and females on such scales rarely fall on opposite sides of the mid-point," an indication of the degree to which most people see women and men as neighboring—not opposite—sexes.[3]

Nevertheless, most of us would agree that the stereotypes still exert an enor-mous prescriptive pull on our lives. We may indeed see ourselves as less gen-der-typed than most members of our sex, but we're not always certain this is something to be proud of. As an undergraduate in the 1960s I was sometimes told by professors, after getting back a paper with a high grade, that I had shown I could "think like a man." Was I to take this as a compliment, an insult or some of both? I was never quite sure. And what are Christian men to make of the research on gender stereotypes showing that men are regarded—both ac-tually and ideally—as less religious than women?[4] If you are a serious Christian who happens to be male, are you to conclude that your masculinity quotient is inversely related to the depth and activity of your faith?

This last finding should prompt Christians of both sexes to think carefully about the social construction of masculinity, regardless of how much they en-dorse the accuracy or desirability of any other gender stereotypes. Although it is quite true that the fruits of the Spirit do not come labeled pink or blue in the Christian Scriptures, the cultural assumption that they are mostly pink is still enough to make a lot of Christian men nervous. On more than a few occasions I have asked largely Christian lecture audiences how they think Christian men deal with the cultural message that strong religiosity means less masculinity. The response—more accurately, the nonresponse—is almost always the same. I see various women nudging their husbands, as if to say, "Good question, George. Why don't you answer it?" George, however, sits stiffly in his seat with a look of veiled panic on his face and volunteers nothing.

---

[2]See Irene H. Frieze and Maureen C. McHugh's edited volume on "Measuring Beliefs About Appropriate Roles for Women and Men," special issue of *Psychology of Women Quarterly*, 21, no. 1 (1997).

[3]Hilary Lips, *Sex and Gender: An Introduction,* 3rd ed. (Mountain View, Calif.: Mayfield, 1997), p. 7.

[4]Inge K. Broverman, Susan R. Vogel, Donald M. Broverman, Frank E. Clarkson and Paul S. Rosenkrantz, "Sex-Role Stereotypes: A Current Appraisal," *Journal of Social Issues* 28, no. 2 (1971): 59-78. These researchers found high agreement about men's greater indifference to religion regardless of the age, sex, educational level, marital status or even religion of the re-spondents.

Indeed in the many years that I have asked that question, I have received only two answers. One was from a male undergraduate who proclaimed that if anyone ever told him he was less masculine for being a Christian, he would "just punch them in the nose." The other was from a recent graduate of an M.B.A. program at a large state university. Midway through that program, he and several male classmates had concluded that their Christian convictions were incompatible with certain questionable practices—such as hostile takeovers and the evasion of environmental regulations—that they were being taught. They agreed that if rejecting such practices meant they would never be part of a Fortune 500 company, then that was a price they would pay, regardless of what others might think it implied about their masculinity.

The Bible: Dictionary, Springboard or Cosmic Drama?

Which of these men's responses was closer to the biblical mandate for masculinity? If there is an answer to that question, how are we to discern it? How are we to determine the significant teachings of a book that is actually a collection of sixty-six books, many with more than one author and/or editor, written and compiled over more than a millennium and gathered into its present canonical form some fifteen hundred years ago?

N. T. Wright, in *The New Testament and the People of God*, mentions three ways Christians have grappled with this question over the past two centuries.[5] The first is to assume we can extract timeless propositions or truth-statements from all parts of the Bible, including rules about gender roles and relations, with little regard for the differing times they were recorded or the genre of the book (epistle, Psalms, Gospel, etc.) where they appear. In its extreme form, this approach turns the Bible into something like a dictionary or encyclopedia, where almost any reference to men and women is grist for a fixed set of gendered behaviors. This tendency to treat the Bible as a "flat book"[6] owes much to the legacy of the fundamentalist-modernist controversy that arose in North America early in the twentieth century. While claiming to challenge "godless science" with a high view of Scripture, fundamentalists still let the positivist norms of modern science dictate the terms of the debate. That is, they uncritically bought the notion that truth could be packaged only in scientifically or

---

[5]N. T. Wright, *The New Testament and the People of God* (Minneapolis: Fortress, 1992), chap. 5.
[6]The term comes from Willard Swartley's book *Slavery, Sabbath, War and Women: Case Studies in Biblical Interpretation* (Scottsdale, Penn.: Herald, 1983).

historically literal form, though they included in the latter category statements inspired by God and recorded in Scripture.[7]

One result of this attitude was a suspicious attitude toward the arts. Thus Clyde Kilby, for many years an English literature professor at a conservative Christian college, recalled a board member asking him why he taught courses involving novels, since (in the board member's mind) novels, being fiction, contained nothing but lies. And with regard to gender roles and relations, the result was a tendency to play what might be called "proof-text poker." For example, in the debate about male headship in marriage, traditionalists and egalitarians would confront one another with their favorite handful of biblical texts (e.g., Gen 3:16; 1 Cor 11:3-10; Eph 5:22 and 2 Tim 2:11-15 for traditionalists; Gen 1:26-28; Job 42:15; Acts 2:17-18 and Gal 3:26-28 for egalitarians). The assumption was that the one with the fullest hand of texts won the argument. But this interpretive strategy, while claiming to represent a very high view of Scripture, really embodies a very questionable view. For it assumes we can impose on the Bible our modern reverence for "factoids" instead of letting the Bible tell *us* how its cumulative story and various ways of speaking embody God's truth and illuminate our present path.[8]

If fundamentalists appropriated post-Enlightenment positivism to flatten the Bible of its historical and literary dimensions, hoping thereby to defend its status as the Word of God, liberal theologians and biblical scholars often did the opposite. Attempting to apply modern notions of scientific "objectivity," they became so concerned with questions of historical context, literary structure and ideology that the texts were often stripped of their authority completely. The "factual" findings of historical scholarship were now to be separated from any values readers might invoke in applying the text to their own lives. One could use the results of biblical scholarship, springboard fashion, to inspire an environmentalist or liberation-theological or feminist or any other social agenda. But the texts themselves were to be analyzed like any other historical documents, not seen as having anything besides natural and human social processes operating therein.

The problem with this approach is that while claiming to imitate the detached objectivity of science, it fails to understand the way science is actually done. Recent philosophers of science have shown that even in the so-called hard sciences there is no such thing as immaculate perception. To do effective science (or any other kind of research) you need to have some prior idea what it is you are

---

[7]For a more detailed history of this positivist approach to Scripture, see George Marsden, *Fundamentalism and American Culture* (New York: Oxford University Press, 1980).

[8]As Wright says, "We have abandoned biblicistic proof-texting as inconsistent with the nature of the texts that we have (and anyone who thinks that this means abandoning biblical authority should ask themselves where the real authority lies in a method that effectively turns the Bible into something else)" (*New Testament and the People of God,* p. 140).

looking for and what it means. "In nature," writes University of Kansas philosopher Ann Cudd, "things do not come with labels saying 'This is data.' In deciding what is data, scientists impose their values. That's what's meant by the social construction of scientific theories."[9]

This does not mean that there is no difference between doing science—or history for that matter—and, say, writing a novel, for neither nature nor our historical sources will indefinitely accommodate distorted theories about them. But as long as we are open to alternative theories and keep gathering relevant data, we have a check against misguided theorizing. Theory and data thus form a kind of feedback loop, while also incorporating values such as the theory's simplicity, elegance and capacity to generate other fruitful research. And if all researchers rely on values, knowingly or not, to help decide what is relevant data and good theory, then other things being equal (such as native ability and good training) scholars in *any* discipline who view their subject matter through the lens of Christian faith are no less "biased" or "unscholarly" than ones who do so through the lens of a naturalistic or Marxist or any other worldview.[10] In fact, it is more honest and fruitful to do scholarship from the standpoint of an acknowledged worldview that can be candidly analyzed and discussed than to presume one is working from a position of impossible neutrality behind which a worldview will be operating anyway.

Thus scholarship and the life of faith are more similar than modern thinkers have generally supposed. In each case, as philosopher Michael Polanyi puts it, "we know more than we can tell."[11] That is why scientific and religious understanding are both advanced by active praxis—in the laboratory for scientists, in engagement with worship and the world for Christians. Both are based on what Augustine called "faith seeking understanding." Both require us to learn from a prior tradition—to "indwell the tradition," Polanyi would say—in order to advance and adapt it in surprising but promising ways. Lesslie Newbigin summa-

---

[9]Quoted in Sharon Begley, "The Science Wars," *Newsweek* 129, no. 6 (1997): 54-57 (quotation from p. 56).

[10]The classic texts concerning this "critical realist" epistemology (which Wright also endorses) include Thomas Kuhn, *The Structure of Scientific Revolutions,* 2nd ed. (Chicago: University of Chicago Press, 1970), and Michael Polanyi, *Personal Knowledge: Towards a Post-critical Philosophy* (Chicago: University of Chicago Press, 1962). See also Richard Rorty, *Philosophy and the Mirror of Nature* (Princeton, N.J.: Princeton University Press, 1979), and Mary Hesse, *Revolutions and Reconstructions in the Philosophy of Science* (Bloomington: Indiana State University Press, 1980). In addition to Wright, the application of a critical-realist approach to biblical and theological studies can be found in Lesslie Newbigin's *The Gospel in a Pluralist Society* (Grand Rapids, Mich.: Eerdmans, 1989). For its appropriation by Christian scholars in psychology, see for example Stanton L. Jones, "A Constructive Relationship for Religion with the Science and Profession of Psychology: Perhaps the Boldest Model Yet," *American Psychologist* 42 (1994): 184-99, and Mary Stewart Van Leeuwen, "Five Uneasy Questions: Or, Will Success Spoil Christian Psychologists?" *Journal of Psychology and Christianity* 15, no. 2 (1996): 150-60.

[11]Polanyi, *Personal Knowledge,* especially chap.4, and also pp. 107, 124, 139-45, 165, 176, 186.

rizes it well: "The holding of a theory is an act of faith in the rationality of the cosmos. The justification—if one may put it so—is by faith; only afterward, as a spin-off, does one find that it is also justified because it works. The analogy with Christian faith hardly needs to be pointed out."[12]

The Unfinished Play

All of this suggests that we need a third and more fruitful way of approaching the Bible as a source of authoritative wisdom about gender roles and relations. We need to understand the Bible—and the story of gender relations within it— as the account of a cosmic drama that is still in progress.[13] N. T. Wright invites us to do the following thought experiment: Consider a group of Shakespeare lovers who have come across a previously unknown play by the bard. The manuscript includes four complete acts but only a few fragments of the fifth. Even so, they can tell from those fragments how the play is to end: it is ultimately a comedy, not a tragedy, with a happy outcome for most of its players. The Shakespeare lovers are naturally eager to see the play staged and discuss at length how to supply the missing parts of the fifth act in a way that the author would endorse as being in keeping with the rest of the play and his own intentions.

They conclude that rather than assigning someone to write the rest of the fifth act, the playwright's goals will best be met if they give the key parts "to highly trained, sensitive and experienced Shakespearean actors, who will immerse themselves in the first four acts, and in the language and culture of Shakespeare's time, *and who would then be told to work out a fifth act for themselves.*"[14] In such an exercise, it is obvious that the first four acts are authoritative: whatever ends up in the fifth act must build on and make sense according to the preceding ones. Yet as Wright notes, such authority does not mean the actors will simply repeat earlier parts of the drama over and over again. Rather, they need to be sensitive to the story's "impetus and forward movement, which demand to be concluded in an appropriate manner . . . with both innovation and consistency." Like laboratory scientists, they will "indwell the tradition"—in this case the first four acts of the play—in order to advance it in ways that are true

---

[12]Newbigin, *Gospel in a Pluralist Society,* p. 96. See also Bert H. Hodges, "Perception, Relativity, and Knowing and Doing the Truth," in *Psychology and the Christian Faith: An Introductory Reader,* ed. Stanton L. Jones (Grand Rapids, Mich.: Baker, 1986), pp. 57-71.

[13]See also Mary Stewart Van Leeuwen, *Gender and Grace: Love, Work and Parenting in a Changing World* (Downers Grove, Ill.: InterVarsity Press, 1990), especially chap. 2.

[14]Wright, *New Testament and the People of God,* p. 140 (his italics).

to the intentions of its creator. Thus "a good fifth act will show a proper final development, not merely a repetition."[15]

The biblical drama is just such an unfinished play, with Christian women and men the ones appointed to live out the last act in a way that shows both continuity and development with regard to the Author's goals. The church as the body of Christ is thus the historical stage for the completion of God's vast cosmic drama. Its first four acts—creation, fall, the story of Israel and the story of Jesus—are recorded in the various books and genres of Scripture, along with many smaller stories and other details in the service of the larger cosmic Story. As the church lives out the fifth act of that Story, it develops appropriate *symbols*—in music, art, liturgy, feasts and so on—as well as ethical *practices* for living justly with each other and the rest of creation. All of these, however imperfectly realized, are meant to recall and build on the first four acts of the biblical drama, and to anticipate the New Creation toward which the fifth act points.

Four Worldview Questions

Story, symbol and practice: Wright notes that these are aspects of *worldviews,* Christian or otherwise. And as I have already noted, no one is without a worldview. Indeed the conviction that "facts" can be completely separated from "values" is part of the modern worldview, according to which the universe, ultimately reducible to matter and energy, "consists of brute facts, and values are only introduced when a subject turns up who has a personal preference."[16] Worldviews also include a set of basic assumptions, often more implicit than explicit, as to how one should answer four ultimate questions: Who are we? Where are we? What's wrong with our world? What's the solution?[17]

To answer the questions *Who are we?* and *Where are we?* adherents of a Christian worldview look to the theme of *creation* within the scriptural record. This record proclaims that men and women have both been made in the im-

---

[15]Ibid., pp. 140-41.
[16]C. Stephen Evans, *Wisdom and Humanness in Psychology: Prospects for a Christian Appoach* (Grand Rapids, Mich.: Baker, 1989), p. 107.
[17]The analysis of worldviews according to story, symbol, praxis and answers to four ultimate questions is developed in Wright, *New Testament and the People of God,* chap. 5. Other treatments of worldview can be found in Ninian Smart, *Worldviews: Cross-Cultural Explorations of Human Belief,* 2nd ed. (New York: Prentice-Hall, 1994); James Sire, *The Universe Next Door: A Basic Worldview Catalog,* 3rd ed. (Downers Grove, Ill.: InterVarsity Press, 1997); Brian J. Walsh and J. Richard Middleton, *The Transforming Vision: Shaping a Christian Worldview* (Downers Grove, Ill.: InterVarsity Press, 1984); and Albert Wolters, *Creation Regained: Biblical Basics for a Reformational World View* (Grand Rapids, Mich.: Eerdmans, 1985).

age of the creator God and given the task of engaging in responsible stewardship and development of the riches of creation. "Humans in general," notes
Wright, "are part of the creator's designed means of looking after his world."[18]
Thus they have the capacity for action, constrained but not overwhelmed by
their biological embodiment and historical location. They are also created for
relationship and community. We humans may not be reflexively good and un-
selfish, but neither are we simply isolated hedonists, as some behaviorists,
economists and evolutionary psychologists contend. And because the image
of God is basic to our humanness, what we share in terms of cognition, personality and purpose is more significant than the variables of ethnicity, class
or gender, and more than the outcome of blind mechanisms like evolutionary
adaptation. As Wright summarizes it, "We are not fundamentally determined
by race, gender, social class, or geographical location; nor are we simply
pawns in a determinist game."[19]

Likewise, the setting of the biblical drama is not a universe reducible to
brute matter, energy and causal laws but one that, in poet Gerard Manley Hopkins's phrase, "is charged with the grandeur of God." The cosmos is not divine
in itself, as pantheists would have us believe, but is the creation of the same
God in whose image humans are made, and is designed to be a welcome and
fitting place for them to carry out their cultural mandate. It is not an alien setting whose material constraints and particularity we need to escape, gnostic
fashion, in order to be saved. It is the *cosmos* of John 3:16, which God "so
loved" along with its inhabitants that he judged it worth redeeming, in spite
of its brokenness from sin. It is a cosmos that we are promised will not disap-
pear but will ultimately be made new by God, along with our own resurrected
bodies.

Thus in reference to the question *What's wrong with our world?* a Christian
worldview rejects any answer that sees physical bodies or the physical world as
inherently evil. It is true that some theologians, influenced by the gender dualism of much Hellenistic thought, have identified men with "spiritual" mind, reason and soul, and women with "fallen" passion and embodiment and hence the
gateway through which sin entered the world.[20] This mistake is matched by
some feminist thinkers, who merely reverse the equation to identify biological
maleness as inherently evil and femaleness as either much less so or even in-

---

[18]Wright, *New Testament and the People of God,* p. 133.
[19]Ibid., p. 132.
[20]Elizabeth A. Johnson, *She Who Is: The Mystery of God in Feminist Theological Discourse* (New
York: Crossroad, 1994), especially chap. 4. See also David F. Noble, *A World Without Women:
The Christian Clerical Culture of Western Science* (New York: Oxford University Press, 1992).

herently good.[21] Against both these distortions, the second act of the biblical drama declares that it is humankind as a whole that rebelled against its Creator by being unwilling to practice freedom within boundaries set by God for the benefit of all.[22]

The distorting results of this rebellion do not negate the goodness of creation or the worth and dignity of all who inhabit it. Still, the fallout of the fall, if we may call it that, is all-pervasive. The entire material world, Paul tells us in a graphic mix of metaphors, "groans in labor pains" and is trapped in "bondage to decay" as a result of it (Rom 8:19-23). And human relations are no less fractured, with sin and injustice marring actions between generations, classes, nations and—of course—the sexes. But to the question *What's the solution?* the biblical drama pointedly rejects the partial answers humans keep trying to impose. We are not to put our trust in princes (or princesses for that matter—Ps 146:2-3) nor in economists, psychotherapists, scientists or political leaders. For despite the good that all these are able to accomplish in their limited spheres of authority, none are able to deal with the deepest root of the problem. For that we need outside help.

What, then, is the solution? "The creator has acted, is acting, and will act within his creation to deal with the weight of evil set up by human rebellion, and to bring his world to the end for which it was made, namely, that it should resonate fully with his own presence and glory. This action . . . is focused upon Jesus and the spirit of the creator."[23] The third and fourth acts of the biblical drama unfold this solution in a complex historical narrative. For centuries, Israel had been telling and retelling the story of creation *(Who are we? Where are we?)* and fall *(What's wrong?)*. They discerned that they had been chosen by the one true God to be a "light to the nations" (Is 42:6; cf. Lk 2:32), and in the first century various Jewish groups—Pharisees, Sadducees, Essenes, nationalist Zealots—competed with each other, each claiming to be the vehicle through which this would happen.

But many of them had forgotten that God's salvation was not meant to be narrowly beneficial to the Jews (or more narrowly to a particular subgroup of them). On the contrary, this was to be the kind of drama in which the original

---

[21]For example, Mary Daly, *Gyn/Ecology: The Metaethics of Radical Feminism* (Boston: Beacon, 1978); Andrea Dworkin, *Our Blood: Prophecies and Discourses on Sexual Politics* (New York: Putnam, 1981); Catharine MacKinnon, *Feminism Unmodified: Disclosures on Life and Law* (Cambridge, Mass.: Harvard University Press, 1987). For a very balanced survey of these and other radical feminist thinkers, see Rosemarie Putnam Tong, *Feminist Thought: A More Comprehensive Introduction*, 2nd ed. (Boulder, Colo.: Westview, 1998), especially chap. 2.

[22]Phyllis Trible, *God and the Rhetoric of Sexuality* (Philadelphia: Fortress, 1978), especially chap. 4.

[23]Wright, *New Testament and the People of God*, p. 133.

cast invites members of the audience, once they have viewed part of the play, to come up and join the actors on stage. The death and resurrection of Jesus were to bring together a worldwide company dedicated to fleshing out the fifth act of the biblical drama until the time when, as C. S. Lewis once put it, the Author walks onto the stage at the end of the play and is recognized by cast and audience alike.[24] It was to be a company where there would be "no longer Jew or Greek, no longer slave or free, no longer male and female" (Gal 3:28). Thus

> the critical thing is that the church, those who worship God in Jesus Christ, should function as a family in which every member is accepted as an equal member, no matter what their social, cultural or moral background. . . . The very existence of a community of love, where before there was mutual suspicion and hatred, is the crucial piece of evidence that . . . God's spirit has been at work.[25]

For Christians this is a mandate to use the power of God's Spirit to achieve right relations among persons and with the rest of creation, while realizing that this task cannot be perfectly fulfilled by still-imperfect human beings. We have been called to set up "pilot plants" demonstrating ways of living that anticipate the full healing that God will eventually bring.[26] And not least important is the mandate to rewrite the story of gender relations in the fifth act of the biblical drama. That cosmic drama, as we have seen, is primarily concerned with persons as generic human beings. But it contains a subplot concerning women and men, and it is to that story within the Story that we now turn.

Principalities, Powers and Gender Stereotypes

Earlier in this chapter I noted in passing that research on gender stereotypes can focus on either their "actual" or "ideal" aspects. Some researchers ask respondents to rate what they think men and women *are* like, while others ask for judgments about what traits (if any) *should* separate the sexes. This is a crucial distinction, since one may conclude—quite accurately—that men on average are more violent than women, or that women are more religious than men, without endorsing either state of affairs. And it is just as important a distinction to make when we study the Bible's account of gender relations. What is norma-

---

[24]C. S. Lewis, *Mere Christianity* (New York: Macmillan, 1943).
[25]N. T. Wright, *What Saint Paul Really Said* (Grand Rapids, Mich.: Eerdmans, 1997), p. 146.
[26]The metaphor is Francis Schaeffer's. See his *The God Who Is There* (Downers Grove, Ill.: InterVarsity Press, 1968).

tive in that account and what is merely descriptive, and in what ways may we have confused the two?[27]

We begin, in the first act of the drama, with the passage quoted at the end of chapter one. "In the image of God he created them; male and female he created them. God blessed them, and God said to them, 'Be fruitful and multiply, and fill the earth and subdue it; and have dominion over the fish of the sea and over the birds of the air and over every living thing that moves upon the earth.'" What is significant here is the shared image of God and the shared cultural mandate. Both man and woman were to exercise *responsible dominion* or stewardship over the rest of creation, and to exercise *responsible community* by forming families together. But though assigned a set of common tasks, they are clearly formed as two sexes, male and female. Is the Genesis statement just a passing recognition of the sexual dimorphism that humans share with other animals? And if not, how are we to understand it as part of the character complication of the biblical drama?

Creation themes are not limited to the Old Testament, and Lesslie Newbigin, in his book *The Gospel in a Pluralist Society,* has traced one such theme in the New Testament that may help us answer this question.[28] There, on almost every page, are words that speak, more or less synonymously, of *powers, authorities, rulers, elements, angelic forces* and *dominions*. While these terms are sometimes used in connection with God's kingdom, more often they are used to refer to *human* rulers or authorities—or, more accurately, to the ambiguous roles, offices or structures that successive human beings have inhabited in history. I believe we can extend Newbigin's biblical analysis to understand manhood and womanhood as being among those ambiguous, universal structures or powers.

Individual rulers may come and go, but "kingship"—or its modern equivalent, such as the office of president or prime minister in a nation—continues as a structure, element or power. Likewise individuals can come and go in a company or a school, but the spirit or elemental authority of the institution endures. Members of a family will live and die, but as any well-trained family therapist can affirm, families as a whole can remain in the grip of certain powers or relational dynamics that keep being played out, for good or ill, from one generation to the next.

So on the one hand we can think of these powers or elements as parts of the

---

[27]See also Miroslav Volf, *Exclusion and Embrace: A Theological Exploration of Identity, Otherness and Reconciliation* (Nashville: Abingdon, 1996), especially chap. 4, which is on gender identity.

[28]Newbigin, *Gospel in a Pluralist Society,* chap. 16. See also Mary Stewart Van Leeuwen, "Principalities, Powers and Gender Relations," *Crux: A Quarterly Journal of Christian Thought and Opinion* 31, no. 3 (1995): 9-16.

creational scaffolding needed for orderly human life. To call them scaffolding is also to affirm that they are not the entire building, whose final shape must surely include other factors, such as the ecological niches people live in and the technical, personal and historical challenges they face. Still, they are the basic forms within which humans are to exercise their stewardship of the earth and of human life. As such they are good creations of God. Moreover, they are "held together" in Christ, as the apostle Paul reminds us when he writes that Jesus "is the image of the invisible God, the firstborn of all creation; for in him all things in heaven and on earth were created, things visible and invisible, whether thrones or dominions or rulers or powers—all things have been created through him and for him. He himself is before all things, and in him all things hold together" (Col 1:15-17).

Thus these elements or powers have a legitimate part to play in the working out of God's kingdom purposes. They are, in the language of Reformed theology, the "creation norms" within which we are called to conduct human life. Can any of us imagine life without structures such as government, family or economic activity? However simple or complex these structures may be, as we will see in a later chapter all cultures and societies have approximations to them. Likewise, sexual complementarity is built into creation as a structure or norm within which persons are to develop the image of God as they engage in responsible stewardship of the earth and create families and communities. That does not mean all women and men must form sexual unions and have children. But it does mean that we cannot adequately serve God, or indeed even be fully human, as half of humankind, male or female. Women and men are written into the biblical drama together, and the drama cannot be completed without their mutual cooperation.

▌ Warped Powers

However, the elements or powers must be understood in light of not just the first but also the second act of the biblical drama. The fall of humankind and the resultant wounding of the rest of creation begin with the primal man and woman's joint refusal to let God be the arbiter of good and evil (Gen 2:9; 2:17; 3:5; 3:22). In wake of this rebellion, their relationship to all the rest of creation is skewed. Work is no longer a naturally satisfying, stewardly activity but often an anxious burden with unpredictable results. Forming families is no longer a smooth and happy progression from sexual attraction to conception to birth and childrearing, but an activity fraught with risk, tension, heartache and ultimately death. And the creational elements or powers, while still good and necessary for human life, become vulnerable to distortion. As Newbigin observes:

> They can come to usurp the place to which they have no right, the place which belongs to Christ and him alone. They can, as we say, become demonic. [Thus] the state power, ordained by God of Romans 13 becomes the beast of Revelation. The Torah, that loving instruction which God gives his people . . . becomes a tyrant from which Christ has to deliver us. Tradition, the handing on of good practice from parent to child, beautifully described in Deuteronomy, becomes an evil power which comes between human beings and the living God.[29]

This biblical list of powers gone wrong is exemplary rather than exhaustive, for it is easy to think of others. *Number,* that element that allows us to measure and quantify (and that Pythagoras claimed to be the irreducible essence of all reality), "can become [an idol] when, as in modern reductionist thinking, it is absolutized and nothing is valued except that which can be measured and quantified."[30] *Money,* a useful and efficient means for facilitating exchange, turns into an idol when we cease to measure human value in terms of real goodness and happiness and measure only in terms of consumer power; hence Jesus' warning about the impossibility of trying to serve both God and Mammon.

Kinship and ethnicity, Newbigin notes, are structures that "play a vital part in the nurturing . . . of authentic humanity," but in South Africa "when this good provision was given an absolute status as part of the order of creation, not subject to Christ, it became the demonic power of Apartheid."[31] *Chance* seems to be a fundamental element of the creation, seen in such processes as the recombination of genes, the random rearrangement of gas molecules, and certain weather patterns. But when we are told that huge differences between rich and poor are the inevitable result of "chance" workings of the market's invisible hand, then "we are no longer responsible to Christ; we are not responsible at all, for economic life has been handed over to the goddess Fortuna"—who was in fact sometimes deliberately set up as an object of worship in times past.[32]

---

[29]Newbigin, *Gospel in a Pluralist Society,* p. 206.
[30]Ibid.
[31]Ibid., p. 207. Indeed it was a distortion of the Calvinist concept of sphere sovereignty that laid the foundation for apartheid in the first place. See Charles Bloomberg, *Christian Nationalism and the Rise of the Afrikaner Broederbond in South Africa, 1918-1948* (Bloomington: Indiana University Press, 1989), and P. J. Strauss, "Abraham Kuyper, Apartheid and Reformed Churches in South Africa in Their Support of Apartheid," *Theological Forum* 23 (March 1995): 4-27.
[32]Newbigin, *Gospel in a Pluralist Society,* pp. 106-7.

Manhood and Womanhood as Powers

How can masculinity and femininity be seen as powers similar to the ones described above? Here let me suggest a slight shift in terminology. By using the terms *manhood* and *womanhood* to refer to examples of what the Bible means by principalities, powers, authorities, elements or forces, I mean to suggest two things that are missing from approaches not based on a Christian worldview. The first, in keeping with the "scaffolding" metaphor, is that manhood and womanhood are neither fixed blueprints for behavior nor arbitrary social constructions, but something in between. It matters that we are embodied male or female, just as it matters that we are born into one family or another, and we cannot become completely human by pretending to ignore either. Gender is never a completely social construction. At the very least it must cooperate with physical and reproductive differences between the sexes as these interact with the settings in which people carry out the cultural mandate. At the same time, these variations in setting mean that just and healthy gender relations may differ in a subsistence hunting and gathering culture as compared to an agricultural one, or in both as compared to an urban industrial society. Indeed within *any* setting healthy gender relations may take different forms at different stages of the life cycle.

But second, in distinguishing manhood and womanhood from masculinity and femininity, I am acknowledging that these powers are at root spiritual, not material.[33] They are not reducible to purely natural processes—to "flesh and blood," as Paul puts it in Ephesians 6. That is why they cannot be completely explained or controlled by the tools of politics, science or human reason. I use the qualifier "not completely" because as a social scientist (and a Calvinist with a high view of the cultural mandate) I have great respect for what God calls humans to discover about the world through the natural and social sciences. But these human tools can take us only so far. Understanding spiritual powers calls for spiritual discernment; and undertaking spiritual warfare when they become distorted requires the weapons of the Spirit. Thus, writes Newbigin,

> the principalities and powers are real. They are invisible and we cannot locate them in space. They do not exist as disembodied entities floating above this world, or lurking within it. They meet us embodied in visible and tangible realities—people, nations and institutions. . . . The language is pictorial, mythological if you like, be-

---

[33]See especially Walter Wink's three-volume work *Naming the Powers: The Language of Power in the New Testament, Unmasking the Powers: The Invisible Powers That Determine Human Existence* and *Engaging the Powers: Discernment and Resistance in a World of Domination* (Minneapolis: Fortress, 1984, 1986, 1992).

cause we have no other language. But [they are] real and are contemporary. They are at the heart of our business as Christians.[34]

Fallen Manhood and Womanhood

How did the powers of manhood and womanhood get warped? Augustine, Aquinas and Luther all claimed that men's rule over women was justified by the fact that Eve supposedly precipitated humankind's fall into sin. But equally careful exegetes of both sexes regard Genesis 3:16—where God says to Eve, "Your desire shall be for your husband, and he shall rule over you"—as descriptive of the tragic consequences of the couple's joint sin and not to be read back into creation. Moreover, this passage suggests that the fallout of the fall may affect men and women differently.

More specifically, postfall man is continually tempted to turn the legitimate, God-imaging *dominion* of Genesis 1:28 into *domination,* and to impose it in illegitimate ways on the earth and on other men but also on woman, his God-mandated partner. In complementary fashion, womanhood as a creational power is warped by the woman's postfall collusion with the man's domination. Her continuing temptation is to turn the creational, God-imaging sociability of Genesis 1:28 into distorted social enmeshment (the fallen "desire" of Gen 3:16) and to use the preservation of existing relationships (however unjust or unhealthy) as a reason not to exercise accountable dominion. It is the temptation to avoid taking personal risks, even to do what is right, if doing so will upset existing relationships, especially those with men.[35]

So durable are these colluding fallen powers that, without using the specific language of the biblical drama, American popular psychologist Laura Schlessinger (herself an Orthodox Jew) has made them chief themes of her books *Ten Stupid Things Women Do to Mess Up Their Lives*[36] and *Ten Stupid Things Men Do to Mess Up Their Lives.*[37] In various chapters she shares case studies of women's "stupid attachment," "stupid devotion" and "stupid subjugation" at different points in the life cycle, and men's corresponding "stupid ambition," "stupid strength" and "stupid independence."

---

[34]Newbigin, *Gospel in a Pluralist Society,* pp. 209-10.
[35]See for example Emil Brunner, *The Divine Imperative: A Study in Christian Ethics* (Philadelphia: Westminster Press, 1947); Gilbert Bilezikian, *Beyond Sex Roles: A Guide for the Study of Female Roles in the Bible* (Grand Rapids, Mich.: Baker, 1985); Judith Plaskow, *Sex, Sin and Grace: Women's Experience and the Theologies of Reinhold Niebuhr and Paul Tillich* (Lanham, Md.: University Press of America, 1980); and Van Leeuwen, *Gender and Grace,* especially chap. 2.
[36]Laura Schlessinger, *Ten Stupid Things Women Do to Mess Up Their Lives* (New York: Random House, 1994).
[37]Laura Schlessinger, *Ten Stupid Things Men Do to Mess Up Their Lives* (New York: HarperCollins, 1997).

It is not that attachment, self-sacrifice and devotion are intrinsically evil in either sex, any more than strength, independence and ambition are. All of them originate in God's image and mandate to fill the earth and subdue it, and neither task could be carried on without them. But if we overascribe these various traits to men or women and endow them with a mystique that empowers or romanticizes one sex more than the other, or creates rigidly separate spheres of activity, then we have allowed the powers of manhood and womanhood to become idols, or "agents of tyranny."[38] What was meant to be mere scaffolding for life risks being turned into the entire building.

Reversing Fallen Gender Relations

In the next chapter I will explore in more detail what the coming of Jesus meant for gender relations in the Mediterranean world into which he was born. I anticipate that discussion by pointing out that to reverse distorted manhood and womanhood, men will often need to be *less* assertive and women *more*. Philip Cary, a philosopher and theologian, put it well when he reminded women that "there is more to biblical morality than the sort of ethic that rebukes our pride and restrains our desires." Women especially need encouragement to start living as God's stewards, heirs and priests, for "there is work to be done—servant's work and healer's work, hard work which nevertheless comes naturally to the heir of God, like fruit ripening on a good tree." But if women need encouragement to *start,* Cary continues, "isn't it time for men to *stop?* Isn't it time for men to acquire a conscience about male prerogatives and use of power? Isn't it time for us to look carefully at the biblical lists of what should *not* be done: hatred, discord, jealousy, fits of rage, [unfettered] ambition, dissension, factions, envy, drunkenness, just to mention a few?"[39]

In the end, Cary rightly concludes, the biblical ethics of *start* and *stop* do not lead to two separate ways of life, for while men may be more prone to the sins of assertiveness and women to those of passivity, we are all quite capable of the full range of character distortion. In the next chapter, as we consider shifting conceptions of masculinity in the Western world and compare them to the trajectory of the biblical drama, we may find ourselves alternately encouraged and disturbed, but in either case possibly led to reconsider some of our own taken-for-granted gender stereotypes.

---

[38]Newbigin, *Gospel in a Pluralist Society,* p. 206.
[39]Cf. Gal 3:19-21. Philip Cary, "Start and Stop: Two Kinds of Ethics," *Daughters of Sarah,* September/October 1989, pp. 8-9 (quotation from p. 9).

3

Masculinity and Honor:
A Mixed Legacy

I<small>N</small> THE EARLY YEARS OF THE twentieth century Otto Weininger, a young friend of Sigmund Freud, wrote a book titled *Sex and Character*. Its main thesis was that all living things combine various proportions of "masculine" and "feminine" elements. Moreover, he argued, the masculine element is honorable, productive and moral while the feminine is shameful, unproductive and amoral. But just as troubling as Weininger's misogyny, given his Jewish background, is the fact that he devoted an entire chapter to denouncing Judaism as feminine and weak, in contrast to the honorable, masculine morality he attributed to Christianity. According to Weininger, whose family had converted to Christianity, Jews and women alike are ruled by sexual passion and emotion and are devoid of true creativity, individuality and self-worth. The Jewish male, he wrote, "is saturated with femininity. The most feminine Aryan is more masculine than the most manly Jew."[1]

It is perhaps unsurprising that Weininger committed suicide at the age of twenty-three, shortly after the publication of *Sex and Character*. Few of us can imagine what it was like to grow up in a society that barred Jews from many occupations, then labeled them "less than men" for laboring under such constraints and resented them for their success in the vocations they were permitted to practice. The distorted powers of gender, ethnicity and tradition, outlined in the last chapter, were hard at work in early-twentieth-century Germany, culminating in World War II and the horror of the Holocaust.[2] And if Weininger actually believed (or even

---

[1]Quoted in Michael S. Kimmel, "Judaism, Masculinity and Feminism," in *Men's Lives,* ed. Michael S. Kimmel and Michael A. Messner, 3rd ed. (Boston: Allyn & Bacon, 1995), pp. 42-44 (quotation from p. 43).

[2]There were, of course, parallel distortions of womanhood in Nazi Germany. See for example Claudia Koonz, *Mothers in the Fatherland: Women, the Family and Nazi Politics* (New York: St. Martin's, 1987).

pretended to, in the interests of self-protection) that masculine honor is associated not just with a certain religion but with some mysterious Aryan essence, then converting to the cultural Christianity of his day may not have been enough to reassure him. In such a no-win situation suicide might tempt many men.

Why was Weininger fixated on a certain kind of masculine "honor," in contrast to the shame or dishonor of being a woman or a womanlike man? What has the concept of male honor meant in the past, and how have Christian ideals supported, adapted or challenged it? I have made that the central question of this chapter because concern for the wrong kind of honor—both in the past and in the present—has been a feature of distorted manhood that has caused great damage to men and women alike. But to set the stage for considering this question, I first need to note some general themes about the cultural construction of masculinity that are illustrated by Weininger's case.

Hegemonic and Other Masculinities

First, masculinity in a given time or place is not necessarily a unitary concept—which is why books, articles and even journal titles in men's studies often contain the plural form *masculinities*.[3] In complex and highly class- or caste-differentiated societies there will develop what sociologists call *hegemonic* and *subordinated* masculinities. *Hegemony* in this context refers to "a social ascendancy achieved in a play of social forces that extends beyond contests of brute power into the organization of private life and cultural processes."[4] More simply, hegemonic masculinity embodies what men in the ruling class aspire to be like and the multiple means by which other groups of men are judged, sorted and "kept in their place."

Weininger's Jewish masculinity was kept subordinate less by random pogroms (though these were always a threat) than by a complex network of legal, cultural and social practices that, when internalized by a given group, are much more efficient as social controls than crude violence. In sociologist Robert Connell's words, "Ascendancy of one group of men over another achieved at the

---

[3]For example, Harry Brod, ed., *The Making of Masculinities: The New Men's Studies* (Boston: Allyn & Unwin, 1987); Michael A. Messner, *Politics of Masculinities: Men in Movements* (Thousand Oaks, Calif.: Sage, 1997); Jacqueline Murray, ed., *Conflicted Identities and Multiple Masculinities: Men in the Medieval West* (New York: Garland, 1999).

[4]Robert W. Connell, *Gender and Power: Society, the Person and Sexual Politics* (Stanford, Calif.: Stanford University Press, 1987), p. 184. See also Kenneth Clatterbaugh, *Contemporary Perspectives on Masculinity: Men, Women and Politics in Modern Society,* 2nd ed. (Boulder, Colo.: Westview, 1997).

point of a gun, or by threat of unemployment, is not [by itself] hegemony. Ascendancy which is embedded in religious doctrine and practice, mass media content, wage structures, the design of housing, welfare/taxation policies and so forth, is."[5] In light of this definition, we can easily think of other examples. For much of American history, especially in the South, black masculinity has been subordinated to the hegemonic white version, but to a lesser degree rural, immigrant and working-class masculinities have been subordinated to urban, upper-class, native-born masculinity as well.

Second, hegemonic masculinity is a cultural ideal that may not correspond very closely even to the lives of the men who seem to enjoy its privileges. But with the help of such things as cultural icons, religious ideology, athletic standards and even fashion norms, it is held up as the goal to which every "real man" should aspire.[6] In societies with little social mobility, those aspirations may be denied realization to all but a select few, but they are still regarded as standards to aim for. Thus in much of nineteenth-century Europe, Jewish men were prohibited from fighting duels, which at that time were part of the culture of honor of hegemonic masculinity. But some of them dreamed of dueling and defeating members of the anti-Semitic establishment, both to erase the stigma of being "less manly" and to move in the same social circles as their adversaries.[7] And in early-twentieth-century America, when finally given a chance to challenge the white heavyweight boxing champion, African American Jack Johnson eagerly climbed into the ring to become what journalists of the time dubbed "the Negroes' Deliverer."[8]

Agency and Change

Third, like the relationship between men and women, the relationship of hegemonic to subordinate masculinities involves mutual dependence and ongoing change. Hegemonic groups—whether based on class, ethnicity, religion or gender—can rarely afford to suppress subordinated groups completely. For one

---

[5]Ibid., p. 184.

[6]On the part played by fashion in the maintenance of hegemonic masculinity, and its counterpart in "emphasized" or "privileged" femininity, see Helen Sterk, "Whatever Happened to the Fig Leaf? Gender Relations and Dress," in Mary Stewart Van Leeuwen, Annelies Knoppers, Margaret L. Koch, Douglas J. Schuurman and Helen M. Sterk, *After Eden: Facing the Challenge of Gender Reconciliation* (Grand Rapids: Eerdmans, 1993), pp. 299-339.

[7]George L. Mosse, *The Image of Man: The Creation of Modern Masculinity* (New York: Oxford University Press, 1996), chap. 2.

[8]Gail Bederman, *Manliness and Civilization: A Cultural History of Gender and Race in the United States, 1880-1917* (Chicago: University of Chicago Press, 1995), chap. 1.

thing, they are usually in a relationship of economic or some other kind of interdependence with them. For another, they are often able to maintain their sense of superior status only by putting up the appearance of a fair contest. Thus, after decades of banning black men from boxing with whites, American sports authorities in 1910 reluctantly allowed Jack Johnson to take on white heavyweight champion Jim Jeffries, popularly known as "The Great White Hope." When Jeffries was decisively trounced by Johnson, it was a bitter pill for white men to swallow (indeed there were postmatch riots in all of the Southern and several Northern states). Even so, Johnson might have been allowed to enjoy his title had he not used his newfound wealth to leverage other perks of hegemonic masculinity, such as marrying a white woman, parading her in expensive clothes before newspaper reporters and moving into a white neighborhood. The result was a concerted campaign by the FBI to convict him of white slavery and prostitution, and eventually he was forced to flee to Cuba, only to return to a jail sentence in the United States in 1920.

Yet Johnson did challenge the system of gender and race relations of his day, at least temporarily. This helped set the stage for the eventual integration of African American men into professional sports, as well as the desegregation of the armed forces, schools and various other institutions. In the words of historian Gail Bederman, "Gender ideology, although coercive, does not preclude human agency. . . . Men and women cannot invent completely new formations of gender, but they can adapt old ones. They can combine and recombine them, exploit the contradictions between them, and work to modify them."[9] Powerful social structures do not completely cancel out human action; indeed they sometimes stimulate people to work successfully for change.

To illustrate this, we might further develop the "canoe" image from chapter one. In a canoe holding several people, all occupants may be paddling diligently, yet they are not strictly equal: the person in the stern, just by virtue of being in the rear "ruddering" position, has more power over the boat's direction. But the hegemonic sternsman cannot push his authority too far, for if the boat is to stay upright and move efficiently, he needs the ongoing cooperation of the crew. As a result temporary changes in position may be negotiated. Occasionally there are even full-blown protests by the crew that may lead to permanent changes of place and authority. Analogous processes are at work during historical shifts within and between various constructions of masculinity.

So far I have noted that masculinity can exist in several versions and that

[9]Ibid., p. 10. See also Annelies Knoppers, "A Critical Theory of Gender Relations," in Van Leeuwen et al., *After Eden*, pp. 225-67.

these are usually arranged hierarchically. The hegemonic masculinity of ruling males is an ideal all men are expected to revere but which few attain, since various social, legal and economic barriers create subordinated masculinities, and even for the hegemonic elite the standards of "true manhood" are multiple and demanding. However, the existing masculinities are in many ways interdependent, and hegemonic masculinity is vulnerable to challenges from below that may lead to a reshuffling of power among the various groups and of accepted definitions of masculinity within them.

With these theoretical concepts in place, we will look at two examples of shifting standards for masculinity, the first recent and the second from the era of the early church. As we do so, male honor and its relationship to Christian ideals will be the central theme.

Honor, Shame and Masculinity

In the provinces of Greece north of Corinth live a sheep-herding people known as the Sarakatsani. The men of this seminomadic group spend the summers grazing their flocks on mountainous slopes several thousand feet above sea level, leaving their families lower down in makeshift huts for days or weeks at a time. In winter they move both families and sheep even farther down to the warmer coastal plains, where they rent grazing land from the permanent inhabitants. The Sarakatsanis' customs and their Greek dialect yield evidence that they have practiced this lifestyle for centuries; indeed some scholars believe they are the direct descendants of the shepherds of preclassical Greece. Yet by confession they are Orthodox Christians, albeit somewhat tenuously attached to the institutional church, having preserved their religious identity even through centuries of Muslim rule during the Ottoman Empire.[10]

By the standards of sedentary Greek villagers, Sarakatsan males, being rough-hewn, unsettled shepherds and largely illiterate, represent a subordinated masculinity. But among themselves—and since they are a tightly kin-bonded culture the Sarakatsani keep very much to themselves—they have their own standards for hegemonic masculinity. The Sarakatsani, observes one of their ethnographers, "are deeply concerned about three things: sheep, children (particularly sons) and honor."[11] What does *honor* mean in this long-

---

[10]J. K. Campbell, *Honour, Family and Patronage: A Study of Institutions and Moral Values in a Greek Mountain Community* (Oxford: Clarendon, 1964).
[11]Ibid., p. 3.

standing rural Mediterranean culture? Answering that question will help us understand both the Greco-Roman context in which the New Testament church emerged and the tensions among cultural, environmental and religious forces in men's lives today.

Among the Sarakatsani personal honor and family honor are tightly inter-twined, as they are in many Mediterranean-area cultures.[12] Both refer to a state of integrity, in the sense of being "untouched" by challenges from unrelated others, ranging from homicide, theft, bodily injury and verbal insults to rape or se-duction of the women in one's family. Moreover, honor is a highly gendered concept, and for Sarakatsan men maintaining it is a very public and active un-dertaking. To be a "real man" requires visible and competitive displays of strength, economic success, self-confidence, practical problem-solving ability, courage and shrewdness. Some of this, we should note, is the predictable result of living in a precarious subsistence-herding economy, in which flocks and graz-ing land must be defended against would-be thieves and intruders.

But masculine *honor* is also contrasted to feminine *shame* in a culture pre-occupied with producing legitimate heirs to carry on the family-based work of herding, milking, and making cheese and wool. "The sexual, reproductive, and working capacities of women belong exclusively to their families, and there is no more certain way of defiling the honor of another family than by seducing one of its women."[13] To ensure that this is unlikely to occur, the lifestyle ideal-ized for Sarakatsan women is almost the inverse of men's. Public activity is strict-ly limited, especially for unmarried adolescent girls, and even when permitted to married women for purposes of household management it includes a prohi-bition on any conversation with unrelated males.

Women's sexual shame requires them to dress with extreme modesty, since even in cases of rape a woman's failure to preserve her chastity places a blot on the family's honor that can never be completely erased. This remains so even if her male relatives kill both her and her attacker. Well before the current wave of feminism, anthropologist J. K. Campbell noted that among the Sarakatsani "the whole burden of the shame of sexual relations is shifted onto the female sex. She is a constant threat to [man's] honor. . . . Since her powers of sexual attraction are [seen to be] of a supernatural order, man in general is unable to resist them."[14]

---

[12]In its contemporary form this theme of Mediterranean male honor has been taken up by pop-ular culture in the many stories about Sicilian Mafia families and their American descendants, such as the *Godfather* movie series and more recently the extremely popular American TV series *The Sopranos*.

[13]Ibid., p. 270.

[14]Ibid., p. 277.

But even women's ideal character profile—fearful, modest, submissive, lacking in resolution—is seen as evidence that God created them the inferior sex, while men's highest traits—courage, pride, shrewdness, success in competition against other men—"provide the ideal virtues of the total community."[15]

Despite the cultural gap separating us from these nomadic, preindustrial shepherds, we should note that modern Western women have labored under a similar double bind: they are enjoined to display stereotypical femininity, while those same feminine traits are used as evidence for their lesser status as mature adults.[16]

Masculine Honor and Christian Ideals

"It is clear," Campbell notes in his study of the Sarakatsani, "that the values of honor are not what they are for any influence of Christian ideals."[17] Indeed the ideals of masculine pride, shrewdness, contempt for and rigid control of women, and competitiveness toward all but a few closely related males do seem quite antithetical to the fruits of the Spirit and the great commandment to love God and neighbor as oneself. Among women in such honor/shame cultures (technically known as *agonistic* or *heroic* cultures), the contradiction is not always so great. Publicly, they must show a shamed reticence that supports the honor of male family members, but within nonpublic spaces, interacting only with each other, women's "invisible" code of honor often stresses honesty, trust, friendship and industriousness.[18] But how do Sarakatsan men reconcile the male code of honor with their Orthodox Christian identity?

The men are evidently aware of the challenge their faith makes to a lifestyle built on male and family honor. One indication is the fact that during Easter week (the most important time in the Orthodox liturgical year, and one of two times annually when all Sarakatsani make confession and take Communion) everyone in the community gives gifts of food to nonrelated—even non-Sarakatsan—neighbors. In addition, each family makes a point of visiting all the Sarakatsan families within easy walking distance. This, notes Campbell, "is probably the only occasion during the year that a man penetrates into the home and

---

[15]Ibid., p. 276.

[16]Inge K. Broverman, Donald M. Broverman, Frank E. Clarkson, Paul S. Rosenkrantz and Susan R. Vogel, "Sex-Role Stereotypes and Clinical Judgments of Mental Health," *Journal of Clinical and Consulting Psychology* 34, no. 1 (1970): 1-7.

[17]Campbell, *Honour, Family and Patronage,* p. 355.

[18]Carolyn Osiek and David L. Balch, *Families in the New Testament World: Households and House Churches* (Louisville, Ky.: Westminster John Knox, 1997), chap. 2.

receives the hospitality of an unrelated shepherd."[19] But even at other times, though there is vocal admiration for the cunning, clannishness and self-aggrandizement demanded by the male code of honor, it is mingled with regret. "If only we could trust one another" is the common mode of expressing this desire for "a more excellent way."[20]

Moreover, in the week before Easter, Lenten fasting extends beyond the group's usual avoidance of meat, fish and dairy products to include avoiding bread and even sexual contact. "For this week, at least, the ancestral sins of sensuality and envy must be suppressed. The community becomes continent and unrelated men behave towards one another with unaccustomed warmth and good will. . . . This yearning for union with other men is always present but it is inevitably inhibited by attitudes of pride and distrust."[21] Significantly, whenever a quarrel leads two men to draw their knives against each other—an event considered of epic importance in heroic cultures—the Sarakatsani observe that "the Devil is dancing in the middle." Campbell concludes that such statements and practices, however infrequent, show that Sarakatsan men realize all is not right in their honor-driven world—"a sentiment that is Christian, not heroic."[22]

The Early Church's Challenge to the Culture of Honor

Sarakatsan men share a Christian heritage with other modern Westerners, though they are very different in their subsistence-herding lifestyle. These contrasting features make them an especially interesting case study in male honor. But masculine honor codes are not restricted to herding cultures, though the demands of such a lifestyle make some of their features more understandable. A code of male honor endures in the American South, where the rate of argument-related homicides among white (but not black) males is higher than in other parts of the country, even when factors such as climate, education, income and gun availability are controlled for.[23] It was a well-defined norm in ancient Greek city-states and among male citizens of the Roman Empire, as

---

[19]Campbell, *Honour, Family and Patronage,* p. 350.

[20]1 Corinthians 12:31—the apostle Paul's introduction to his famous passage on the gifts of faith, hope, and love. See also Cambell, *Honour, Family and Patronage,* p. 329.

[21]Campbell, *Honour, Family and Patronage,* pp. 353, 351.

[22]Ibid., p. 336.

[23]Richard E. Nisbett and Dov Cohen, *Culture of Honor: The Psychology of Violence in the South* (Boulder, Colo.: Westview, 1996). See also Bertram Wyatt-Brown, *Southern Honor* (Oxford: Oxford University Press, 1982).

we will see presently. A similarly heightened concern for public respect is common on the streets of inner-city America, where some young men fight and die over what most of us would regard as quite trivial affronts.[24]

There are, as we might expect, differences among male codes of honor in various times and places. For example, the American version—whether in the South or in the inner cities of the East Coast—seems to emphasize individualism and self-reliance more than those of Mediterranean cultures, both past and present. But there is a core of more or less common features—masculine competition, family and tribal loyalty, disdain for and control of women—that crosses geographic and historical boundaries. And many men, Christians not excluded, will admit to the attractions of male cultures of honor. Such ambivalent attraction may help account for the reluctance of Christian men, noted in the previous chapter, to discuss their fear of being feminized by virtue of being Christian. Psychologists Richard Nisbett and Dov Cohen point out that there is a romantic allure in mythic characters such as the Mafia godfather, the Masai warrior and the Scottish chieftain to which few are completely immune.[25] It even extends to a fascination for men with antisocial personality disorder, such as Hannibal Lecter in Thomas Harris's novel *The Silence of the Lambs,* who commits his crimes with a paranoid concern for his own dignity but a complete absence of remorse or regard for wider social norms.[26] And because even Christian men harbor a mixed attraction to such figures, it will be useful to examine how the early church dealt with the Greco-Roman culture of honor, but also the latter's influence on the church.[27]

The Jews who returned to Palestine after the Babylonian exile and whose

---

[24]Elijah Anderson, "The Code of the Streets," *Atlantic Monthly* 5, no. 5 (1994): 81-94.

[25]Nisbett and Cohen, *Culture of Honor,* p. 94. In Sue Miller's novel *The Distinguished Guest* (New York: Wheeler, 1995) the main character is the aging widow of a man who had been minister of a large Protestant church in Chicago following the civil rights movement of the 1960s. She describes her husband as having been so eager to participate vicariously in the glamour of armed struggle that he allowed armed black activists to store their weapons illegally in his church. In this way, she believed, he was trying to transmute his self-image from bland church bureaucrat to heroic male, regardless of the cost to their marriage.

[26]Persons with antisocial personality disorder were until recently called psychopaths or sociopaths. For a thorough analysis of this syndrome, see Donald W. Black and C. Lindon Larson, *Bad Boys, Bad Men: Confronting Antisocial Personality Disorder* (New York: Oxford University Press, 1999). On pp. 52-53 they describe the case of a convicted murderer who forged a relationship of mutual admiration with author Norman Mailer, whose efforts aided his early release from prison, shortly after which he committed yet another murder.

[27]This analysis draws primarily from Osiek and Balch, *Families in the New Testament World,* and from Don S. Browning, Bonnie J. Miller-McLemore, Pamela D. Couture, K. Brynolf Lyon and Robert M. Franklin, *From Culture Wars to Common Ground: Religion and the American Family Debate* (Louisville, Ky.: Westminster John Knox, 1997), especially chap. 5; and from Jerome H. Neyrey, ed., *The Social World of Luke-Acts: Models for Interpretation* (Peabody, Mass.: Hendrickson, 1991), especially chap. 2 by Bruce J. Malina and Jerome H. Neyrey, "Honor and Shame in Luke-Acts: Pivotal Values of the Mediterranean World," pp. 25-65.

descendants formed the nucleus of the early Mediterranean-area church, were not unlike the Sarakatsani in several ways. Their families were arranged in patriarchal clans, and blood relationships were highly valued, often putting families and clans in tension with each other and with the more inclusive nation of Israel. Family arrangements were patrilocal (the bride moving into or near the groom's household of birth), and marriages tended to take place among people of the same clan, a relational unit larger than the extended family household but smaller than the tribe. From the beginning of the postexilic period, however, most marriages were monogamous, in part because there was a concern to prevent men from divorcing their Hebrew wives in favor of wealthier non-Jewish women from the families that had occupied Israel during the exile.

Living mainly as subsistence herders and farmers, postexilic Jews discerned "that they lived in a world of limited goods for which they needed to compete, and were generally distrustful of other clans, tribes and nations. Such families were political-religious entities, centers of cultic worship, deeply concerned with their own honor."[28] Thus despite differences in religion and their status as a subordinate people in the Roman Empire, first-century Jews shared some features of a gender-based honor/shame ethic with their Greco-Roman neighbors. Developed in Aristotle's *Politics* and *Nicomachean Ethics* and later reinforced by the Roman emperor Augustus, this ethic was summarized by the Stoic writer Arius Didymus as follows: "The man has rule of [the] household by nature, for the deliberative faculty in a woman is inferior, in children it does not yet exist, and in the case of slaves, it is completely absent."[29] Moreover, despite efforts to center Roman men's allegiance on the larger Empire, the honor-based values of hierarchy, binding family loyalty and competition for personal prestige remained very strong.

It was this honor- and bloodline-preoccupied familial structure—whether Jewish or Greco-Roman—that Jesus challenged in the teachings recorded in passages such as Matthew 12:46-49 and Luke 14:25-33. He insisted that allegiance to God's kingdom might divide families and that his true family consisted of those who do the will of God. That Jesus was not trying to subvert marital fidelity and the responsible nurturing of children is made quite clear in other passages in which he preaches against divorce and warns against those who would ignore children or lead them astray. As one group of scholars puts it,

> These passages are not attacks on families in any simple sense, and certainly not attacks on the conjugal couple or the nuclear family. . . . They were, first of all,

---

[28]Browning et al., *From Culture Wars,* p. 133.
[29]Quoted by Osiek and Balch, *Families in the New Testament World,* p. 119.

criticisms of ancient family clans that functioned as religio-political units that inhibited their members from becoming a part of the kingdom that Jesus was proclaiming. . . . The records of the early church present Jesus as wanting families, and individuals within them, to submit their lives to the rule of the kingdom of God rather than to the codes and cults that were the center of family clans. . . . This tension between loyalty to household or clans and loyalty to the kingdom of God has been pervasive throughout Christian history.[30]

A Message
to Men

In the Greco-Roman setting of the early church, patriarchal control of wives, slaves and children was so strong that it was even reflected in household architecture. Where finances permitted, houses were divided into men's and women's quarters, with the latter having less access to the outside world, and even dining took place in sex-segregated fashion.[31] One of the things we need to note about male codes of honor is that to the extent that they project sexual danger, dishonor and license onto women, they will include rules for keeping men's and women's activities rigidly segregated. Women are sequestered as much as possible within the domestic realm, while men control public areas such as the fields, the marketplace, the academy and the political forum. Ironically, the fact that this is economically impossible for poorer people—who need all adults in the fields or the marketplace to support the family—means that there is often more functional gender equality among them than among the wealthy.[32]

The culture in which the early church arose was thus agonistic to the core, presenting a constant challenge for men to keep their own resources—family members, slaves, land, animals—untouched, while at the same time working to decrease other men's honor quotient in favor of their own. As the authors of

---

[30]Browning et al., *From Culture Wars,* p. 134.

[31]Osiek and Balch, *Families in the New Testament World,* chaps. 1-2.

[32]Thus in India, where a certain percentage of village council seats must now be set aside for women and for lower-caste candidates, it is largely the Dalit (formerly known as Untouchable) caste women who have successfully taken seats. This is largely because their history of poverty has required them to be active in the public sphere (at the same time it has been taken as an indicator of the shame of being a lower-caste woman). By contrast, upper-caste women have been so sequestered that they—not to mention their husbands—find the idea of being active in public (let alone campaigning for political office) too "shameful" to their feminine identity to embrace very easily. See Mary Anne Weaver, "Gandhi's Daughters: India's Poorest Women Embark on an Epic Social Experiment," *The New Yorker* 75, no. 41 (2000): 50-61. For a more general discussion see Jean Bethke Elshtain, *Public Man, Private Woman: Women in Social and Political Thought* (Princeton, N.J.: Princeton University Press, 1981).

From Culture Wars to Common Ground observe, "Males could with ease have [sexual] access to female slaves, possibly young boys, or even their neighbor's wife if they were clever enough to go unchallenged. It was a sign of their agency and dominance to enjoy these relations and intrude on the private areas of others."[33] In relation to their own families men adhered to the Aristotelian household code. Slaves were objects of tyranny, because they existed for the benefit of their masters. Fathers ruled as monarchs over their children, supposedly for their benefit. The relationship of husband to wife involved "constitutional aristocracy": women had their own sphere of domestic authority but still required male rule because of their diminished cognitive and governing abilities. While love between husband and wife was not discouraged, it could never be a love between equals, since according to Aristotle the man, being endowed with more excellent virtues, should naturally receive more love and honor from his wife than he was required to give.

It was precisely this arrangement of gender, family and social relations that the New Testament writers challenged with their vision of God's kingdom as a discipleship of equal regard. Matthew's Gospel shows how Jesus reversed men's unilateral divorce privileges, used children as models for faith, and urged his disciples to set aside the habitual quest for prestige and wealth and instead, like slaves, to embrace an attitude of service. As the church described in the book of Acts gathered in people's houses, the usual architectural and social barriers between slaves and masters and between the sexes and generations became irrelevant. The writer of the letter to the Ephesians subverts the culture's heroic preoccupation with war by telling readers to embrace instead "the whole armor of God," including "the breastplate of righteousness . . . the gospel of peace . . . the shield of faith . . . the helmet of salvation and the sword of the Spirit, which is the word of God" (Eph 6:10-17).

Although the apostle Paul still uses the language of husbandly headship, his statement in 1 Corinthians 7 to the effect that wives and husbands have equal authority over each other's body is virtually without precedent in the Greco-Roman world. The same is true of Paul's admonition to men in Ephesians 5 to love their wives "as they do their own bodies"—an unthinkable symmetry in the Aristotelian view of gender relations. In short, in the embryonic church "hierarchy and status [were] replaced by a new equality between husband and wife, rich and poor, and a new respect for childhood."[34]

---

[33]Browning et al., *From Culture Wars*, p. 142.
[34]Ibid., p. 136.

Compromise with the Culture of Honor

Scholars note that the shared leadership that developed in house churches probably spilled over to give Christian women greater freedom in the public sphere
generally.[35] That this was regarded as upsetting to the hegemonic male honor
code can be seen in the stance of compromise taken by various New Testament
writers. Other literature of the period shows Greco-Roman authorities being critical of *any* religious or philosophical group that questioned the total rule of
male householders over slaves, wives and children.[36] Thus for the sake of
spreading the gospel, Paul writes to the Corinthians, Christians should adhere
publicly to the honor- and shame-based norms of their setting. Slaves should
remain slaves, and women should submit to husbands and not be too assertive
in worship settings, despite their equal status in Christ. Christian women should
even remain with non-Christian husbands if the latter are willing. The practical
need for external conformity, Paul writes, is less important than the deeper unity
in Christ shared by all believers (1 Cor 7:17-24).

Paul "hoped to earn Christians protection from outside hostility by advising
them to conform to the public honor codes of the Greco-Roman world. At the
same time he subverted this very world by developing ideas that led Christians
to contradict this code in their private lives."[37] In its subsequent history the
church has continued this ambiguous relationship to male honor codes. Some
Christian groups, as I noted previously, continue to see the New Testament ad-
monitions about women's silence and submissiveness as creation norms hardly
less binding than the Ten Commandments. Other Christians, including me, see
these first-century compromises as the pragmatic response of a young church
striving to perform the final act of the biblical drama by balancing Christian freedom and mutuality between women and men with the norms of a hegemonic
culture committed to neither.

Many subsequent legal changes in gender relations can be seen as cumulative
attempts to eliminate residual aspects of the male honor code. That women can

---

[35]For example, Stephen Barton, "Paul's Sense of Place: An Anthropological Approach to Community Formation in Corinth," *New Testament Studies* 32 (1986): 74. A contemporary analogue
to this process can be found in the house church-centered evangelical and Pentecostal movements in Latin America, where the language of male headship is belied by the functional
equality of men's and women's groups within the congregation and the men's rejection of the
agonistic *machismo* lifestyle. See for example Elizabeth Brusco, *The Reformation of Machismo: Evangelical Conversion and Gender in Colombia* (Austin: University of Texas Press,
1995).

[36]See David Balch, *Let Wives Be Submissive: The Domestic Code in 1 Peter* (Atlanta: Scholars
Press, 1981).

[37]Browning et al., *From Culture Wars*, p. 139.

vote, hold property in their own name after marrying, not have to tolerate being raped by their husbands, and qualify for the custody of children after divorce are things that most of us take for granted as matters of simple justice. But all of these shifts were accompanied by struggle and controversy, with Christians lined up both on the side of change and on the side of male hegemony and female dependence and confinement. Similar tensions are evident in the record of the early church. Nevertheless, we need to see that record for its remarkable contrast to Greco-Roman norms of the time. Christianity "inspired heightened degrees of female equality, a chastened patriarchy, higher levels of male responsibility and servanthood, less of a double standard in sexual ethics, and deeper respect for children." That this was accomplished "with ambivalence, hesitation, compromise and some defensiveness"[38] should not blind us to the radical shift at the heart of the New Testament away from the male culture of honor.

Honor in the Old Testament

But does not the concept of honor (with related terms like *glory, splendor, weight* and *majesty*) appear frequently in the pages of both the Hebrew and Christian Scriptures? This is quite true, so we need to see how its treatment in the Bible differs from the male cultures of honor I have been discussing. I have already noted that subsistence-herding and farming groups may be under pressure to develop gendered codes of honor and shame simply by virtue of the material and economic risks they must face. This will be addressed further in a later chapter when we explore masculinity in other premodern cultures. The Old Testament writers understandably make some concessions to those challenges. Children are to honor parents; Sarah calls her husband, Abraham, "lord"; families are assumed to be patriarchal, with male householders controlling the family's land, animals, servants and offspring, as well as its religious activities.

However, we should regard these practices not as endorsements of some immutable male sexism at the heart of biblical faith but as evidence for its historical and incarnational nature. God calls people to participation in the cosmic drama not by ignoring the survival challenges of their environment in pursuit of a disembodied "spiritual" existence—that idea is a Gnostic heresy—but by gradually pointing them to "a more excellent way."

Seen in this light, the Bible's challenge to the culture of honor is quite striking. To begin with, personal honor in the Hebrew Scriptures is regarded as a

---

[38]Ibid., p. 131.

gift from God, who is the source of all glory and the only appropriate object of worship. It is not something to be earned or lost in competition with others (for example, Ps 8:5; 62:7; 71:21). And though it may sometimes (but by no means always) include the signs of visible wealth and property, honor is best evidenced in obedience to God and in the wisdom, justice and righteousness that build up the life of an entire community. The book of Proverbs warns that fools are not fit for honor (no matter what their pedigree or material assets) and that heeding "a word aptly spoken" is a better index of honor than competing for social status among the powerful (Prov 26:1; 25:2-12).[39] Men who try to build up honor for themselves are roundly denounced by the prophets (for example, Is 1:23; Amos 5:11-12; 8:4-5).

Challenges to the specifically gendered aspects of male honor codes are equally striking. It is tempting to see the Decalogue's prohibition on coveting a neighbor's wife, slave or donkey simply as evidence of the chattel status of women. But in light of prevailing male honor codes it is actually a stern moral challenge. In classic cultures of honor, anything a man can get away with taking from an unrelated male is not only fair game but an addition to his honor quotient. Since honor, like everything else, is seen as a limited resource, it must be built up at someone else's expense. But in the Hebrew Scriptures men are called to a larger sense of community and to reject honor-driven acquisitiveness—by limiting not just their actions but even what they entertain in their thoughts.

It is important to bear in mind that in the earlier scenes of the biblical drama Israel too is a "pilot plant" or work in progress. It is striving to hear God's word for a pastoral-agricultural society whose material survival requires them quite literally to "be fruitful and multiply" while avoiding the sexual and other idolatries of their pagan neighbors. Thus while divorce and polygamy are permitted, they are not seen as ideal and are bluntly repudiated by the prophet Malachi, followed by Jesus and the early church.[40] In addition, the hymn to the capable woman of Proverbs 31 can be seen as a pointed corrective to the more common Near Eastern focus on women mainly as erotic objects. It is arguably "an implicit attack on the ancient (and modern) valuations of women only according to their external beauty and sex appeal."[41] And in contrast to the culture-of-honor prac-

---

[39]See also Raymond C. Van Leeuwen, *The Book of Proverbs: Introduction, Commentary and Reflections,* vol. 5 of *New Interpreters Bible* (Nashville: Abingdon, 1997).

[40]For a treatment of the pertinent passages, including Genesis 1-3 and Malachi 2:10-16, see John J. Collins, "Marriage, Divorce and Family in Second Temple Judaism," in Leo G. Perdue, Joseph Blenkinsopp, John J. Collins and Carol Meyers, *Families in Ancient Israel* (Louisville, Ky.: Westminster John Knox, 1997), pp. 104-62.

[41]Van Leeuwen, *Book of Proverbs,* p. 263.

tice of regarding widows and orphans as being without status due to their loss of a male protector, the law and the prophets regard generous support of both as an indication of true honor. Open-handed hospitality is to be extended even to total strangers, in gratitude for God's deliverance of Israel, "for you were aliens in the land of Egypt" (Ex 23:9; see also, for example, Ex 22:22-23; Deut 10:17-19; Is 1:17; Jer 7:5-7).

Honor in the New Testament

When we come to the Christian Scriptures we find their writers repeatedly turning the prevailing male honor code upside down. This is most clearly shown in the many passages emphasizing Jesus' humiliating death as the vehicle of humans' salvation, and the requirement that Christians not be ashamed to identify with it. As Paul wrote to the Corinthian church, "God chose what is foolish in the world to shame the wise; God chose what is weak in the world to shame the strong; God chose what is low and despised . . . so that no one might boast in the presence of God" (1 Cor 1:27-29; cf. Mk 8:34-38; Rom 1:16-17; Phil 2:5-11; 2 Tim 1:8-13). Moreover, salvation is a matter of personal faith responding to God's grace; unlike human honor, it can neither be inherited—via "blue blood"—nor earned by public performance. Any resulting good works are meant to be tokens of gratitude for that salvation, not showy attempts to build up human (let alone heavenly) honor for the self.

The gospel message also turned upside down the ambiguous speech codes of the male culture of honor. These included giving an oath on one's "word of honor" to reassure outsiders of one's sincerity. Yet given the blood- and status-linked nature of honor, there was no firm requirement to tell the truth to outsiders at all. As New Testament scholars Bruce Malina and Jerome Neyrey point out, in the Mediterranean culture of honor "loyalty was to blood and kin; people were not obligated to tell the truth to everyone, only to kin. . . . The right to truth exists only where respect is due, that is, to the family and superiors, but not necessarily to equals with whom one competes or to inferiors."[42] Over against such practices, Jesus (followed by the apostle James) commands his hearers not to use oaths at all but to "let your word be 'Yes, Yes' or 'No, No'; anything more than this comes from the evil one" (Mt 5:33-37; cf. Jas 5:12).

The New Testament thus overturned the preoccupation with prestige and com-

---

[42]Malina and Neyrey, "Honor and Shame in Luke-Acts," p. 36.

petition at the heart of the male honor code. But it also challenged the practice of equating women's honor mainly with sexual shame, constricted mobility and their reproductive value to the family. This challenge begins with Anna the prophet, widowed as a young woman, who instead of remarrying kept a highly public vigil in the temple in Jerusalem until she identified the infant Jesus as Israel's redeemer in her eighty-fifth year (Lk 2:36-39). It continues with Jesus' relationship to Mary and Martha of Bethany, whom he accepts as honorable single women and encourages to learn from him side by side with the male disciples when he stays at their house (Lk 10:38-41). It is seen in Jesus' public healing of the woman with a longstanding hemorrhage that had made her ritually impure, and in his inclusion of women in his company of itinerant disciples (Mt 9:20-22; Lk 8:1-3).

Paul continues this trajectory by treating marriage as an individual decision and not something binding on every adult, as was the norm in ancient Judaism. His letters clearly indicate that for both sexes there are honorable Christian vocations that do not involve marrying and raising a family. And as the early church continued into the era of post-Constantinian Christendom, the emergence of celibate religious orders enabled many women to reject the demands of families preoccupied with their marriage and reproductive potential and to pursue instead a life dedicated to God and others. Even as aspects of the culture of honor reasserted themselves in the church—for example, during the Crusades—women and men alike used the resources of Christian teaching to carve out lives outside of its confines.[43]

In sum, the New Testament, building on the foundation of the Hebrew Scriptures, takes male honor away from "the court of public opinion and the reputation which that court bestows"[44] and relocates it in persons' relationship to God, the integrity of their character and their acts of unobtrusive service. Moreover, it stresses that the kingdom of God to which both men and women are invited is not a win-or-lose game in which the elevation of one requires the deflation of another. True kingdom-building, said Jesus, works like yeast, expanding the lump of dough rather than keeping it a fixed size. Or like a mustard seed: when planted in the right soil it becomes an ever-growing tree with resources for all that reside in it. At its best, the kingdom of God is a win-win endeavor, in which

---

[43]See for example Anne Carr and Mary Stewart Van Leeuwen, eds., *Religion, Feminism and the Family* (Louisville, Ky.: Westminster John Knox, 1996), particularly the chapters by Robert Sweetman, "Christianity, Women and the Medieval Family" (pp. 127-48), and Merry E. Wiesner, "The Early Modern Period: Religion, the Family and Women's Public Roles" (pp. 149-65). See also Elizabeth Abbott, *A History of Celibacy from Athena to Elizabeth I, Leonardo Da Vinci, Florence Nightingale, Gandhi and Cher* (New York: Scribner, 2000).

[44]Malina and Neyrey, "Honor and Shame in Luke-Acts," p. 36.

the growth of the whole enhances the growth of each person in it, at the same time as persons make their individual contributions and sacrifices for the whole. This is a message of true liberation for men caught up in the never-ending performance demands of male codes of honor, and for women whose performance capacities have been greatly limited by those same codes.

Embodiment and Beyond

In later chapters we will consider other historical themes and variations in masculinity, particularly those that preceded and accompanied two great manifestations of modernity: the rise of sovereign states and the coming of the Industrial Revolution. But in the meantime I am going to shift focus from the bigger worldview-based picture that has provided a Christian foundation for this study of masculinity to the more specialized disciplines of biology, developmental psychology and cultural anthropology. In doing so I will be guided by another important Reformed theological concept: the doctrine of common grace. In lay terms, common grace is the notion that God restrains evil and accomplishes kingdom goals through whomever God pleases to use, even people who may not recognize God's sovereignty. This is so often the case that Reformed theologian and statesman Abraham Kuyper wryly observed a century ago that "the world often does better than expected and the church worse."[45]

The doctrine of common grace follows directly from the Reformed emphasis on God's cultural mandate to subdue and fill the earth and to unfold the rich potential of creation. That mandate was given at creation to humankind as a whole, not just to an isolated cohort of (as yet nonexistent) Christians. And so we should expect to find valid insights about human functioning in any discipline with high standards for its practitioners and a commitment to careful and honest research. Indeed this chapter's analysis of cultures of honor obviously owes much to ongoing work in anthropology, sociology and social psychology. Thus the next three chapters will focus on the constraints that nature and nurture place on sexed and gendered human bodies. At the same time, I will be careful not to succumb to the reductionism of any analysis that denies the possibility of those bodies' coming alive to God. For that, as the Westminster Catechism reminds us, is "the chief end of man"—both generically and gender-specifically.

---

[45]Quoted in G. C. Berkouwer, *Man: The Image of God* (Grand Rapids, Mich.: Eerdmans, 1962), p. 186.

PART TWO

DISCIPLINARY

PERSPECTIVES

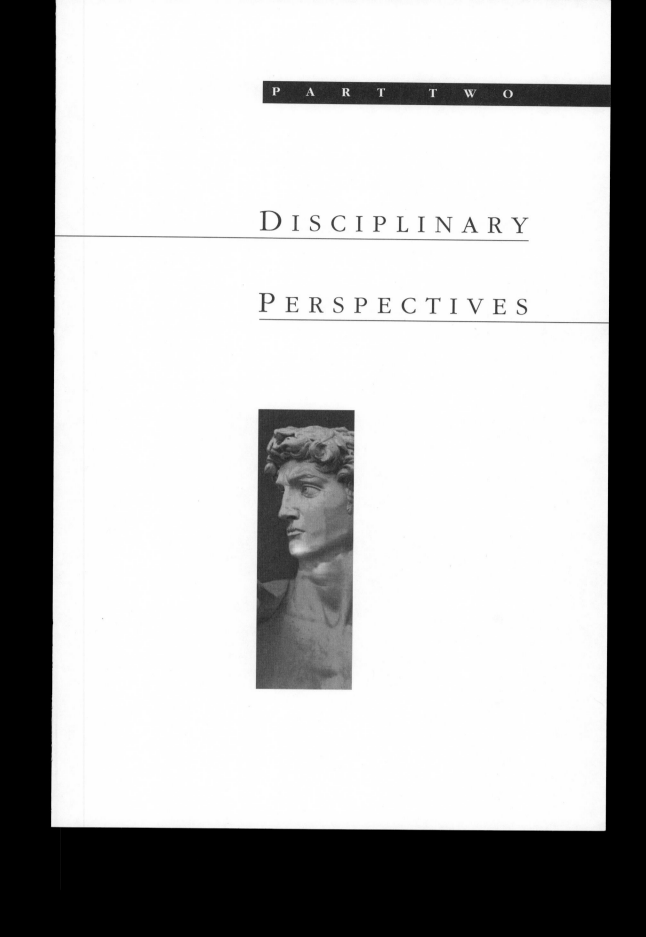

What Can We Learn
from Biology?

Each year I teach a college-level course on the psychology of gender. My students are always fascinated (and sometimes bewildered) by two case studies we examine in the section on the biology of maleness and femaleness. The two young people represented by these cases are very courageous for their willingness to make their stories public, in the hope that others will benefit from the knowledge they have generated. In this chapter I will use their stories to shed light on the complex interaction of nature and nurture in shaping that moving target we call masculinity.

Normally we cannot separate out the effects of biology from those of socialization, since humans carry both together through life. However, occasionally an accident of nature or history allows us to disentangle the two somewhat and thus shed a little more light on the relative importance of each. That is what these two case studies help us to do.

Questionable Chromosomes

The first story concerns a young Spanish track star, María Patiño, who competed during the 1980s at the national and international level, frequently winning the sixty-meter women's hurdles event that was her specialty. Prior to competing at the 1985 World University Games in Japan she had to undergo a test, used only on female athletes, known as a buccal smear. This involved scraping some large cells from the inside of her cheek, staining them, then doing a microscopic check to see if her sex chromosomes showed the XX pattern typical for females or the XY pattern typical for males. At that time the test was used routinely as a way of (supposedly) eliminating unfair competition: sports officials reasoned that male athletes disguised as women would be unmasked at the microbiological level by an examination of their sex chromosomes.

By the standards of the buccal smear test, María Patiño failed to make it as a female, because she was repeatedly shown to have the XY chromosome pattern. That she had breasts, female genitalia and a vagina, as well as a clearly female voice, hair pattern, bone and muscle structure, made no difference. Nor did the fact that she was a self-identified heterosexual female with a boyfriend (who promptly deserted her when her ambiguous sexual status was made public). She was forced to withdraw from competition, and her previous wins as a female athlete were stricken from the record. However, subsequent follow-up examinations showed that her male chromosomes gave her no strength advantage. Indeed her bone and muscle structures were less affected by circulating testosterone than a normal XX female's would be, even though she had normal male-range levels of the hormone! Finally, in 1988, María Patiño was officially recertified as a woman and went on to set a new national record for the indoor hurdles. But although she affirmed that the day of her reinstatement was the happiest of her life, she also said that the intervening psychological trauma "was like being raped."[1]

Sex Reassignment

The second case study concerns a pair of identical twin boys, Bruce and Brian Reimer, born in Manitoba in 1966. At the age of eight months the babies developed a condition known as phimosis, in which the foreskin of the penis begins to seal over at the tip, making urination painful. The problem could easily be remedied by circumcision. However, as baby Bruce was being operated on, a problem in the electrical cauterizing device caused his penis to be burned away beyond repair. Unsure how to handle this tragedy, his distraught young parents were eventually referred to the psychohormonal research unit of Johns Hopkins University in Baltimore, which had been studying and helping families with aberrations of sex chromosomes, hormones and genitalia since the early 1950s.

Previous research by the unit's best-known psychologist, John Money, seemed to show that with appropriate surgery and hormonal therapy, children with ambiguous genitals could be reared as either sex. The crucial qualifiers

---

[1] Alison Carlson, "When Is a Woman Not a Woman?" *Women's Sports and Fitness,* March 1991, pp. 24-29; quotation from p. 29.

were that such reassignment should take place before the critical psychological period for developing gender identity ended at around two years of age and that the child be treated as unambiguously boy or girl by its caretakers thereafter. Given the difficulty at that time of reconstructing a seminormal penis by plastic surgery, the parents after much heart-searching chose surgical reconstruction for Bruce as a passable girl. This meant immediate removal of the testes and surgical resculpting of the external genitals. At puberty, oral estrogen treatment would be added to induce breast development, and once the child was full-grown, "she" would have an artificial vagina constructed. Without functioning ovaries, childbearing would be out of the question, but marriage and adoption would still be entirely possible.

Thus did baby Bruce become baby Brenda, who then proceeded to take part in one of the most famous unplanned experiments in the history of sex research. To begin with, the child had been born as an unambiguous male in all known respects. Furthermore, after the accident and sex reassignment, "she" still had an identical male twin who had not been reassigned. It seemed to be the perfect test for proving the origin of behavioral sex differences. If Brenda, after being dressed, coifed and reared as a girl, arrived at adolescence feeling and acting pretty unambiguously like a girl, while twin Brian was raised as a boy and maintained that gender identity, it would be a strong argument for the power of nurture to override or at least strongly redirect nature.

Six years into the experiment, nurture seemed to have won. According to the parents' reports to the Johns Hopkins clinic, Brenda enjoyed having long hair and wearing dresses, preferred dolls to trucks, played with other girls and happily joined her mother in domestic activities. Any tomboyism in her behavior was judged to be within the normal range for girls. Her brother, meanwhile, had acquired many of the tastes, mannerisms and activities typical of North American boys in the 1970s. The case continued to be cited as affirming the power of nurture to override nature after its description in a 1972 book by Money and another colleague.[2]

However, in the 1980s word began to filter out that Brenda was not adjusting to her female status as smoothly as her doctors had asserted, and in the mid-1990s *Rolling Stone* magazine assigned a reporter, John Colapinto, to investigate. The resulting 1998 article won its author a national journalism award, and with the Reimer family's cooperation it was later expanded into a book. Colapinto reviewed the literature associated with Brenda's case (plus

---

[2]The case study as reported by the clinicians at Johns Hopkins, including follow-up until the boy's eighth year of age, can be found in John Money and Anke A. Ehrhardt, *Man and Woman, Boy and Girl* (Baltimore: Johns Hopkins University Press, 1972), pp. 123-28.

others from the Johns Hopkins archives) and interviewed family members, teachers and other people who had known the twins growing up.[3] In sum, the reports of Brenda's adjustment as a girl had been highly overrated. In fact "she" was even more inclined to physical aggression and rough-and-tumble play than her intact brother. No one outside her immediate family regarded her as anything like an average girl, even by the somewhat relaxed gender-role standards of western Canada.

Neither child had been told the actual story of the accident—only that Brenda's female anatomy was "not quite normal" and hence needed medical intervention. Both twins came to dislike their annual follow-up visits to psychologist Money in Baltimore (especially since, as they reported in adulthood, these interviews were often highly and inappropriately sexualized), and Brenda in particular became less and less cooperative. She resisted taking estrogen as an adolescent and disliked the breasts that developed as a result. She had rarely played well with other girls, yet being officially a "girl" she was not accepted by boys either. As a result her social life was very limited, and her schoolwork suffered constantly. But so great was Money's reputation as psychologist of sex and gender anomalies that local therapists and medical doctors in Winnipeg felt they must continue working to consolidate Brenda's female gender identity.

However, as Brenda approached the age at which an artificial vagina was to be constructed for her, two therapists newly assigned to her case were brave enough to contend that she should be told about her childhood accident and allowed to choose her own future. Although understandably stunned and angry when the truth was revealed to her at age fourteen, Brenda felt mainly relief: she now knew that her "odd" ways were not the result of some inherent moral defect. With the agreement of her parents and doctors, she declined artificial vagina construction at age fourteen, began taking oral testosterone instead of estrogen, and opted for a double mastectomy two years later. Advancements in genital surgery now made possible the reconstruction of a penislike appendage from nerves and skin removed from the inner thigh.

Rather than reclaiming the name Bruce, this restored young man chose the name David, because of its association with the biblical boy who against all odds slew a giant. In his early twenties, now financially self-sufficient with a factory job, David Reimer married a woman with young children from a previous relationship, having told her the entire story of his life.

---

[3]John Colapinto, *As Nature Made Him: The Boy Who Was Raised As a Girl* (New York: Harper-Collins, 2000).

▌ *Genes, Hormones and Male Development*

You can see why the stories of María and Bruce/Brenda/David, told back to back, might well bewilder my students. Both were conceived with the standard male XY pair of sex chromosomes. But María developed bodily and psychologically as a female and was eventually reclassified as one despite her male chromosome pattern. David (as he was later named) was born with the internal and external anatomy of a normal male but because of his accident had his testicles removed and was raised as a girl—unsuccessfully, despite the loss of his main source of testosterone in infancy and the addition of estrogen therapy at the time of puberty.

What's going on here? Why should the same sex-chromosomal pattern lead to two such different results? And what can these unusual cases teach us about the relative power of nature and nurture to influence both behavioral preferences and masculine gender identity—that is, the enduring, internal sense that one is (and wants to be) a male? To answer these questions we will first take a look at how male bodily *structures* develop pre- and postnatally. Then we will examine the *functions* that are associated with that much-studied (and much-maligned) hormone testosterone. In both cases we will see that things are considerably more complex than popular accounts about the origins of masculinity usually tell us.

Perhaps the best place to start is to note that several biological factors must co-operate to produce a male or female whose chromosomes, gonads, hormone ratios, and internal and external sexual anatomy all point in the same direction.[4] We can think of pre- and postnatal sexual development in terms of a road that has several successive forks in it, with one or another direction needing to be taken at each fork. If the preliminary genetic fork points in the male direction, normally all subsequent forks will continue to take that slant. But for a variety of reasons, reversals of direction can occur at any fork. Taken together, the resulting anomalies total only one in several hundred live births (and it is estimated that an even higher proportion are spontaneously miscarried). Nevertheless, their existence has taught us to speak of biological sex in terms of at least six successive stages, or biological road forks, that occur from conception through adult maturation.[5]

---

[4]Two good sources for more technical details about pre- and postnatal male sexual development are Janet Shibley Hyde, *Understanding Human Sexuality,* 5th ed. (New York: McGraw-Hill, 1994), especially chap. 5, and *Scientific American Presents* 10, no. 2 (1999), a special issue titled *Men: The Scientific Truth About Their Work, Play, Health and Passions,* especially the article by Bruce T. Lahn and Karin Jegalian, "The Key to Masculinity," pp. 20-25, and the article by Doreen Kimura, "Sex Differences and the Brain," pp. 26-31.

[5]John Money and Patricia Tucker, *Sexual Signatures: On Being a Man or a Woman* (Boston: Little, Brown, 1975).

In normal fetal development the first fork, occurring right at conception, determines *chromosomal sex* (XY for males or XX for females), which in turn determines the second fork of *gonadal sex* (testes for males or ovaries for females). The gonads then heavily influence the third fork, *hormonal sex,* which refers to the relative amounts of various sex hormones the gonads start producing by about the twelfth week after conception. People commonly speak of "male" hormones (testosterone and other types of androgens) in contrast to "female" ones (such as estrogen and progesterone), but in reality both types of hormones are produced by both the ovaries and testes, both in the fetus and in sexually mature adults. Lesser amounts are also produced by the adrenal glands, located on top of the kidneys in both males and females. As we will see shortly, what is significant for the directionality of the remaining three developmental forks is not the absolute but the *relative* amounts of "male" and "female" hormones available for uptake by the baby's body as its organs continue to differentiate after the twelfth week.

A Tiny Male Chromosome

Much has been learned about the structure and action of the Y chromosome in recent years. It is so small that until the beginning of the twentieth century it had not yet been seen under the microscope. (I find it a nice irony that it was finally spotted in male insect cells by biologist Nettie Stevens of Bryn Mawr, a famous women's college in the Philadelphia suburbs where I live). The Y chromosome harbors very little genetic material compared to the X and to the other twenty-two chromosome pairs that human body cells share. Only twenty-one genes had been identified on it by the late 1990s, of a probable total of no more than forty, in contrast to the many thousands of genes that are present on every other chromosome. Ten of those Y-chromosome genes are concerned with routine "housekeeping" functions in the body's cells, and another ten are involved in sperm production in adult males. One single gene appears to be the "master switch" (known as sex-determining region Y, or SRY) that begins the series of forks resulting in complete male anatomy and physiology.

The importance of SRY became evident when researchers discovered that about one in every twenty thousand individuals is "sex reversed." That is to say, they have an XX chromosomal pattern but are anatomically male, or have an XY chromosomal pattern but are anatomically female.[6] With the help of molec-

---

[6]These sex-reversed individuals are always infertile in adulthood, and it is their infertility that normally brings them for help; before that time many are quite unaware of their condition.

ular analysis, it was shown in the 1980s that the sex chromosomes in many sex-reversed individuals had undergone genetic rearrangements not previously detectable under a microscope. More specifically, in many "XX males" one of the X chromosomes had a tiny piece of Y chromosome abnormally attached to it. By contrast, in many "XY females" the Y chromosome was missing a minute fragment. By 1990 researchers had verified that this fragment contained SRY, the gene that appears to be the factor controlling male development in all mammals, including humans. Its absence alone can send most of the remaining developmental forks in the female direction.[7]

Critical Hormone Ratios

From what I have just said, you might conclude that María Patiño, our first case study, is an example of sex reversal—an XY male whose missing SRY gene pushed her development largely toward becoming a female. But in fact hers was a more complex anomaly, because she was not even anatomically a complete female, though she did not know it until research was done on her in light of her disputed athletic status.[8] So far I have listed the first three forks of normal male fetal development—chromosomal, gonadal and hormonal; it was at the hormonal, not the chromosomal, fork that María Patiño's development took a reverse turn.

That her Y chromosome included the normal SRY "master switch" is confirmed by the fact that she did have testicles—though unknown to anyone, including herself, since they had remained undescended within her pelvis. That these testicles produced testosterone within the normal adult male range was confirmed by hormone analysis of her urine and blood. Why then would she have breasts, a vaginal passage and normal female genitals? Just as mysteriously, why did her normal male levels of testosterone not produce the voice, hair, bone and muscle patterns generally typical of adult males? The answer lies in a genetic anomaly quite different from the absence of SRY on the Y chromosome. This anomaly, known as androgen insensitivity syndrome, or AIS, makes body

---

[7]Lahn and Jegalian, "Key to Masculinity." It should be noted, however, that sex-reversed individuals are infertile, like almost all sex-anomalous persons. (Indeed they would have to be infertile, since they have only the SRY gene and not the ten others from the Y chromosome that have been identified as essential for sperm production.) As noted, it is their infertility as adults that often brings their condition to the attention of researchers.

[8]María Patiño claimed to be completely surprised by her XY chromosomal status when it was revealed to her in her early twenties. Yet lacking ovaries and uterus, she would never have menstruated, so it is difficult to believe that she had no sense that something was amiss. See Carlson, "When Is a Woman Not a Woman?"

cells incapable of being influenced by testosterone, no matter how much is being produced.

Both during fetal development and after puberty, Maria Patiño had testosterone levels in the normal male range. But due to her AIS abnormality, she functionally had *no* testosterone. And once gonadal sex is laid down around the twelfth week of pregnancy, further development of male internal and external structures (including the penis and scrotal sac) requires a high ratio of testosterone as compared to other hormones that are produced in lesser amounts.[9] These structures result from the fourth and fifth forks, which occur between the twelfth and sixteenth weeks of fetal development, and thus allow us to speak of *internal accessory organ sex* and *external genital sex.*

Because María Patiño had no *usable* testosterone, her body responded instead to the small amounts of estrogen produced by males and took the female direction for the fourth and fifth forks. This resulted in a female-type urethra, a short vagina (but no uterus or ovaries) and a female external genital appearance at birth.[10] Finally, when she reached puberty the hidden testes began producing more testosterone, as they normally do in male bodies at the sixth developmental fork, *pubertal hormonal sex.*[11] But again AIS prevented the uptake of testosterone in María's cells, so her secondary sex characteristics became those of an adult woman.

No doubt you can now see why she should never have been classified as a male athlete. Her circulating testosterone gave her no "male" advantage in terms of bone structure or upper-body strength. Indeed normal XX females, whose ovaries produce small amounts of usable testosterone, would have more advantage from that hormone that she did!

▌ Brain and Behavioral Sex: The Controversial Forks

To summarize what Maria Patiño's case shows us, at least six successive developmental forks must be negotiated to form a complete male anatomy and phys-

---

[9]The internal structures that depend on crucial ratios of testosterone for their differentiation in the male direction include the epididymis, the vas deferens and the seminal vesicles—all structures that mediate between the testes and the penis for the production and transport of sperm-bearing semen.

[10]Cases such as Maria Patiño's are called "pseudo-hermaphrodites"; the term "true hermaphrodite" is reserved for those extremely rare cases in which *both* testicular and ovarian tissues are present in the body.

[11]From shortly after birth until just before puberty, both boys and girls produce so few sex hormones that their urine and blood cannot be distinguished on this basis. Childhood thus represents a "latency period" not only as Freud saw it in terms of psychosexual development but hormonally as well.

iology. These include the chromosomal fork (requiring a Y chromosome with the crucial SRY gene), the gonadal fork (resulting in the formation of testes), the hormonal fork (leading to greater "male" than "female" hormonal production by the testes), the internal accessory fork (producing structures that will connect the testes to the penis), the external genital fork (resulting in the formation of the penis and scrotal sac) and finally the pubertal hormonal fork that leads to male secondary sex characteristics.

These six stages—the first five prenatal and the last during puberty—are relatively well understood and uncontroversial, in part because of what has been learned from anomalous cases such as María Patiño's. But when we look at David Reimer's case—and particularly his postnatal psychological development—we enter into much more tendentious scientific turf. For prenatal hormone ratios bathe not only the developing internal and external sex organs but also bathe the developing brain. Is it possible, then, that to the six prenatal forks we need to add a seventh? Perhaps as normal internal and external sexual structures are differentiating in the "male" direction, so too is "brain sex," thus placing limits on the extent to which early childrearing can tilt gender identity in the female direction. Is this the lesson to be learned from David Reimer's case?

Some researchers believe that the answer to that question is yes. Indeed as long ago as the 1960s even John Money acknowledged the possible influence of hormones on behavior, in his exploration of a syndrome that is in many ways the opposite of María Patiño's androgen insensitivity—namely, adrenogenital syndrome, or AGS. In this anomaly an XX female fetus begins to produce abnormally high amounts of androgens from their secondary source, the adrenal cortex, beginning after the ovaries and uterus are laid down prenatally. Hence the subsequent fork for external genital development may result in partially or almost fully masculinized genitals at birth.

Without cortisone therapy to neutralize the continuing production of these adrenal androgens, pubertal development would also result in male secondary sex characteristics.[12] Hence when the syndrome is identified at birth (which it usually is), surgical refeminization of the genitals usually takes place, accompanied soon after by cortisone therapy. However, even though they are XX females raised as girls, these AGS children tend to prefer vigorous outdoor activity, games and competition. They are less interested

---

[12]This syndrome can also occur in XY males, but in either case puberty occurs too early, sometimes around the age of seven or eight years. Hence cortisone therapy is also used in AGS boys, to cancel out the excess adrenal androgens and allow the body to wait until normal testicular testosterone can produce male secondary sex characteristics during the normal pubertal age range.

in self-adornment, domestic games and romance, and while they are as likely to be heterosexual in adulthood as any other female, they tend to postpone marriage in favor of career development.[13] These behaviors seem to
some scientists to provide some evidence for the power of prenatal testosterone to "masculinize" the brain. By contrast (on this theory) even though she
was conceived as an XY male, because María Patiño lacked the capacity to
make use of testosterone in *any* part of her body, her brain—and later her
gender identity and preferred behaviors—quite logically developed in a
more feminine direction. Indeed her brain would be even less "masculinized" than that of a normal female fetus that produces a small amount of usable testosterone—arguably another good reason for supporting her
reclassification as a female in her mid-twenties.[14]

Nature, Nurture or Both?

But if María Patiño, despite her XY chromosomes, was so thoroughly "feminized" by her functional absence of testosterone, it might also be the case that
David Reimer, exposed to normal male amounts of testosterone before birth,
had a brain so normally "masculinized" that even the deprivation of his testicles
after birth could not tilt his gender identity in the female direction. Why then
did his doctors and therapists bet on the power of early gender socialization to
turn him into a girl? The decision was based on earlier studies of children born
with ambiguous genitals. Those studies seemed to show that regardless of genetic sex, such children could grow up comfortably male *or* female, provided
that their genitals had appropriate plastic surgery and provided that consistent
gender socialization began before about age two. In Money's estimation, it was
therefore logical to conclude that a baby boy with ambiguous genitals cased by
an accident could be dealt with in a similar fashion.

Not everyone agreed, despite the fact that the Reimer case became a land-

---

[13]Money and Ehrhardt, *Man and Woman, Boy and Girl,* chap. 1.

[14]Controlled experimental work on small mammals such as rats and guinea pigs yields even
more dramatic behavioral results. Female rat pups administered large doses of testosterone
in utero are more active than normal females, and at sexual maturity they display the
mounting behavior of males rather than the receptive "lordosis" behavior of females. How
much one can generalize these results to the more environmentally flexible brains of humans is a matter of ongoing controversy. See Charles Phoenix, Robert Goy and J. A. Resko,
"Psychosexual Differentiation as a Function of Androgenic Stimulation," in *Reproduction
and Sexual Behavior,* ed. Milton Diamond (Bloomington: Indiana University Press, 1968).
For a more extensive but accessible treatment of these issues, see Deborah Blum, *Sex on
the Brain: The Biological Differences Between Men and Women* (New York: Viking Penguin,
1997).

mark one for the apparent power of nurture to override nature. Neuropsychologist Milton Diamond pointed out repeatedly that children born with ambiguous genitals by definition must have had a more ambiguous mix of hormones than normal during their fetal development—which might account for their more fluid gender identity. He agreed that humans have much greater role flexibility and adaptability than other mammals, whose behavior is more closely tied to their hormonal history and cycles. Nevertheless Diamond continued to be skeptical that a boy such as Bruce/Brenda—an intact male at birth with a presumably standard male hormonal history beforehand—could be resocialized as a girl, with or without genital surgery, no matter how early the process began.

Even follow-up studies of children born with ambiguous genitals had shown that they, like David, did not always accept the gender identity they had been assigned. Diamond and his colleague Keith Sigmundson (who had been one of David Reimer's later therapists) saw this as a strong argument against surgically interfering with babies' ambiguous genitals in order to bolster what parents and others decided should be a child's socialized gender identity. They agreed that such children should be raised either boys or girls, at least in terms of hair length, clothing and name. But any surgical intervention should be delayed until they were old enough to express which gender identity they felt closer to; otherwise they risked being consigned to the private hell that had been David Reimer's for so many years.[15] The best compromise, as Diamond summarized it, would be "to rear the child in a consistent gender, but keep away the knife."[16]

Testosterone and Aggression

Both our case studies suggest that biology in general and hormone ratios in particular may play a role in determining male gender identity—the sense that one is, and

---

[15]Milton Diamond and H. Keith Sigmundson, "Sex Reassignment at Birth: Long-Term Review and Clinical Implications," *Archives of Pediatrics and Adolescent Medicine* 151, no. 3 (1997): 298-304.

[16]Quoted in Colapinto, *As Nature Made Him,* p. 210. Colapinto also discovered that as part of his doctoral requirements, Money had written a monograph in the 1950s reviewing the psychological adjustment of no fewer than 250 "intersexed" people who had received *no* surgical intervention as children. Despite their continuing genital sexual ambiguity, almost all went on to lead productive and satisfied lives. That Money never again referred to this study suggests that by the late 1960s he had become firmly wedded to his socialization hypothesis—and perhaps that when its "ideal test" came along in the form of the identical Reimer twins, he pressed their parents much more than he otherwise would have to surgically reassign the damaged twin as a girl.

wants to be, a male.[17] But this is not the main reason for testosterone's current no-toriety. David Reimer did not just *feel* like a boy in his childhood incarnation as Brenda; he apparently *acted* like a boy—or at least like some boys, some of the time—in the sense of being quick to pick a fight and preferring vigorous activity and object-oriented play over more relational and domestic games. Is this evidence for the capacity of prenatal testosterone to affect not just male gender identity but certain stereotypical male behaviors? And if aggression is one of those behaviors, are we justified, in the face of high levels of male violence, in speaking of "testosterone poisoning" the way that some prefeminist males used to appeal to women's "raging female hormones" as a reason to keep them out of certain jobs?[18]

Clearly this is too simple. It is true that males commit the vast majority of vi-olent crimes and that they are especially likely to do so in the young adult years when, as biologist Robert Sapolsky puts it, they are "swimming in testosterone" relative to earlier and later developmental stages.[19] But if testosterone is the root cause of male violence, how are we to explain why homicide rates by young males are higher in the United States than in other industrialized countries—ten times greater than even in neighboring Canada? Or why the homicide rate by American adolescent *girls*—who average about ten times less testosterone than their brothers—surpasses that of Japanese and Scandivanian *boys?* Other factors must somehow be interacting with nature.[20] Just how does this happen?

To begin with, it is true that normal-range levels of testosterone appear to be necessary to bring out male aggression. This is particularly obvious if we look at extreme cases: compared to castrated males[21]—especially those castrated at a

---

[17]However, it needs to be said that the David Reimer case still has some unanswered questions. For one thing, since "Brenda" and Brian were identical male twins at birth, how does one account for the fact that "Brenda" was always the more aggressive of the two (relatives re-ported that "Brenda" regularly bested her brother in physical fights and protected him in his chronic reluctance to fight with other boys)? In addition—and even more puzzling—despite testicular castration as an infant, Brenda's voice began to deepen rapidly at puberty, and this only partly reversed when she (reluctantly) began to take oral estrogen.

[18]Here as in psychology generally, aggression is defined as any physical or verbal behavior in-tended to hurt or destroy, whether out of hostility to another or as a means to achieve other goals. See Mary Stewart Van Leeuwen, *Gender and Grace: Love, Work and Parenting in a Changing World* (Downers Grove, Ill.: InterVarsity Press, 1990), chap. 5, for further commen-tary on "hormonal stereotypes" of men and women.

[19]Robert M. Sapolsky, *The Trouble with Testosterone, and Other Essays on the Biology of the Hu-man Predicament* (New York: Touchstone, 1997), p. 150.

[20]James Garbarino, *Lost Boys: Why Our Sons Turn Violent and How We Can Save Them* (New York: Free Press, 1999), chap. 1.

[21]Some of this data comes from India, where there are estimated to be anywhere from 50,000 to 500,000 *hijras*—men who voluntarily undergo removal of all or part of their genitals and adopt female dress and some other aspects of female behavior, including dedication to one of the mother goddesses worshiped throughout India. See Serena Nanda, "The Hijras of India: Cultural and Individual Dimensions of an Institutionalized Third Gender Role," in *Culture and Human Sexuality*, ed. David N. Suggs and Andrew W. Miracle (Pacific Grove, Calif.: Brooks/ Cole, 1993), pp. 279-93.

young age—men who are pumped up with four times their normal level of testosterone (athletes on anabolic steroids, for example) are overwhelmingly likely to be the more aggressive ones. (That David Reimer, in his castrated incarnation as Brenda, remained much more aggressive than his intact identical twin was a puzzle to his doctors, as was the deepening of his voice at puberty in the absence of testicular testosterone. Some believe he may have had the male version of AGS—that is, he was getting abnormal amounts of androgens from his adrenal glands.)[22] But such extremes do not tell us much about the everyday world. In that world even the baseline level of testosterone shows considerable variability from man to man. This might lead us to wonder whether, within the normal range of testosterone, men with higher levels tend to be more aggressive.

The answer to that question is yes—but it still does not settle the question of causality. Do aggression levels positively correlate with testosterone levels because testosterone secretion causes aggression? Or could it be the opposite—that aggressive behavior causes testosterone secretion to rise? Although our first impulse might be to assume that testosterone rises precede aggression, the opposite seems to be the case. Sapolsky observes that "when you examine testosterone levels when males are first placed together in a social group, [those] levels predict nothing about who is going to be aggressive. The subsequent behavioral differences drive the hormonal changes, rather than the other way around."[23] So differences among men in normal-range, baseline testosterone levels don't predict later differences in aggressive behavior. Moreover, neither do fluctuations of testosterone within men themselves. "Get a hiccup in testosterone secretion one afternoon," says Sapolsky, "and that's not when the guy goes postal."[24]

Competition and Coparenting

What we do know is that men's testosterone levels generally rise in anticipation of competition and drop when they lose a contest. For example, in studies of male tennis and chess players, the levels in both contestants rise just before a game, then settle down somewhat as it proceeds. At the end of the game, the losing player's testosterone continues to go down while that of the winner rises

---

[22]Colapinto, *As Nature Made Him,* pp. 131-32. This conjecture still does not explain why David's identical male twin would not also have been susceptible to adrenal overproduction of androgens.

[23]Sapolsky, *Trouble with Testosterone,* pp. 151-52.

[24]Ibid., p. 153.

again.[25] And you don't even have to be a player to experience this effect. By taking saliva samples from male soccer fans before and after the Italy-Brazil match in 1994, psychologist James Dabbs and his students found a comparable rise or fall, depending on whether the individual fan's team had won or lost![26]

If hormonal patterns are in part the result of humans' early survival challenges, this makes some sense. Science writer Deborah Blum suggests that "high testosterone is the hormonal equivalent of cockiness. The winner is primed to take on all comers. . . . The loser? The last thing he wants is some pushy little hormone shoving him into battle when he's had no time to recover. Low testosterone is the hormonal equivalent of licking one's wounds."[27]

So a normal-range rise in testosterone level does not produce aggression directly. But the sense of well-being and success that accompanies it may help men to be more ready for aggression if they believe a situation demands it. The crucial qualifier here is the matter of belief. Researchers do find high levels of testosterone among prisoners convicted of violent crimes, but they find similar levels just as often among successful, law-abiding men. And in either group, the chosen activity is more likely to be affecting testosterone secretion than the reverse. The self-confidence and readiness to take risks that seem to go with a rise in testosterone may account for why one boy, attending an all-male prep school in my neighborhood, called it the "cool hormone."[28] But that rise clearly does not have to result in criminal behavior and murderous anger. As Blum puts it, "There are many ways to channel a pushy and competitive personality."[29]

Interestingly, in both the tennis and chess studies, if the winner of the match viewed his victory as the result of luck rather than skill, his testosterone level

---

[25]Political columnist Charles Krauthammer, writing about his own passion for chess, recounts that Soviet-era dissident Natan Sharansky played chess in his head while confined to prison in the gulag. It not only kept him sane, Sharansky noted, but had the added benefit of providing him with a lift. "I always won," he recalls cheerfully. See Krauthammer, "Drinking Aftershave: A Confession," *Time* 155, no. 11 (2000): 102.

[26]See James McBride Dabbs, *Heroes, Rogues and Lovers: Testosterone and Behavior* (New York: McGraw-Hill, 2000), chap. 4.

[27]Blum, *Sex on the Brain*, p. 168. The authors of the study on testosterone levels in football fans also speculated—and it is only speculation—that the "hormonal cockiness" of winning-team fans may help explain their temptation (too often acted out) to trash the losing team's goalposts and other symbolic spaces, such as pubs and streets.

[28]See Michael Sokolove, "What Men Are Made Of: Helping Boys Find New Paths to Manhood," *Philadelphia Inquirer Magazine,* June 8, 1997, pp. 12-16, 30; quotation from p. 15.

[29]Blum, *Sex on the Brain*, p. 176. She further notes that "aggressive hockey players tend to be high in testosterone; so do virtuoso criminal lawyers. Ministers, interestingly, tend to have fairly low levels" (p. 176). Her point is that value choices influence how testosterone is managed vocationally. But since such studies are based on purely correlational data, we have to allow for the possibility that those very vocational activities may tend the men who have chosen them toward elevated or lowered testosterone!

did *not* rise afterward. And this too makes sense, Blum concludes. "If you were an early human, battling it out in some ancient forest, and you won, say, only because your opponent fell over a rock, you might not want to challenge the rest of the tribe."[30] A later chapter will explore in more detail the pros and cons of such appeals to evolutionary psychology. But for now, the empirical (as opposed to the speculative) point emerging from these studies is that there is a complex feedback loop between thought processes and hormones. Although they cannot reliably predict aggression, testosterone levels may somehow nuance how men think and feel. But more important, how men think, feel and behave clearly affects their testosterone levels.[31]

Complex feedback loops involving testosterone show up in other areas of life too. A later chapter will look more specifically at its role in sexual desire and activity. But testosterone levels also predict and respond to the quality of one's marital and family life. A 1993 study found that high-testosterone men (however they got that way) were less likely to be married, and when they did marry were far more likely to be divorced, often because they had a pattern of being unfaithful or abusive to their wives. In addition, the same study found that on average, single men had higher testosterone levels than men who were contentedly married, and when those married men became fathers they tended to experience a further decrease, though again staying within the normal range.[32]

For what it's worth (and we must generalize only cautiously from other species to humans), this process plays out in spades among birds. Testosterone secretion is the most flexible among monogamous species whose males share parental care, decreasing most during the times when chicks are in the nest. By contrast, the males of polygamous bird species have testosterone levels with both a higher baseline and less responsiveness to the presence of others. Since testosterone level is a better predictor of aggression in birds than in people, Blum speculates that "a male bird that takes no role in raising young can be consistently more aggressive. But a dad that is crucial to the survival of his offspring can't be so edgy that he's dangerous to them. . . . What he needs is a system that will tend towards calm, except in times of danger or instability. Then a jolt of testosterone could be

---

[30]Ibid., pp. 171-72.

[31]But here again it needs to be repeated that within and even well beyond normal ranges, testosterone shifts have no power to predict aggression. The brain apparently cannot distinguish among shifts anywhere from about 20 percent to 200 percent of normal average levels. This is technically known as a hormonal "permissive effect" (see Sapolsky, *Trouble with Testosterone,* chap. 11).

[32]By contrast, as the level of conflict and instability rises in a marriage, so do testosterone levels in husbands—but the direction of causality is still uncertain. See Alan Booth and James M. Dabbs Jr., "Testosterone and Men's Marriages," *Social Forces* 72, no. 2 (1993): 463-77.

very useful."[33] Regardless of testosterone's role in birds, what's intriguing in the case of humans is the apparent feedback loop between men's willing assumption of nurturing responsibilities and the modest drop in testosterone level.

A Common
Legacy

This examination of testosterone, complex though that hormone's activity is, has actually been rather limited. For one thing, testosterone is only one among several androgens (and I haven't discussed the others) even though it may be the most important one in terms of its role over men's life span. In addition, male brains can convert testosterone into estradiol, which is the chief form of estrogen, and researchers are still trying to figure out when and why this occurs. All this serves to underline a point made early in this chapter: we have mistakenly labeled certain hormones male or female when in fact they really belong to the entire human species.[34]

This might lead us to wonder whether testosterone plays a role in women's emotions and behavior, even though its usual secretion is only about a tenth of that in men. There's some evidence that women athletes on high doses of synthetic testosterone can get grouchy and obnoxious, though they are not as likely as pumped-up men to get physically aggressive. But as with men, such findings don't tell us much about the average woman who isn't obsessed with muscle building. In this realm, the few studies correlating women's attitudes and lifestyles with their testosterone levels have found it difficult to disentangle cause and effect. Women in higher-status jobs (as our culture defines them, in terms of education, power and income) tend to have higher testosterone levels within the normal female range than those in more traditional women's roles such as domestic, clerical and sales-clerking jobs. But lower-status jobs are more stressful, no matter who occupies them, and high levels of stress can lower testosterone secretion, so it's hard to know what is causing what in these studies.[35]

---

[33]Blum, *Sex on the Brain*, p. 173. By contrast she notes (p. 117) that male birds with higher and steadier levels of testosterone are "dedicated polygamists." And among those with "screamingly high testosterone levels" a single "super-macho, alpha-type male may account for 90 percent of the young in a single breeding season. But he's so stunningly successful only for a very brief time, a true live-fast-and-die profile. Most of the 'screamers' last about two breeding seasons tops, before the hatred of other males runs them off, or they drop dead of infection (since high testosterone can shred the immune system), or, possibly, of exhaustion."

[34]The biochemical conversion of hormones from so-called male to female ones is actually fairly uncomplicated, as all are derivatives of cholesterol. In Blum's words, "All the steroid hormones are stepchildren of cholesterol, an indirect reminder that for all we worry about having too much of that stuff, we can't do without it" (*Sex on the Brain*, p. 160).

[35]Francis Purifoy and Lambert Koopmans, "Androstenedione, Testosterone and Free Testosterone Concentration in Women of Various Occupations," *Social Biology* 26 (1980): 179-88.

To complicate things further, some researchers suspect that women's testosterone levels are not influenced by competitive scenarios in the same way men's are—elevated less by winning but at the same time not decreased as much by losing. If so, women might often be the emotionally steadier sex in a high-stakes situation. Others have found (specifically in a study of women basketball players) that it is not their testosterone that responds to competitive challenge but cortisol, another steroid hormone that is made in the adrenal glands. The best women players became calm and focused before a game, correlating with a drop in cortisol—the same hormone that rises in young children when they are left in a new situation (such as the first day of kindergarten) and drops as they adapt. The authors of this study speculate—and at this point it is only speculation—that this sex difference reflects the fact that women, who tend to be more inclined to nurturing behavior, require a different adaptation from men in order to get into the competitive mode. Once there, they practice largely the same skills as men—but hormonally they may have gotten there by a somewhat different route.[36]

Our Choices Matter

Our brief tour through the complexities of male biological development has shown that as human beings we are indeed "fearfully and wonderfully made" (Ps 139:14). Our bodies—male, female or very occasionally ambiguous—do set certain limits as over a lifetime we develop the image of God in ourselves. But we have also seen that those limits are not as causally constraining as many popular accounts would have us believe. Blum summarizes the situation well when she asserts that "it is not insulting to either sex to suggest that hormones influence our reactions, especially if how we behave—even how we choose to behave—can influence the hormones. . . . As testosterone's variable nature should remind us, people can change."[37]

We have seen, for example, that competitive activity in males is a two-edged sword: winning may produce a testosterone-mediated sense of confidence and well-being, but losing, even vicariously, can have quite the opposite effect. To this I should add that for all its immediate benefits, there is evidence that when testosterone levels remain unusually high they have the effect of suppressing

---

[36]Alan Booth and James M. Dabbs Jr., "Cortisol, Testosterone and Competition Among Women," unpublished manuscript, Pennsylvania State University, 1996. See also Blum, *Sex on the Brain,* chap. 6.

[37]Blum, *Sex on the Brain,* p. 188.

the immune system. And as I have also noted, the testosterone rise that comes from engaging in strenuous activities can reverse rather dramatically if stress levels get too high. This is one of the unhappy ironies not only of bodybuilding but of other stressful lifestyles undertaken by many men, such as basic army training. In both cases, pushing the body *too* hard can be counterproductive, forcing testosterone levels to an abnormal low and leading to a muscle loss that then tempts men to take steroids, in spite of the long-term health hazards involved in doing so. Our choices affect our bodies at least as much as our bodies affect our choices.[38]

It is possible that there is a connection between the complexities of testosterone and the male cultures of honor that we encountered in the previous chapter. Such cultures generally require a continuous stance of competition between males, with little sense that there might also be times when cooperation would yield gains for everyone. Yet the euphoria of high-stakes competition is a decidedly mixed blessing, as the Sarakatsani shepherds recognize every year during Lent, when they are temporarily given a liturgical reprieve from its demands.

This observation is not meant to malign competitiveness per se; few people of either sex, I'm sure, would want to see a permanent moratorium placed on chess games or athletic matches. But we also saw in our study of the New Testament's challenge to the culture of honor that the gospel calls men to submit their competitive impulses to a larger kingdom vision. "Athletes exercise self-control in all things," Paul wrote to the young Corinthian church. "They do it to receive a perishable wreath, but we an imperishable one" (1 Cor 9:25). How we understand that kingdom vision, and its mandate for males and females, will have a great deal of influence on how we socialize our children, including our sons.

Here too we have a steady accumulation of social science research to help us along. To this body of literature, with a particular emphasis on the development of boys, we turn in the following chapter.

---

[38]Alan Booth, Allan C. Mazur and James M. Dabbs Jr., "Endogenous Testosterone and Competition: the Effect on Fasting," *Steroids* 58 (August 1993): 348-50.

What Can We Learn from Developmental Psychology?

In THE SECOND OR THIRD CENTURY A.D. a lengthy epistle was written by an unknown person to a man named Diognetus, possibly a Roman citizen. It included a discussion of pagan and Jewish religions, a summary of the Christian faith and a description of the lifestyle led by early Christians. In dealing with the last of these, the writer noted that "the distinction between Christians and other men is neither in country nor language nor customs. For they do not dwell in cities in some place of their own, nor do they use any strange variety of dialect, nor practice an extraordinary life. Yet," the author continues,

> while living in Greek and barbarian cities, according as each has obtained his lot, and following the local customs, they show forth the wonderful and confessedly strange character of the constitution of their citizenship. They dwell in their own fatherlands, but as if sojourners in them; they share all things as citizens, and suffer all things as strangers. . . . They marry as all men do, they bear children, but they do not expose their offspring. . . . They obey the appointed laws, and they surpass the laws in their own lives.[1]

Then as now, Christians struggled to be in the world but not of it as they lived out the claims of the gospel. Not only did they not expose their own children; at times they raised biologically unrelated infants who had been abandoned on the orders of Roman fathers with absolute power over their children's lives. This abiding concern for children was apparently so unusual in the classical Mediterranean culture of honor, with its elevation of male citizens and their public lives over the concerns of women, children and slaves, that it merited

---

[1]*Epistle to Diognetus,* in *The Apostolic Fathers,* 2nd ed., trans. J. B. Lightfoot and J. R. Harmer, rev. Michael W. Holmes (Grand Rapids, Mich.: Baker, 1989), pp. 291-306; quotation from p. 299.

special mention in this letter to an elite man of the Empire.

Now, nearly two millennia later, Christians share with others the challenge of raising children in a world beset by rapid social, intellectual and technological changes. Not least of these is the long-delayed acknowledgment by developmental psychologists that parenting is more than mothering and thus that fatherhood is worthy of study. Another is the recognition that boys as well as girls bear scars from being raised in a society that still promotes a male culture of honor in some ways like the one in which Diognetus lived. We may not literally expose infants to the physical elements anymore, as happened to some children in ancient Rome. But we have other ways of traumatizing boys in the process of introducing them to accepted standards of masculinity.

In this chapter I offer some insights for adults who care about developing the image of God and concern for others in children of both sexes, and boys in particular. I will concentrate on children's development in industrial and (increasingly) postindustrial societies. The next chapter will focus on what can be learned from crosscultural researchers studying groups of people who, by virtue of their lifestyle, are still classified as preindustrial.

Gender Asymmetry

Some years ago a researcher was exploring career aspirations and the way these interacted with children's gender stereotypes. Her method was to ask each of her young respondents what they would do in adulthood if they grew up as a member of the other sex. One little girl confided that her ambition was to "fly like a bird" but that this would probably not happen because she wasn't a boy. And a boy in the same study concluded that if he were a girl he would just grow up "to be nothing."[2]

In a more recent study in Michigan, elementary school children were asked: "If you woke up tomorrow and discovered you were the other gender, how would your life be different?'" Most of the girls stated that they'd rather remain female but readily listed positive features of being a boy. ("I could shoot hoops after breakfast," "I'd hunt and fish with my dad," "I'd be picked in gym to demonstrate how to play a game.") But the majority of boys were horrified by even the imaginary prospect of becoming girls. Some envisaged taking their life as a result. ("I would stab myself in the heart fifty times with a dull butter knife," "I'd

---

[2]Marion N. Libby and Elizabeth Aries, "Gender Differences in Preschool Children's Narrative Fantasy," *Psychology of Women Quarterly* 13 (1989): 293-306. See also Hilary M. Lips, *Sex and Gender: An Introduction,* 3rd ed. (Mountain View, Calif.: Mayfield, 1997), chap. 10.

take a whole bottle of aspirin.") Others portrayed what they saw as the draw-backs—but almost never any advantages—of being female. ("I couldn't play any good sports," "I'd have to stay home," "I'd be weak, a pansy, a wimp.")[3]

Studies like these underline an important point about boys and girls growing up in our culture: their socialization as children is not merely complementary but often *asymmetrical.* That is to say, the amount, the timing and the results of social-izing influences directed at boys and girls are not necessarily the same at all ages. For example, in the above-mentioned studies, preadolescent boys and girls both agreed that boys have it better in terms of the kinds of activities they can engage in. As another example, North American parents on average still invest more re-sources (such as teaching and sports equipment, private schooling, special lessons or summer camp experiences) on behalf of their sons than of their daughters.[4]

However, the asymmetry does not always favor boys. It is true that females continue to struggle with various kinds of discrimination, both while growing up and as adults. But at least in the years prior to adolescence girls do not need to be as careful as boys to avoid the clothing, toys and games normally associ-ated with the other sex.[5] Close to two-thirds of U.S. women report that they were tomboys as children, and young tomboys, far from being ostracized, are usually popular with peers of both sexes. Boys, on the other hand, are more narrowly socialized into the masculine script, and the social costs of deviating from it are much higher in terms of peer rejection and adult disapproval.

One result of this male gender-role rigidity was described by *Generation X* author Douglas Coupland, who is also a trained artist. "My first day of art school," he recalls wryly, "was the first day in my life I could pick up an object and say 'That's so beautiful' without getting beaten up."[6] In the same vein, ther-apists Dan Kindlon and Michael Thompson recall a fifty-two-year-old male pa-tient who described his hurt and bewilderment when, on graduating at the top of his class at an elite university, he told his parents he wanted to apply his gifts to teaching. His father's only response was "You mean after all that, you want to be a teacher? Why can't you get a *man's* job?"[7]

---

[3]Office for Sex Equity in Education, "Influence of Gender Role Socialization upon the Percep-tions of Children." (Lansing: Michigan Department of Education, 1989).

[4]Carole R. Beal, *Boys and Girls: The Development of Gender Roles* (New York: McGraw-Hill, 1994), chaps. 1-2.

[5]This changes rather drastically in adolescence, however. See for example Mary Pipher, *Reviv-ing Ophelia: Saving the Lives of Adolescent Girls* (New York: Grosset/Putnam, 1994), and Jill McLean Taylor, Carol Gilligan and Amy M. Sullivan, *Between Voice and Silence: Women and Girls, Race and Relationship* (Cambridge, Mass.: Harvard University Press, 1995).

[6]Quoted in Fred Bernstein, "Blame Canada: Bottling Gen X Style," *New York Times,* March 30, 2000, pp. F1, F8; quotation from p. F8.

[7]Dan Kindlon and Michael Thompson, *Raising Cain: Protecting the Emotional Life of Boys* (New York: Ballantine, 1999), p. 112.

Unlike these two men, most boys choose not to pay the price of deviating very far from the requirements of cultural masculinity. In the Michigan study, you will notice that the boys saw the idea of waking up female as not just inconvenient or disadvantageous but a source of panic and even pollution.[8] In part, as I have noted, this is because our society promotes a male culture of honor not unlike ones we met in an earlier chapter. In such cultures hegemonic masculinity, though accompanied by power and status, is hard-won, precarious and subject to escalating performance demands. Consequently it is something many males (both younger and older) fear losing. As we will see shortly, this fear begins early in life and leads most boys to base the security of their gender identity as much—if not more—on avoiding the feminine as on embracing the masculine.[9]

But we should also note that children acquire notions about gender even when adults bend over backwards to make sure this doesn't happen. Fifty years ago, under the sway of Freud's dictum that anatomy is destiny, parents worried if their children didn't conform to traditional notions of what males and females should be like. Now, a few decades after the advent of second-wave feminism, some parents are upset—or at least bewildered—when their children *do* adhere, often quite extremely, to the gender stereotypes their parents were so careful not to teach them. A five-year-old boy whose mother is a practicing physician nonetheless insists that only men can be doctors. A four-year-old girl asserts that it is her mother who vacuums the carpets, even though this task is routinely done by her father. A three-year-old girl is dressed in blue pajamas by her mother one night, only to sneak out of bed and exchange them for her pink pair once her mother has left the room. How do little girls and boys acquire such ideas and behaviors? In part through patterns

---

[8]On boys' treatment of girls and girl-associated things as polluting, see for example Barrie Thorne, "Girls and Boys Together . . . but Mostly Apart: Gender Arrangements in Elementary Schools," in *The Gender and Psychology Reader*, ed. Blythe McVicker Clinchy and Julie K. Norem (New York: New York University Press, 1998), pp. 667-83. Boys' almost panicked resistance to engaging in "girl play" persists even when they are encouraged by influential adults to do so. In one study, preschool children of both sexes were able to select a small toy as a prize, and most selected a gender-typical one. Then the child's favorite teacher was recruited to come and see the toy, but then to give several strong reasons for trading it in for a gender-atypical one. Both boys and girls resisted this suggestion, but while most girls were content just to say that they preferred the girls' toy, the boys appeared extremely uncomfortable, argued actively with the (favorite) teacher, and even tried to discredit her advice by saying that she must be ill or overworked or she would never have urged them to swap a truck for a necklace! See Dorthea M Ross and Sheila A. Ross, "Resistance by Preschool Boys to Sex-Inappropriate Behavior," *Journal of Educational Psychology* 63 (1972): 342-46.

[9]For an earlier analysis of this tendency, see Deborah S. David and Robert Brannon, *The Forty-nine Percent Majority: The Male Sex Role* (Reading, Mass.: Addison-Wesley, 1976). For a variety of more recent reflections, see Larry May, Robert Strickwerda and Patrick D. Hopkins, eds., *Rethinking Masculinity: Philosophical Explorations in Light of Feminism,* 2nd ed. (Lanham, Md.: Rowman and Littlefield, 1996).

of role modeling and reinforcement by parents and others, but also through the children's own attempts to make cognitive sense of their social world. Let's look at each of these processes in turn.[10]

Raising Cain

The asymmetry of boys' and girls' paths begins with an obvious but often underappreciated fact: in industrialized societies, from infancy through at least middle childhood, most boys have much less access than girls to same-sex role models. Girls are literally surrounded by adult women from birth on, since most infants are cared for by mothers or other female caretakers, and most preschool and elementary school teachers are women. As a result girls tend to feel reasonably confident that they are "getting it right" in terms of learning their gender script, though sooner or later they also learn that in many ways it is a culturally devalued script relative to boys'.

But with asymmetrical caretaking boys get double messages as well. Most female teachers and caretakers want boys to be culturally masculine but also self-controlled and deferential. On the other hand, their fathers and male peers are likely to encourage self-assertion, independence and vigorous play. Thus as psychologist Carole Beal puts it, "the little boy is faced with figuring out whether he should be like Cary Grant or Hulk Hogan."[11] And in contrast to his sister, he has fewer same-sex adults around to reassure him that he's getting his gender script right—or that perhaps it's not such a big deal even if he isn't. Small wonder that panic and fears of pollution surface at the least suggestion of being girlish. The boy is supposedly getting ready to join the more powerful half of the adult human race, but for much of his childhood he lacks close, regular contact with male mentors who can help him on this path or encourage him to seek an alternate one.[12]

Independence training for boys starts young. From the first few weeks of life on, mothers on average look at, hold, touch and cuddle daughters more than sons—even though boys actually startle, cry and fuss more readily than

---

[10]See also Eleanor E. Maccoby, *The Two Sexes: Growing Up Apart, Coming Together* (Cambridge, Mass.: Harvard University Press, 1998).

[11]Beal, *Boys and Girls,* p. 10.

[12]For a detailed theoretical treatment of this asymmetry and its consequences for both sexes, see Nancy Chodorow, *The Reproduction of Mothering: Psychoanalysis and the Sociology of Gender* (Berkeley: University of California Press, 1978). For an applied, clinical perspective, see for example Frank Pittman, *Man Enough: Fathers, Sons and the Search for Masculinity* (New York: Putnam, 1993).

girls during the first months of life.[13] But mothers also cut boys more slack when they resist attempts to control them, in effect allowing sons to set the style of interaction, on the assumption that boys should learn to assert themselves. With girls, by contrast, mothers usually try to create and sustain a more mutual pattern of exchange. We should note that the direction of causality here may run both ways: infant boys do appear to be more stressed than girls by intense social interaction, so in some ways they may be training mothers to keep their distance. But either way it is a mixed blessing: Children's later capacity to express healthy independence depends on large doses of responsive caregiving which help the child feel that the world is predictable and thus worthy of progressively greater risk-taking, both physically and emotionally. At the same time, the early concession to boys' self-assertiveness, if not combined with reasonable limits, often means that as they get older they are treated (using terms coined by two therapists who work with boys) either as "Wild Animals" who cannot be controlled or as "Entitled Princes" who should not be.[14]

As early as one year of age, when given the choice boys and girls alike gravitate towards gender-typical toys. Longitudinal studies have shown that this behavior follows, rather than precedes, parents' expressed enthusiasm for the child's interaction with these "appropriate" toys, which suggests that such behavioral tendencies are more the result of nurture than of nature.[15] But again the reactions of parents are not symmetrical: mothers on average are fairly tolerant of cross-gender play in daughters or sons, but fathers are much less so, especially when boys play with "feminine" toys.

In one study, preschool children were taken to a playroom while their parents were being interviewed, and were asked to play with either gender-typical or gender-atypical toys. When a parent later joined the child, his or her reactions were observed. Parents of both sexes reacted positively to daughters' playing with a kitchen set and with only mild negativity when they played with a toy gas station. But boys got mixed messages: Mothers were generally positive toward whatever toy the sons played with, often sitting down and joining them. Most fathers, however, responded positively to sons' playing with "masculine" toys but *very* negatively to play with "feminine" ones: they frowned, made sarcastic comments and in some cases even picked up the

---

[13]William Pollack, *Real Boys: Rescuing Our Sons from the Myths of Boyhood* (New York: Random House, 1998), chap. 2.

[14]Kindlon and Thompson, *Raising Cain,* chap. 2; Beal, *Boys and Girls,* chap. 3.

[15]Eleanor E. Maccoby and Carol N. Jacklin, *The Psychology of Sex Differences* (Stanford, Calif.: Stanford University Press, 1974).

child and moved him away from the kitchen set.[16] Again, whatever biological priming boys and girls may bring to their play styles, it is magnified greatly—and asymmetrically—by socialization.

Gender Chauvinism

By the time children are about five years old, much of their play is so thoroughly gender-typed that parents no longer need to monitor it. But gender typing happens not just because children passively absorb parental preferences, influential though these are. Once they pass through infancy and early toddlerhood, it also happens because of children's own need to develop a clear self-concept. This leads to (among other things) the formation of gender identity which, as we saw in the last chapter, refers to a sense of oneself as being male or female. Once established, gender identity provides a strong motivation to identify with same-sex role models and to learn from them by observation. Moreover, the growing realization that one is either a boy or a girl—and permanently so—becomes a powerful tool with which to make sense of the child's social world. Gender becomes an organizing principle, a cognitive category or (more technically) a schema that children use to understand and judge people's behavior.[17]

The development of a gender identity and a gender schema helps us to understand why many younger children apply gender stereotypes to themselves and others even when adults consciously work against this tendency. Developmental psychologist Carol Beal summarizes it well: "Because gender is thought to be an either-or category, children resist the notion that males and females might sometimes behave in similar ways, are critical of others who deviate from traditional gender roles, and exaggerate the differences between the sexes."[18] Regardless of who does what in their own home, children survey their entire social landscape—including, of course, the media images that surround them—and draw general correlations between perceived sex on the one hand and behavior, appearance and personality traits on the other. They then turn the resulting stereotypes into moral imperatives about what males and females can and should do.

---

[16]Judith H. Langlois and A. Chris Downs, "Mothers, Fathers and Peers as Socialization Agents of Sex-Typed Play Behavior in Young Children," *Child Development* 51 (1980): 1217-47. See also Beal, *Boys and Girls,* chap. 5, for related studies.

[17]See especially Lawrence Kohlberg, "A Cognitive-Developmental Analysis of Children's Sex-Role Concepts and Attitudes," in *The Development of Sex Differences,* ed. Eleanor E. Maccoby (Stanford, Calif.: Stanford University Press, 1966), pp. 82-173, and Sandra L. Bem, *The Lenses of Gender* (New Haven, Conn.: Yale University Press, 1993).

[18]Beal, *Boys and Girls,* p. 102.

It's as if the child in the preschool and early elementary school years is saying, "Look, I've just figured out this girl-and-boy thing. Don't complicate it by telling me that the boundaries are sometimes movable." This stance highlights the cognitive strength of all stereotypes: they reduce the mental strain that would occur if we were to regard every person and situation as unique. In Hilary Lips's words, both boys and girls at this stage "seem to be trying to solidify a sense of gender identity by renouncing any form of ambiguity."[19] And it is shortly after this that they often become spontaneous gender chauvinists. The early school years are the ones when "boys versus girls" contests are common, when children segregate themselves by sex at tables in the school cafeteria, and when the chant "Girls rule, boys drool" is matched by "Boys reign, girls are a pain." In the continuing process of consolidating gender identity, each sex insists that it is the best.

I must be careful not to overdraw this picture: boys and girls at this age also do a lot of what sociologist Barrie Thorne calls "border work." They make calculated forays into each other's playground territory, engage in ritualized chasing games with each other and even remain happily capable of mixed-sex activities in a variety of settings. This is especially the case when adults take responsibility for organizing such activities (in well-run church youth groups, for example) and when the task is an absorbing one that encourages cooperation and deemphasizes gender, such as producing a school newspaper or play, or participating in a service project.[20] Furthermore, adults who want children to focus more on their common humanity than on their gender differences can take heart from the fact that the intolerance for ambiguity may start to decrease as early as seven to ten years of age. Throughout this period children—though girls sooner and more often than boys—begin to think it might be acceptable if they, their friends and their families are not always rigidly gender-typed, and that the extent to which they are might be as much the result of custom as of biology.[21]

Schematizing and Its Costs

In sum, children learn to view their social world through the lens of gender in at least two ways. They do so first as a result of reinforcement and role-modeling patterns by adults and others of both sexes. But in the case of boys, the relative

[19]Lips, *Sex and Gender,* p. 64.
[20]Thorne, "Girls and Boys Together," pp. 678-79.
[21]Beale, *Boys and Girls,* chap. 6.

lack of access to adult males who are flexible role models makes them more likely to absorb stereotyped and narrow images of masculinity, and more doubtful about their success in doing so. In addition, children develop and apply gender schemas because of a cognitive need to make sense of a world in which they have come to understand that they themselves are male or female. As noted in the last chapter, these processes may get a boost from preexisting biological factors, especially when the latter point in the same direction as early gender socialization. But children are also active thinkers—if not completely mature and rational ones—about their physical and social worlds. They are not just passive responders to biological and social imperatives.

Much of what results is innocuous, temporary and developmentally inevitable—which is why it is wise for adults not to make too much of the phase when children seem to become such gender chauvinists. But there is a dark side to these processes as well, one that caters to the fallen powers of gender that we met in chapter two. For although children of both sexes practice gender chauvinism, girls must tolerate more cognitive dissonance in order to do so: the little girl who starts out believing girls are better soon realizes that many feminine traits and activities are less valued in her culture.[22] This asymmetry may explain why girls acquire certain gender stereotypes more slowly than boys do and why on average they leave the gender chauvinist stage earlier. "Girls," observes Carole Beal, "are generally more flexible and more aware of the costs of rigid stereotyping than boys. Since boys' beliefs that they are superior to girls are reinforced by their observations of the surrounding culture, they have little motivation to change."[23] This may also help explain why mothers are generally less concerned than fathers to reinforce gender typing in their children.

Lest we be tempted to dismiss this asymmetry with the thought that boys will be boys (or to conclude that girls are always the more tolerant and flexible sex), we should note that a similar process takes place with regard to ethnicity. Children develop ethnic as well as gender schemas, and a corresponding belief that their own group is the best one. But white children of both sexes become "race chauvinists" earlier than children of color, and they hold on to assumptions about their ethnic superiority more stubbornly than children of other groups, since these tendencies are also reinforced by the surrounding culture.[24] Moreover, children with the most strongly developed race schemas

---

[22]See Lips, *Sex and Gender,* chap. 1, which reviews the literature on evaluative aspects of gender stereotypes.
[23]Ibid., p. 107.
[24]Frances Aboud, *Children and Prejudice* (New York: Blackwell, 1988).

are the ones most likely to distort or forget positive information about people from other groups.[25]

Ethnic and gender schemas are useful—and to some extent inevitable—devices that we use to reduce information overload and give us a sense of place and community. But they also keep us from seeing individual differences and evaluating people by more diverse criteria such as ability, experience and character. As noted in an earlier chapter, it is a human weakness—not simply a male one—to see one's own group as the standard by which all others are judged. But if we wish to discourage this tendency among children in its ethnic form, then we should be no less concerned when we see it occurring on the basis of gender. Social psychologist Sandra Bem points out that while children make sense of their social world by appropriating and applying schemas, it is adults in the end who decide which schemas will be treated as the most important ones.[26] They can encourage children to see males and females as opposite sexes destined for quite different (and differently valued) places in the world, or as neighboring sexes sharing a common humanity and tasks, many of which can be flexibly assigned. Following the former path, as we will see, leads to troubling consequences for boys as well as for girls.[27]

Fragile Loyalties

Dan Kindlon and Michael Thompson are psychologists who work in all-boys as well as coed schools in Boston, in addition to having private therapy practices. In their book *Raising Cain* they describe an adult client they call Gary, who recalled cooperating as a boy with a juvenile version of the male culture of honor and in turn becoming its victim. As a fifth-grader Gary had a best friend named Peter, with whom he studied, talked, and played hunting and tracking games in the woods. Peter was a reasonably good athlete but also happened to be the shortest boy in the class. In sixth grade he became the target of teasing, which both boys at first tried to ignore or brush aside. But one day in the locker room

---

[25]Rebecca S. Bigler and Lynn S. Liben, "A Cognitive-Developmental Approach to Racial Stereotyping and Reconstructive Memory in Euro-American Children," *Child Development* 64 (1993): 1507-18.

[26]Sandra Bem, "Gender Schema Theory and Its Implications for Child Development: Raising Gender Aschematic Children in a Gender Schematic Society," *Signs* 8 (1983): 598-616.

[27]Interestingly, religion as a schema is now less emphasized in North America than it was when I was a child being taught to sing anti-Catholic ditties. However, I have a theological colleague from Northern Ireland who discovered at the height of that country's religious troubles that many of his compatriots were willing to label themselves Catholic or Protestant but not *Christian,* because they knew that to embrace this broader schema would require them to take part in the peace process rather than keep fighting.

several boys formed a ring around Peter and started snapping their towels at his crotch and mocking him. While struggling into his pants and trying to protect his anatomy, Peter glanced over at Gary as he stood by his own locker. He was "not exactly pleading for help, but checking to see what I was going to do. What I did," Gary recalled, "was finish getting dressed and walk out of the locker room. We never talked about it, but that was the end of our friendship. To be honest, he had become a liability for me, and I didn't have the guts to deal with it."[28]

Gary soon acquired a new best friend, Lee, a top student, athlete and school leader with whom he even traded clothing as a symbol of mutual allegiance. But in seventh grade Gary—a Jewish boy in a largely non-Jewish school—began preparing for his bar mitzvah, and though his Jewish identity had not previously been a matter for comment, it now became the butt of jokes. Uncertain whether to ignore these or to fight back, Gary (like Peter before him) looked to his best friend for help, only to see him regularly laughing along with the rest of his mockers. Later, when he invited half a dozen boys, including Lee, to his bar mitzvah, none of them showed up. Lee admitted that he and his classmates had decided that none of them wanted to go to the synagogue because they would have to wear "kike caps" during the service. Gary's conclusion: "That's what becoming a man meant to me when I got Bar Mitzvahed: I realized I was on my own. I never had a best friend again."[29]

The "Boy Code" and the Culture of Honor

Gary, Peter and Lee shared with most other boys in our society a systematic process of induction—some of it deliberate, much of it unwitting—into what psychologist William Pollack calls the "Boy Code."[30] This is a set of requirements for all who aspire to a contemporary version of the male culture of honor. We saw that in its classical form the culture of honor requires a man to resist challenges from other men, while advancing his own prestige and social ranking by a continuous display of cool-headedness, shrewdness, and verbal and physical dominance. In an article that has become something of a classic in men's studies, social scientists Robert Brannon and Deborah David have outlined its four imperatives for boys growing up in North America today.[31]

---

[28]Kindlon and Thompson, *Raising Cain,* p. 91.
[29]Ibid., p. 91.
[30]Pollack, *Real Boys,* chap. 2.
[31]Deborah David and Robert Brannon, "The Male Sex Role: Our Culture's Blueprint of Manhood, and What It's Done for Us Lately," in David and Brannon, *Forty-nine Percent Majority,* pp. 1-45.

First, there must be *no sissy stuff.* Any display of behavior or emotion associated with the feminine may become an occasion for shaming or even physical abuse, unless a boy is lucky enough to be raised in a subculture where adults—and especially men—model such emotions and don't punish boys for doing so. Empathy is feminine, so a boy like Gary, though he feels conflicted about it, does not stand up for a friend who is being mocked and abused. Religion is feminine and Jews are a vulnerable minority, so Gary's classmates will not let themselves be seen in "kike caps" even for a short time in a restricted setting. Being small is feminine, so Peter is considered fair game for boys higher up in the pecking order. And since showing distress is feminine, Peter must simply grit his teeth, make light of his torment and hope for a speedy exit from the locker room. In an earlier culture of honor Peter's brothers and other male kin might be a ready-made network to protect or avenge him. In its modern incarnation, even this safety net cannot be counted on, and the "rule of law" that is supposed to have replaced it is often inconsistently enforced by adults responsible for children's welfare. Boys, it is assumed, will sort these things out among themselves.

Recognizing these dark tendencies does not mean we should one-sidedly demonize boys or men. Girls may not be physical bullies as often as boys, but they are quite capable of using ostracism and verbal cruelty to construct their own hierarchies.[32] The difference is that when girls suffer emotional distress, they are not as often discouraged from expressing it. Most parents of both sexes respond with warmth and concern to girls' fears, encouraging them to "talk it out" as an acceptable expression of femininity. But they use fewer emotion-words with sons, expecting them instead to limit their expression of vulnerability. Fathers are especially apt to use scorn and teasing to toughen up their sons in the face of fear or sadness. Indeed one emotion-word that fathers are far more likely to use with sons than with daughters is *disgust.*[33]

This illustrates the second imperative of the Boy Code: he must learn to become *a sturdy oak*—that is, stable, stoical and self-reliant. If he can't always be on top of the heap, he should at least "take it like a man" when adversity comes his way. He should even look for occasions to practice this virtue. In the movie *Lawrence of Arabia* the hero at one point demonstrates how he can let a match burn right down to his fingertips. "Of course it hurts," he says with a smile. "The trick, you see, is not to *care* that it hurts." This, David and Brannon observe,

---

[32]Among others, Margaret Atwood, in her novel *Cat's Eye* (New York: Doubleday, 1989), has painted a graphic picture of little girls' capacity for cruelty. See also Beal, *Boys and Girls,* chap. 7.

[33]Pollack, *Real Boys,* chap. 2.

"goes far beyond the mere avoidance of feminine emotionality: it's the cultivation of a stoic, imperturbable persona. . . . A 'real man' never worries about
death or loses his manly cool."[34] It also helps to explain why Christianity is so
often stereotyped as an unmanly endeavor: to the extent that it calls on men to
admit that they are not self-sufficient but need the grace of God and the support
of other believers, Christian faith and lifestyle challenge the sturdy oak image.

Closely related to that image is a third imperative. A boy must learn, in David
and Brannon's words, to be *a big wheel*—to cultivate success and status and provoke envy and admiration in others. Athletic prowess is perhaps the most acknowledged way to do this, as well as (with the onset of adolescence) the ability
to attract girls. But there are class and subcultural differences. The studious boy
who would be seen as a masculine cop-out in the inner city will be pressed to
study even harder in the suburbs, in order to make it into an elite university and
thence to a prestigious and high-paying career. The zealous Christian boy who
is the butt of jokes in his public school setting may aspire to become a minister
or evangelist who will compete as an adult for fame and followers.

What links these various expressions is something they all share with classic
cultures of honor: by definition "big wheel" status is a limited commodity that
not every male can achieve, and that even those who do are in constant danger
of losing.[35] As one of Kindlon and Thompson's young informants put it, "Everyone thinks you've got it so easy when you're on top, but being on top just means
you have to worry all the time about slipping. . . . All it takes is one mistake or
a bad day, and all sorts of people are waiting to take you down."[36] Pollack notes
that it is this aspect of the code that makes some boys push themselves to unhealthy limits in athletic or other kinds of competition. It is also what leads many
boys to prefer girls who massage their egos (in Virginia Woolf's memorable
phrase, who "reflect them at twice their natural size") to those who see them in
all their human ambiguity and insist on a more genuine partnership.[37]

Lastly, in its extreme form the imperative to be a big wheel becomes, in David
and Brannon's words, the mandate to *give 'em hell*. Violence performed by other
than legally mandated persons is, of course, officially condemned in Western society. At the same time, it is modeled incessantly in the media and often encouraged in boys with a wink and a nod. At the very least, boys are often urged to
defend themselves vigorously when attacked. And given the mystique that vio-

---

[34]David and Brannon, "Male Sex-Role," p. 25.
[35]Ibid., p. 19.
[36]Kindlon and Thompson, *Raising Cain,* p. 75.
[37]Virginia Woolf, *A Room of One's Own* (1929; reprint, San Diego: Harcourt Brace Jovanovich,
1957); Pollack, *Real Boys,* chap. 2.

lence has in popular culture, "the line between self-defense and aggression for the sheer fun of it is narrow in theory and often ignored in practice, especially among older boys out of sight of adults, where the rule that 'might makes right' usually reigns supreme."[38] Alternately, boys may be tempted to engage in behaviors risky to themselves, such as driving too fast or taking drugs, often on an implicit or explicit dare from which they feel they cannot back down.

Emotional Impoverishment

From all this we see that boys are expected to embrace a masculine ideal emphasizing self-reliance, stoicism, competition and power. It is important to point out that these are not inherently pathological traits. In the right contexts and the right amounts, they are virtues *all* human beings can draw on to serve their communities and unfold the potential of creation. What is problematic about them for boys as compared to girls is that they are often emphasized to the exclusion of other equally valuable traits and are linked to performance standards that can never finally be met—if, as the Boy Code holds, it is only by staying on top that one's masculinity can be fully assured. The behavioral rigidity and anxiety this generates are made worse by the fact that most boys have less access than girls to same-sex adult role models— especially to ones who practice a fully human range of emotion and behavior and who refuse to link masculine worth to a never-ending performance treadmill.

In their extreme form, such asymmetries contribute to the dramatic social problems we have come to associate more with boys than girls: homicide, suicide, property crime and various forms of violence. And when we nuance this picture by class and ethnicity, it becomes even more complex, since boys of color often face additional challenges from the Boy Code. Many live in situations of limited economic opportunity and thus feel doubly shamed (or tempted) by the code's demand for material success. In neighborhoods of high father absence, there may be few adult males to model alternative ways of being masculine—though many African American churches do a superb job of providing such models for young people willing to take advantage of them.[39] Moreover, in communities where the rule of law has broken down

---

[38]David and Brannon, "Male Sex-Role," p. 29.
[39]For some pertinent examples see K. Brynolf Lyon and Archie Smith Jr., eds., *Tending the Flock: Congregations and Family Ministry* (Louisville, Ky.: Westminster John Knox, 1998).

and normal city services are inconsistently provided, the temptation to form gangs and channel one's sense of honor and achievement through them is very strong.[40]

But even for boys who do not resort to such behaviors there is an emotional price to be paid. We have seen that boys are pushed from an early age to suppress fearful or sad feelings and are often shamed when they fail to do so. But they *are* often encouraged to express one strong feeling: anger. Indeed when parents tell their children stories or teach them how to manage conflict, they are likely to stress empathy and harmony for their daughters but the use of anger for their sons.[41] As a result, anger can become the single pathway or "emotional funnel" through which boys channel the forbidden, softer feelings. From his work with men and boys Pollack concludes that "the more tender feelings seem too shameful to show, and thus boys turn to anger. . . . It is very challenging for most men to express or experience emotions other than anger, since as boys they were encouraged to use their rage to express the full range of their emotional experience."[42]

The long-term physical consequences of such emotional narrowing—increased risk of ulcers, high blood pressure and other somatic problems—are serious enough, but the relational consequences are equally troubling. This past year, for example, I found myself smiling—but rather ruefully—over a news item about dozens of check-out clerks who complained to their grocery store chain owners about the requirement that they make a constant effort to be friendly to customers. Their professional courtesy was frequently interpreted as a sexual invitation by customers of the other sex, whose persistent attentions then became annoying and occasionally even dangerous. Though both sexes had received exactly the same customer service training, only the women clerks faced this problem. This failure on the part of many men to correctly read others' emotional intentions in voice and facial expression—and their tendency to get angry when their mistaken reading is rejected—has also been found in various laboratory studies.[43]

Part of this asymmetry is due to status differences: lower-status groups—including women and, in America, blacks of both sexes—are generally better at decoding nonverbal cues than the higher-status groups to whom they have

---

[40]See for example Ronald B. Mincy, ed., *Nurturing Young Black Males* (Washington, D.C.: Urban Institute, 1994), and James Garbarino, *Lost Boys: Why Our Sons Turn Violent and How We Can Save Them* (New York: Free Press, 1999).

[41]Pollack, *Real Boys,* chap. 2.

[42]Ibid., p. 44.

[43]See Lips, *Sex and Gender,* chap. 4, for a review of the pertinent research literature.

had to defer for so long. But boys' early training in suppressing or ignoring their own feelings undoubtedly plays a part as well. Clinical psychologist Ronald Levant has coined the term *alexithymia* to describe this truncated ability to feel and express a wide range of human emotions. He has also devised ways for men with stress and relationship problems to relearn how to monitor their bodily states and accurately identify a wider range of feelings.[44] But it would be better for all of us if the emotional narrowing did not occur in the first place.

Raising Real Boys

The psychologists we have met in this chapter who specialize in work with boys show remarkable agreement as to what changes are needed. Boys need freedom to stay attached to parents longer than our culture has allowed them to. They need to be accepted not just for their strengths but with all their fears and doubts, not shamed into denying them or taught always to mask them with anger and bravado. They need academic and cocurricular experiences that challenge but also respect their limits, and that put as much stress on mutual encouragement and skill building as on winning. They need loving but firm limits—to be treated neither as Wild Animals nor Entitled Princes but as persons in whom the fullness of God's image requires wise cultivation.

Many Christian families, churches and parachurch groups, intuitively seeing the New Testament's message of freedom from the male culture of honor, have provided such an environment for boys as well as for girls. Others, interpreting Paul's accommodations to that culture as an unchanging set of gender norms, do not, or do so only ambivalently. Some anxious gender traditionalists worry that the changes suggested above will end up effectively turning boys into girls—although after several decades of gains for women we seldom worry that girls' expanded opportunities are turning them all into men. We might recall that not so very long ago higher education for girls was seen as an activity that would inevitably shrink their ovaries![45]

In point of fact, the psychologists who want to expand boys' emotional and behavioral horizons are aware that boys have some unique developmental challenges that need to be taken seriously but often are not. For example, in early

---

[44]Ronald F. Levant and Gina Kopecky, *Masculinity Reconstructed: Changing the Rules of Manhood at Work, in Relationships and in Family Life* (New York: Dutton, 1995).

[45]See for example Barbara Ehrenreich and Deirdre English, *For Her Own Good: 150 Years of the Experts' Advice to Women* (Garden City, N.Y.: Anchor, 1979).

childhood boys can lag behind girls in their acquisition of language skills by as much as one to two years—yet we insist on keeping both sexes to the same timetable in learning to read and write.[46] In addition, many (though not all) young boys seem to thrive in large spaces that allow for physically active team games with clear rules. By contrast, girls often (though again not always—remember all those tomboys!) prefer one-on-one activities confined to smaller spaces. The point is not that one style is better than the other but that individual differences need to be accommodated, even as we challenge children to stretch their horizons to include the activities and learning styles that they usually associate with the other sex.

The Power of Nurturant Fathering

At various points in this chapter I have noted that the absence of role-flexible men from boys' lives can lead them to overinvest in the Boy Code in order to convince themselves that they are adequately masculine. What happens when this situation is reversed—when boys have regular access to male caretakers who model a wide range of feeling and behavior, accept the same in boys, and establish age-appropriate boundaries in a consistent and nurturing way? These are questions Yale psychiatrist Kyle Pruett has been asking for over a decade while following almost twenty working- and middle-class families in which fathers have been the primary caretakers of children from infancy on and mothers have been the family's primary wage earners.[47] This ongoing study is significant because it compares fathering styles with mothering styles under roughly comparable conditions—that is, when one parent is the primary caretaker while the other is less accessible due to wage-earning responsibilities. Do fathers act just like mothers in such circumstances? And how does their children's development differ from that of children raised primarily by mothers?

When the firstborns of these families were assessed as infants, they were at or above national norms on standardized cognitive tests and ahead of schedule in personal and social skills. Regardless of sex, they seemed unusually attuned to and comfortable with whatever physical or social environment they were in. By age four, "they were avid explorers of their backyards, bus stops and grocery

---

[46]Kindlon and Thompson, *Raising Cain,* chap. 2; Pollack, *Real Boys,* chap. 10.
[47]Kyle D. Pruett, *The Nurturing Father* (New York: Warner, 1987), and *Fatherneed: Why Father Care Is as Essential as Mother Care for Your Child* (New York: Free Press, 2000). Note that 1999 U.S. Census Bureau data listed some two million fathers as primary caretakers of children in two-parent families.

stores, confident that something interesting would always turn up."[48] Pruett also
noted the ease with which they moved between boys' and girls' play: "While
their peers were concentrating on joining the 'gender gang' they were moving
comfortably back and forth between gender groupings at day care, playgrounds
and birthday parties."[49] Their imaginary play was particularly rich with images
of caring fathers, yet not to the exclusion of mothers. These children clearly regarded both parents as procreators and nurturers of human beings.

By age eight, most of the children were involved in nurturing activities themselves—raising or breeding a variety of plants and pets, helping to care for
younger siblings, taking responsibility for various household chores. Because
most of their mothers remained highly involved, Pruett surmised that "having a
father *and* a mother devoted to the nurturing of a child was a pervasive culture
in these families. Children identified early on with nurturing as a valued, powerful skill and role, and wanted to explore their competence in this area."[50] By
ages ten to twelve, they continued to interact comfortably with friends of both
genders. At an age when most youngsters are becoming more sexually self-con-
scious, these children enjoyed cross-sex friendships that included birthday parties and community and religious events, and they preferred friends who shared
their less restrictive view of gender roles. Pruett concludes that having two highly involved parents produces "a bedrock trust and comfort with male and female
relationships, so that [their] gendered aspects may be less salient than their overall quality."[51]

A Plea for Change

My point in sharing this research is not to suggest that role reversal is the only
way for fathers to be better involved with their children, and particularly their
sons. But it does allow us to ask whether there something distinctive about the
way fathers parent in these families, and in others where they are highly involved, even if not as the primary caretaking parent. As it turns out, when children are very tiny, fathers and mothers respond in quite similar ways, both
physiologically and in the ways they handle, comfort and interact with them.
But with older infants and toddlers, fathers do tend to have a somewhat different interaction style than mothers—a little less verbal and more physical, more

---

[48]Pruett, *Fatherneed,* p. 62.
[49]Ibid., p. 62.
[50]Ibid., p. 64.
[51]Ibid., p. 72.

exploratory and somewhat more tolerant of children's attempts at independence. These differences are not absolute, and it is next to impossible to determine how much they are rooted in nature, nurture or both. But whatever its origins, involved fathering is a strong predictor of enhanced verbal and math performance and of independence and healthy assertiveness in both sons and daughters.[52]

One theory is that done correctly, fathers' more challenging interaction style (including what is called "controlled rough-housing") helps teach children spatial skills but also emotion management: the ability to see when playfulness crosses the line into obnoxiousness or violence and to monitor their own responses accordingly. The crucial qualifier is the phrase "done correctly." Both quantity and quality of fathers' involvement matter. Ross Parke, a researcher of fathering for over thirty years, notes that "too many fathers are unavailable to their children because of their work schedules, travel, or lack of interest." Even more significant, "kids whose fathers are cold and authoritarian, derogatory and intrusive have the hardest time with grades and social relationships. They are even worse off than kids who live in homes with no father at all."[53]

A later chapter will return to the topic of marriage and family. But from what has been discussed so far, it seems that while girls' horizons have expanded over the past few decades, boys' range of feeling and action has remained limited by the demands of the Boy Code. I have tried to show that all of us stand to gain if we are willing to challenge that code in a way that respects boys' full humanity while attending to the particular developmental hurdles they face. While such practices may be slow to catch on, we have seen evidence of their power to make boys' lives richer and healthier. In such a healing endeavor, as in the time of Diognetus, Christians might well lead the way.

---

[52]Ross D. Parke and Armin A. Brott, *Throwaway Dads: The Myths and Barriers That Keep Men from Being the Fathers They Want to Be* (Boston: Houghton Mifflin, 1999).
[53]Ibid, pp. 9-10.

What Can We Learn
from Other Cultures?

IN THE POPULAR IMAGINATION OF today's Westerners, there are two premodern cultures, among others, that seem particularly romantic and fascinating. These are the small !Kung Bushmen of the Kalahari Desert (the exclamation mark indicates the famous "click" sound of their language) and the tall, Nilo-Hamitic Masai who inhabit the hills around the Kenya-Tanzania border. Each of these grapples with a challenging physical environment in the company of a closely knit tribal group. Each practices a lifestyle largely impervious to Western technological influence, the Bushmen as hunter-gatherers and the Masai as cattle herders. And each has been the target of recent research by cultural anthropologists studying the roots of gendered behavior and gender inequality.[1]

Traditionally, adult Masai men do not eat with women, even though it is women who do the milking of cows for the group's primary form of nourishment. In the minds of Masai men, the mere presence of women at the time of eating will pollute any food in the vicinity. Polygamy is the common form of marriage for Masai women, who have little formal status on their own. While men's primary identity is with the clan-based warrior age group into which they are socialized, women are attached to the men they marry outside their own clan, and by extension to their husband's age group.[2] Circumcision is performed on both Masai boys and girls. For young men the operation involves the remov-

---

[1]For an ethnographic account of the Bushmen, see Richard Lee, *The !Kung San: Men, Women and Work in a Foraging Society* (Cambridge: Cambridge University Press, 1979). On the Masai, see for example Melissa Llewelyn-Davies, "Women, Warriors and Patriarchs," in *Sexual Meanings,* ed. Sherry B. Ortner and Harriet Whitehead (Cambridge: Cambridge University Press, 1981), pp. 330-58. On gender relations in both groups, see also David Gilmore, *Manhood in the Making: Cultural Concepts of Masculinity* (New Haven, Conn.: Yale University Press, 1990).

[2]Vincent Donovan, *Christianity Rediscovered* (Maryknoll, N.Y.: Orbis, 1987), chaps. 2, 7.

al of the foreskin and is seen as an act of bravery that marks initiation into a warrior age group of peers who will eventually be tribal elders. In young women, however, both the clitoris and labia minora are excised to remove most sexual sensation, supposedly as a way of ensuring women's fidelity to their husbands. It is not uncommon to see females crying and struggling during circumcision, while male warriors hold them down.[3]

By contrast, in both behavior and attitudes the !Kung hunter-gatherers display a degree of status and role equality found in few societies at any level of development. Richard Lee, who did anthropological field work among them for over twenty years, reports that if one asks Bushmen who really has the power and strength in their society, many men will say, "Oh, the women have the strength—they are the strong ones, we are the weak ones." And the women will say, "Oh no, the men have the strength, not us." "That is their story," Lee and his colleague Richard Daly write, "and they stick to it."[4] Although !Kung men are generally hunters while women gather plants, the sexual division of labor is not rigid, as members of each sex often join the others to get a job done. And in terms of social influence, Lee and Daly note, "!Kung women's participation in group discussions and decision-making is probably greater that that of women in most tribal, peasant, and industrial societies."[5] Circumcision is not performed on young people of either sex. Indeed violence of any kind is rare among the Bushmen, and when it does occur, women are almost never its targets. Rape, a common form of violence against women in about one-fifth of band and tribal societies, is extremely rare among the !Kung.[6]

In an earlier chapter I anticipated our crosscultural study of masculinity when I described the seminomadic Sarakatsan shepherds of Greece. Together with the Masai and the !Kung, they remind us of an important research requirement in social science: any theory about human nature or development that makes universal claims must be tested across a wide range of cultures. Taking this truism as their starting point, gender studies researchers who step outside the confines of Western industrialized societies have focused on two large questions. The first is the perennial question of nature versus nurture. Is there some irreducible essence or deep structure to masculinity or femininity that can be discerned in all cultures regardless of their location or level of complexity, or are these concepts

---

[3]Llewelyn-Davies, "Women, Warriors and Patriarchs," p. 351.
[4]Richard Lee and Richard Daly, "Man's Dominion, Women's Oppression," in *Beyond Patriarchy: Essays by Men on Pleasure, Power and Change,* ed. Michael Kaufman (Toronto: Oxford University Press), p. 33.
[5]Ibid., p. 36.
[6]Peggy Sanday, "The Sociocultural Context of Rape," *Journal of Social Issues* 37 (1981): 5-27.

so driven by environmental and ideological forces that their expression is almost infinitely plastic? The second question concerns status and power: Regardless of where gender differences originate, do they inevitably result in men's dominance over women? If so why, and what (if anything) should we do to change such a state of affairs?

Some Cautionary Notes

Crosscultural settings would seem to provide the ideal "natural laboratory" for exploring at least the empirical side of such questions. Male biology and female biology are basically the same everywhere, and taking humankind as a whole, the minor degree of genetic variation that exists among ethnic groups is far less than the amount of variation found within any given group.[7] Moreover, the *most* important genetic legacy of all humans is a flexible cerebral cortex that allows them to be the culture-making, problem-solving, adaptive creatures they have always been. "[Human] behavioral variation is tremendous," observes evolutionary theorist Barbara Smuts, "and it is rooted in biology. Flexibility is itself the adaptation."[8] Thus if gender roles and status vary across cultures, it would seem logical to conclude that both are more influenced by social, historical and environmental forces than by differences in male and female biology.

But although my preliminary comparison of the !Kung and Masai seems to support this conclusion, there are other factors complicating any attempt to sort out the origins of gender roles and gender status differences—let alone make moral judgments about what we find. Before focusing more directly on masculinity in crosscultural perspective, I need to acknowledge some of these factors.

The first has to do with the reliability of the database. Like the other social sciences, cultural anthropology emerged as a formal discipline only in the late nineteenth century. From that time until the 1960s, when second-wave feminism began, most ethnographic studies were done by male scholars (or occasionally females trained by them) who collected information mainly from and about men in the cultures they visited. As summarized by a contemporary woman anthropologist, the picture that emerged was "that culture is created by and for men between the ages of puberty and late middle age, with children, women and the aged as residual categories . . . portrayed, at best, as providing support for

---

[7]L. Luca Cavalli-Sforza, *Genes, People and Languages,* trans. Mark Seielstad (New York: North Point Press, 2000).
[8]Quoted in Natalie Angier, *Women: An Intimate Geography* (New York: Houghton Mifflin, 1999), pp. 346-47.

the activities of [adult] men."[9] This might not seem problematic if we are interested in looking only at masculinity crossculturally—until we remember that masculinity and femininity are relational concepts that cannot be studied in isolation. If we picture culture as a canoe in which both men and women are paddling, then the actions of each group affect—and are affected by—the actions of the other, even if not always in a symmetrical way. So women and men should be studied together, and in equal detail.

Men's and women's behavior is also affected by other factors that we easily overlook because mainstream Western social norms are so different. For example, in more traditional societies, gender interacts in complex ways with age status and kinship practices. In a 1951 study unusual for its early sensitivity to these issues, University of Chicago sociologist Fred Strodtbeck examined husband-wife disagreements in three cultures, including one, the Navajo, which was matrilocal (meaning that the husband moves to his wife's family location upon marrying). After analyzing dozens of taped interactions in each culture, he found that residence pattern was a good predictor of the outcome of spousal disagreements: among the matrilocal Navajo, it was more often the husband who deferred to the wife, whereas the reverse was true among the other groups.[10] Kin-group proximity can thus be a check against the possible misuse of spousal power.

Strodtbeck's study highlights another methodological issue, which is that the earlier male-centered biases of many anthropologists can be offset by studies with more carefully defined behavioral measures and more representative sampling.[11] But despite those historical biases, there *are* behaviorally rich descriptions of gender relations in preindustrial cultures—enough, as we will see later, to allow for the testing of interesting hypotheses when these descriptions are collected and coded into various databases, such as those known as the Human Relations Area Files and the Ethnographic Atlas.[12] A further advantage of doing research in premodern cultures is that since they are less complex and stratified

[9]Alice Schlegel, *Sexual Stratification: A Cross-Cultural View* (New York: Columbia University Press, 1977), p. 2. See also Margo I. Duley and Mary I. Edwards, eds., *The Cross-Cultural Study of Women: A Comprehensive Guide* (New York: Feminist Press, 1986).

[10]Fred Strodtbeck, "Husband-Wife Interaction over Revealed Differences," *American Sociological Review* 16 (1951): 468-73. Strodtbeck's other two groups were American Mormons and American middle-class Texans.

[11]For an introduction to methodological issues in crosscultural research, see Harry C. Triandis, *Culture and Social Behavior* (New York: McGraw-Hill, 1994), especially chap. 3.

[12]See Herbert Barry, "Description and Uses of the Human Relations Area Files," in *Handbook of Cross-Cultural Psychology,* ed. Harry C. Triandis and John W. Berry (Boston: Allyn & Bacon, 1980), 2:445-78. See also George P. Murdock, *Ethnographic Atlas* (Pittsburgh: University of Pittsburgh Press, 1967), from which the Standard Cross-Cultural Sample of 186 preindustrial cultures has been drawn.

than our own, their expressions of masculinity and femininity are often more unitary. One is less likely to find the gradations of hegemonic and subordinated masculinities that I noted in earlier discussions of Western societies, so it is easier to see what other cultural factors contribute to a given expression of masculinity.

Creation, Culture and Sin

One final point needs to be made before we embark on a more detailed study of masculinity crossculturally. Even if we *were* to find some universal pattern of masculinity, this would not necessarily make it the standard all males should aim for. As Princeton Seminary ethicist Max Stackhouse reminds us, the Reformed tradition in Christianity emphasizes that because what we call "nature" is fallen, we cannot directly argue from "what is" to "what is best." "The purposes intended by God are contorted, garbled, or made ambiguous in the actual operation of things," Stackhouse writes. "What we examine when we study what is 'natural' is what is distorted, incomplete, or contingent, even if it bears traces of God's grace in its capacity to be reformed toward order, purpose, and reliable relationship."[13] The goodness of creation and the negative effects of sin are complexly intertwined everywhere, and we must hold both truths in balanced tension.

In chapter two, for example, I referred to certain powers, elements or structures that in biblical perspective are the scaffolding of human life everywhere—structures such as kinship, government, economic activity and education. Though the details of their expression vary, these and many other practices show up in cultures at all levels of complexity. Donald Brown, in his 1991 book *Human Universals,* concludes that all known human groups have, among other things, religious beliefs, family and kin structures, artistic practices, mythologies, rules of hygiene, symbolically important meals, some form of government, and ways of training children and organizing a common economic life.[14] This broad commonality of human cultural activity affirms what early-twentieth-century anthropologists called "the psychic unity of mankind."

It is also consistent with the flexibility that accompanies the cultural mandate described in the opening chapters of Genesis. Human fitness to carry out that

---

[13]Max L. Stackhouse, *Covenant and Commitments: Faith, Family and Economic Life* (Louisville, Ky.: Westminster John Knox, 1997), p. 21.

[14]Donald E. Brown, *Human Universals* (Philadelphia: Temple University Press, 1991). Cross-cultural psychologists refer to such universals as "cultural etics" and to variations as "cultural emics." Thus, for example, the existence of kinship patterns is a cultural etic, but whether such patterns are organized along matrilineal or patrilineal lines would be a cultural emic.

mandate is only secondarily the result of biological adaptation. Made in God's image, and as God's regents throughout the world, human beings are endowed with the capacities to perform that calling and have considerable freedom, both as individuals and groups, in how they do it. They are put "in the garden of Eden to till it and keep it" (Gen 2:15) and told to name the animals (Gen 2:19-20)—broad mandates representative of a longer list of tasks God calls *Homo sapiens* to undertake. But Donald Brown also found that virtually all cultures engage in warfare—although with differing frequencies and degrees of ferocity—and few of us would be inclined to see this as an unmitigated blessing. On the contrary, to argue directly from what *is* the case to what *ought* to be so—to conclude that "whatever is, is right"—is to commit what philosophers call the naturalistic fallacy.

In terms of biblical theology, as Stackhouse reminds us, cultural practices must be judged not just in terms of creation but in light of the fallen tendencies that distort all creation, including all human groups. We are not to romanticize life in other cultures simply because they are "other" and seemingly less spoiled by incursions of modernity. As accountable creatures, humans are to exercise dominion and establish just and flourishing communities within limits set down by God. And all groups, even if they do not explicitly acknowledge the God of the Bible, are capable of doing cultural work that has God's blessing, including the work of crafting relations that make for just and orderly life in a given time and place. That is what common grace is all about. But just as surely, all cultures can and do fall woefully short of those standards. Although we are quite right to avoid an ethnocentric privileging of our own culture, there is no biblical warrant for bracketing all moral sensibilities when we look at other cultures. Therefore we must both understand and critically evaluate what we discover about masculinity crossculturally. And clearly we must understand before we evaluate.

▌ *Are There Masculine Universals?*

David Gilmore of the State University of New York believes he has found something that approximates a universal form of masculinity, which he describes in his book *Manhood in the Making*.[15] Now the fact that he subtitles the volume *Cultural Concepts of Masculinity*—plural, not singular—indicates that he is pulling his punches somewhat on this issue. "Is there a global archetype of manli-

---

[15]David D. Gilmore, *Manhood in the Making: Cultural Concepts of Masculinity* (New Haven, Conn.: Yale University Press, 1990).

ness?" Gilmore asks, and at the end of his book he replies: "I do not think there is a conclusive answer to that question. Perhaps I should give the reader a 'definite maybe,' as the cartoonist Walt Kelly used to say about the really big questions."[16] Yet despite this equivocation Gilmore has probably done the most detailed research into this question of any contemporary anthropologist, and the results of his study merit our attention.

Gilmore's method was to make a detailed survey of anthropological work done on gender in about a dozen cultures at varying levels of complexity, with varying modes of subsistence and in various parts of the world. Included were both the !Kung and the Masai, as well as a group among whom Gilmore himself has done ethnographic work, the Andalusians of southern Spain. In addition, he makes cross-references to historical cultures such as the ancient Greeks and modern subcultures such as American Jews and English gentry who send their sons to boarding schools. His basic thesis is that in most cultures (though, as it turns out, not all) masculinity differs from femininity in being something that must be achieved and maintained through stressful testing. He suggests that such testing—which takes different forms in different cultures but gets built into the gender ideology of each—takes place because of certain biological, environmental and psychological constraints that in most settings affect males in distinct ways.

What are these constraints? Gilmore begins with the observation that men are, in a very basic sense, more expendable than women—especially in subsistence cultures whose survival calls for physical risks to resist predators and extract food from a challenging environment. It is true that in terms of sheer physical effort women work at least as hard as men and contribute as much or more to the food pool in virtually every culture.[17] But that work must be organized around the repeated demands of bearing and nursing infants, each of whom takes nine months to gestate and another couple of years to wean. Giving women the most risky tasks would thus endanger not just them but their capacity to reproduce the children on whom the flourishing of the group depends. By reproductive default, as it were, men must do much of the really dangerous stuff.

Environments, of course, differ in the degree of risk they present: life is more precarious if you are a Masai cattle herder competing with lions and leopards than if you are a Tahitian who fishes in quiet lagoons and has access to plenty of arable land. But when life-threatening activities must be undertaken for the group's welfare, men are the more obvious candidates for the job. Gilmore in no way believes

---

[16]Ibid., p. 220.
[17]See Frances Dahlberg, ed., *Woman the Gatherer* (New Haven, Conn.: Yale University Press, 1981).

that males are born nobly ready to embrace such a fate. On the contrary, he suggests, it is precisely because it is natural for all human beings to avoid life-threatening risks that men must be pushed (and if necessary shamed) into taking them and promised certain rewards for their compliance.

Of course females also need to learn discipline and self-sacrifice; these are part of the process of growing up anywhere. But two things set them apart from males in this regard. First, what is arguably their biggest risk—childbirth—is something that comes with their bodily territory; it generally cannot be avoided as long as a woman is fertile and living in a subsistence culture that requires constant replenishment of its labor supply. Second, by virtue of their greater strength men in most cultures control women more than they control each other, so they can often coerce women into self-sacrificial behavior in the rare instances where social conditioning doesn't work. So even though women and men paddle the cultural canoe together, men are more likely to be in the sternsman's position, with somewhat more control over the direction of the canoe and more opportunity to jab the other paddlers in a way that they cannot easily reciprocate.

Thus in contrast to women, it is relatively easier for men to go their own individual ways if they so choose—to become, in Gilmore's words, cultural Peter Pans who resist putting the welfare of family and tribe ahead of their own immediate desires. For this reason, he suggests, becoming certifiably masculine is made difficult in most societies. It often involves physically challenging rites of passage directly related to risks posed by the surrounding environment—rites that, if not successfully passed, result in men's social ostracism or at least marginalization. In this way males are literally forced to grow up:

> It is clear that manhood cults are directly related to the degree of hardiness and self-discipline required for the male role. Perhaps what [their] frequency shows is [just] that life in most places is hard and demanding, and that since men are usually given the "dangerous" jobs because of their anatomy, they have to be prodded into action. Manhood ideologies force men to shape up on penalty of being robbed of their identity, a threat apparently worse than death.[18]

Thus among the Sambia of the east New Guinea highlands, a young man who is an incompetent hunter may be denied the privilege of marrying, or may lose his wife to a better hunter, while a good hunting record can lead to multiple wives and mistresses. Among the aboriginal Mehinaku of the Brazilian rainforest, who practice tough slash-and-burn horticulture and fish in risky lakes and rivers, boys who resist joining their fathers in these activities are

---

[18]Gilmore, *Manhood in the Making*, pp. 220-221. See also Triandis, *Culture and Social Behavior*, chap. 5.

branded as "little girls" or "lovers of infants' games" and warned that no woman will want them when they grow up. Among the cattle-herding Samburu (who are cultural and linguistic cousins to the Masai), there are dancing and musical gatherings where unmarried girls mock and challenge the young men until each goes off on a solitary cattle-rustling expedition to prove he is deserving of their sexual favors.[19]

By contrast, in the lush and benign environment of Tahiti there is no tradition of "pressured manhood," and men and women differ little from each other in personalities and roles. And among the Malaysian Semai, who rely on slash-and-burn horticulture, land is so plentiful that no one's turf really needs to be defended. Here too gender roles and temperaments overlap almost completely. We could say that both the Tahitians and the Semai have only the most minimal of gender schemas organizing their material and symbolic worlds.[20] Cultures like these are exceptions to the "stressed" or conditional nature of masculinity—its "iffy heroism," in Gilmore's words.[21] But he concludes that it is more accurate to think of "stressed" versus "relaxed" (or "hard" versus "soft") masculine socialization not as a duality but as a continuum that matches the range of environmental challenges, from harsh to benign, faced by various cultures.

█ Hegemony and Heroics: Are They Inevitable?

Gilmore is clearly not trying to paint a picture of males as the naturally superior sex. He is simply suggesting that survival in many places is a tenuous proposition and that prodding reluctant males to take the bigger risks usually makes practical sense. But there are feminists of both sexes—in particular those working in the critical theory tradition that we met in chapter three—who question whether the resulting sacrifices burden men as much as Gilmore thinks they do. On the contrary, these critics argue, the glorification of male heroism and its associated manhood rituals function to maintain male hegemony and to keep women from sharing cultural resources and influence on a level that matches their contributions to the common good.[22]

---

[19]Gilmore, *Manhood in the Making,* chaps. 4, 6, 7.
[20]Ibid., chap. 9.
[21]Ibid., p. 18.
[22]See for example Gayle Rubin, "The Traffic in Women: Notes Towards a Political Economy of Sex," in *Toward an Anthropology of Women,* ed. Rayna Reiter (New York: Monthly Review, 1975), pp. 157-210; Robert W. Connell, *Gender and Power* (Stanford, Calif.: Stanford University Press, 1986); and Frances E. Mascia-Lees and Nancy Johnson Black, *Gender and Anthropology* (Prospect Heights, Ill.: Waveland, 2000), especially chaps. 5-6.

Gilmore agrees that this argument has empirical merit: "Male rites and cults occur most commonly in patriarchal societies where the sexes are strongly differentiated and ranked," he acknowledges. "These rites often lend a certain mystique to men that makes them 'superior' to women, or they enhance male unity, which in turn can bolster this sense of superiority."[23] Thus groups such as the Samburu, the Masai, the Sambia and the Mehinaku, who embrace pressured manhood, are among the cultures in which women have the least voice and the fewest choices. However, pressured manhood is not always accompanied by male dominance. For example, both the !Kung and the Pygmy have a high degree of gender equality and gender-role overlap, yet both have rites of passage for young males which feature the hunting skills that are important for group survival. These rites do not include gratuitous cruelty, such as the flogging and bloodletting that characterize manhood cults in some other groups. But they do involve arduous weeks in the bush during which boys must show both that they understand their native habitat and can bring home game meat from it. Only when he has passed this test can a !Kung man marry and start a family.[24]

But if cruelty to boys and heavy-handedness toward women are not necessary accompaniments of pressured manhood, why do they still occur more often than not among groups who live in challenging physical environments? Here Gilmore appropriates some of the same post-Freudian psychoanalytic insights that I appealed to in the chapter on developmental psychology. In most cultures, he notes, young children grow up asymmetrically parented: that is to say, their primary caretaker (the mother) is the same-sex parent in the case of girls but the other-sex parent in the case of boys. This in turn produces asymmetrical difficulties in the process of growing up male or female.

Now it is true that becoming a separate person and learning to stand on one's own two feet is in many ways the same for girls and boys. All of us must gradually give up the fantasy of being able to flee back to a parent who will always be there to meet our every need—in more technical terms, the fantasy of regressing to an earlier stage where we can avoid or postpone responsibility by merging with a primal caretaker. But for boys there is the added complication that this separation begins at the same time their sense of having a male gender identity starts to consolidate. Girls too must eventually separate from their mothers, but they do not simultaneously have to figure out how to function with a different gender identity. We saw in the last chapter (and know from our own experience) that little girls are almost always surrounded by female role models

---

[23]Gilmore, *Manhood in the Making,* pp. 166-67.
[24]Ibid., chap. 8.

from birth on, while boys in most cultures have few adult males close at hand to look to as they figure out what it means to become culturally masculine. As Gilmore puts it, "In most societies, the little boy's sense of self as independent must include a sense of the self as different from his mother, as separate from her both in ego-identity and social role. Thus for the boy the task of separation and individuation carries an added burden and peril."[25]

I also noted in the last chapter that this dearth of same-sex role models can lead males to doubt their own capacity to become and stay certifiably masculine. Thus they may come to define masculinity negatively, in terms of avoiding whatever they perceive to be feminine. Gilmore believes that manhood rituals in all cultures are not just ways of toughening up males to take physical risks for the welfare of the group—a practice, we should note, that becomes less urgent as cultures become more adept at inventing technology. They are also men's ways of reassuring themselves that they *have* separated from their mothers and the feminine world they represent. Gilmore even borrows theological language to make this essentially psychological point: "The struggle for masculinity is a battle against these regressive wishes and fantasies, a hard-fought renunciation of the longings for the prelapsarian idyll of childhood. . . . The blissful experience of oneness with the mother is what draws the boy back so powerfully toward childhood and away from the challenge of autonomous manhood."[26]

This is not a completely new insight. In her 1949 book *Male and Female* Margaret Mead suggested that men create exclusive male activities and devalue those associated with women because of an ongoing need to define themselves as different from their mothers.[27] And beginning in the 1950s John and Beatrice Whiting and their colleagues observed that harsh male initiation rites occur mainly in cultures that allow children to stay close to and unweaned from their mothers for several years.[28] But the important point is really not the duration of the nursing period—which can also be very long among gentle groups like the !Kung and the Pygmy. *A crucial factor in the formation of a culture that neither oppresses women nor resorts to extreme cruelty to form responsible men is the*

---

[25]Ibid., p. 27.

[26]Ibid., pp. 28-29. Two other books that view masculine identity as in part a process of overcoming mother-son symbiosis (this time in Western society) are R. William Betcher and William S. Pollock, *In a Time of Fallen Heroes: The Re-creation of Masculinity* (New York: Guilford, 1993), and Stephen R. Boyd, *The Men We Long to Be: Beyond Domination to a New Christian Understanding of Manhood* (San Francisco: HarperSanFrancisco, 1995).

[27]Margaret Mead, *Male and Female* (New York: Morrow, 1949).

[28]John M. W. Whiting, Richard Kluckhohn and Albert Anthony, "The Function of Male Initiation Ceremonies at Puberty," in *Readings in Social Psychology,* 3rd ed., ed. Eleanor E. Maccoby, Theodore M. Newcomb and F. L. Hartley (New York: Holt, Rinehart and Winston, 1958), pp. 359-70; Beatrice Whiting and John Whiting, *Children of Six Cultures: A Psycho-cultural Analysis* (Cambridge, Mass.: Harvard University Press, 1975).

presence of nurturing fathers during children's early years. Despite his many insights into the roots of masculinity worldwide, this is a point that David Gilmore seems to have missed in *Manhood in the Making.* Therefore we need to turn to another body of crosscultural research that tests this hypothesis about the importance of nurturant fathering.

Adding Quantitative to Qualitative Studies

Gilmore's method was the standard anthropological one of looking at a small number of cultures in detail. This yields rich, multifaceted descriptions of life in the groups studied, but it is limited in its power to test hypotheses about universal human behavior, since describing cultures in depth necessarily means that the actual number of cultures sampled is few. In recent decades crosscultural researchers have tried to overcome this limitation by collecting hundreds of ethnographic accounts published by past researchers and finding ways to numerically code the behaviors they describe. As a result there are now computerized archives or databanks of behavioral measures, such as the Human Relations Area Files and the Ethnographic Atlas, from which large, worldwide samples of cultures can be drawn.

These databanks can be used either simply to survey the frequency of certain practices across cultures or to see what behaviors regularly appear together and hence might be causally related to each other. Thus, for example, when David Levinson studied family violence using the Human Relations Area Files, he found that wife beating was noted in 84 percent of the listed societies, physical punishment of children in 74 percent and frequent fighting between siblings in 44 percent.[29] Robert Watson used the same databank to explore what correlated with particularly vicious behavior (torture, deliberate maiming) on the part of soldiers during war. The best predictor was what social psychologists call "deindividuation," the loss or muting of a soldier's individual identity—and by implication responsibility—through the use of uniforms, masks or war paint.[30] Data archives have also been used to test hypotheses

---

[29]David Levinson, *Family Violence in Cross-Cultural Perspective* (Newberry Park, Calif.: Sage, 1989). By making statistical allowances for the possibility of missing data from some cultures, these computer searches are able to make reasonably accurate assessments of the frequency of a given behavior worldwide.

[30]Robert I. Watson Jr., "Investigation into Deindividuation Using a Cross-Cultural Survey Technique," *Journal of Personality and Social Psychology* 25 (1973): 342-45. Clearly both Levinson's and Watson's studies underline the importance of not committing the naturalistic fallacy of arguing from "what is" to "what is morally right"!

about the origins of gender-role distinctions and gender inequality, and it is two of these studies that we now consider.

University of California sociologist Scott Coltrane has looked at relationships among three cultural factors that are of interest here and that previous researchers have not studied quantitatively on a worldwide basis: women's status and influence, men's adherence to culture of honor practices, and the degree to which fathers interact with young children in a nurturing way. His data base was two separate samples of almost a hundred preindustrial cultures from all areas of the world whose ethnographies had been collected and coded in the Ethnographic Atlas. Based on observations originally recorded from the mid-nineteenth through the mid-twentieth centuries, the samples included hunter-gatherer, horticultural, pa toral and subsistence agricultural groups. This "Standard Cross-Cultural Sar le," as it is called, is the most representative and complete sample of pre   ern cultures available for cross-cultural analysis, and Coltrane's use of ι is a helpful addition to Gilmore's more qualitative work.[31]

Nurturant Fathering and Women's Status

In his first study Coltrane looked at relationships among several cultural factors in a sample of ninety premodern groups, about a third of which were hunter-gatherers and the rest simple horticulturalists, herders or subsistence farmers. He was particularly interested in factors that would predict gender egalitarian relationships, so he began by selecting ratings of women's status in his sample of cultures. These included the extent to which women had a voice in domestic and public decision making; whether formal positions of influence were open to women as well as men; and the extent to which women featured positively in the origin myths of each culture. He guessed that women's status was related to men's involvement with childcare—that is, that males would have less need to engage in activities that limit or devalue women if they were less exclusively cared for by women as young children. Again, this is not a new hypothesis, but Coltrane's systematic sta-

---

[31]Coltrane's first study actually predates Gilmore's book by a couple of years, so it is a little puzzling that Gilmore does not refer to it. See Scott Coltrane, "Father-Child Relationships and the Status of Women: A Cross-Cultural Study," *American Journal of Sociology* 93, no. 5 (1988): 1060-95, and "The Micropolitics of Gender in Nonindustrial Societies," *Gender and Society* 6, no. 1 (March 1992): 86-107. For an expansion of his analysis to the North American context, see Scott Coltrane, *Family Man: Fatherhood, Housework and Gender Equity* (New York: Oxford University Press, 1996).

tistical testing of it on a worldwide basis is unique.[32] He included ratings of father involvement from each culture, measures such as the amount of time men spend in proximity to their young children, the degree to which fathers share in children's routine caretaking, and ratings of the culture's overall degree of paternal affection.[33]

Since the advent of second-wave feminism, several other theories have been advanced about the origins of male dominance and women's relative lack of power in premodern cultures. Some anthropologists theorize that men's involvement in warfare exaggerates existing physical sex differences and leads to male-dominated social structures, or that male preoccupation with war limits their involvement in childcare and thereby promotes the adoption of activities aimed at shoring up insecure male identities. Some argue that men in hunting cultures are more likely to bond together, ignoring children and excluding women from other nondomestic activities. Others say the opposite: that hunter-gatherer cultures, by virtue of their small size, nomadic existence and lack of accumulation, tend to be egalitarian. It is when settled populations start farming crops and trading their food surplus that roles begin to differentiate sharply and men take control of resources, to the detriment of women. Still others argue that it is certain male-oriented social structures, such as patrilocal residence (which requires wives to live near their husbands' kin) and patrilineal kinship and inheritance systems that disadvantage women most.[34]

Coltrane enhanced his study greatly by including behavioral measures for each of these competing theories and testing their relative strength against measures supporting his theory about the importance of involved fathering.[35] Having done so, he found that the strongest empirical link was in fact between fathering activity and women's status:

> In those societies with high levels of father-child proximity, women tend to be active participants in community decision-making. Similarly, societies with significant paternal involvement in routine child care are more likely than father-absent societies to include women in public decisions and to allow women access to positions of authority. Societies that couple frequent father-child contact with high levels of

---

[32]Earlier theoretical treatments, beside that of Margaret Mead, include Dorothy Dinnerstein, *The Mermaid and the Minotaur* (New York: Harper & Row, 1976), and Nancy Chodorow, *The Reproduction of Mothering* (Berkeley: University of California Press, 1978). See also Mary Stewart Van Leeuwen, *Gender and Grace: Love, Work and Parenting in a Changing World* (Downers Grove, Ill.: InterVarsity Press, 1990), chaps. 7-8.

[33]Coltrane, "Father-Child Relationships."

[34]See ibid. for pertinent references on these competing theories.

[35]Ibid., for details of his statistical technique (multiple regression analysis) in weighing these factors.

father-child affection are the most likely to exhibit significant female public authority and status.[36]

This relationship remained significant even when other factors were taken
into account—factors such as the culture's mode of subsistence, its warfare habits, and its type of kinship and residence rules. But this last factor also proved
somewhat important. Paternal involvement combined with the relative absence
of male-dominated social structures (such as patrilocality and patrilineal de-
scent) accounted for almost all the variance in women's status, with things like
subsistence practices and warfare habits contributing very little to differences
across the ninety cultures Coltrane sampled.

Nurturant Fathering and Culture of Honor Practices

Because studies like Coltrane's are based only on correlational data, it is not
strictly possible to say what the direction of causality is. Does women's enhanced cultural influence come first, enabling them to lobby successfully for
men's greater participation in childrearing? Or is it men's willingness to be involved with children that both frees up women for other cultural tasks *and*
makes men less likely to engage in women-devaluing activities (because they
have had parents of both sexes involved in their early caretaking)? Of course it
would be nice to know the answer to this question. But even though we can't
answer it at this time, Coltrane's work is very important, for it suggests that just
and mutually supportive relationships between the sexes are possible in a wide
range of cultures with a wide range of task assignments between women and
men. It does not require rigid androgyny—even though it is true that gender
roles tend to be more flexible in cultures whose men are more active in the care
of young children. What it does require is that fathers be routinely involved in
childrearing in ways that set appropriate limits yet remain warm and affirming.[37]
As we saw in the last chapter, this kind of coparenting yields positive developmental results for children of both sexes, as well as for women.

However, from a Christian point of view it would be good to know not just
whether involved fathering is associated with positive outcomes for women and
children but whether it increases the possibility of peaceful and less aggressive
relations *among men,* both within and between cultures. Here we can refer to

---

[36]Ibid., p. 1085.
[37]For one very detailed case study of paternal nurturance in a hunter-gatherer culture, see Barry
    S. Hewlett, *Intimate Fathers: The Nature and Context of Aka Pygmy Paternal Infant Care* (Ann
    Arbor: University of Michigan Press, 1992).

another study conducted by Coltrane on a second sample of cultures from the Ethnographic Atlas. In this study he again used measures of fatherly involvement *but also* measures of men's adherence to a male culture of honor. He included ratings of men's public displays of aggression, strength and sexual potency; measures of norms regarding women's deferential behavior toward men (e.g., whether wives are forbidden to challenge husbands' decisions or to be seated in men's presence); measures of the extent to which husbands dominate wives; and the degree to which each culture had a stated view of women's inferiority. He also used measures of women's control of resources in each of the ninety-three cultures in his sample, including the extent to which women can inherit property, own or control dwellings, and have a say about the use of the products of their own—and men's—labor.[38]

These quite specific measures capture aspects of male honor codes that I have described previously: men's preoccupation with competition among themselves, their corresponding efforts to confine women's activities, and the existence of a double standard of sexual morality. Coltrane wanted to see what cultural practices are most strongly associated with a decrease in men's adherence to such codes of honor. And as in his first study, he found that the *most consistent predictor* was men's routine, nurturant involvement in childcare. This was followed by a second strong factor: significant control of resources by women. All other factors, such as modes of subsistence, participation in warfare, and types of social structures (e.g., matrilocality and matrilineality), were either nonsignificant or only modestly significant predictors of the absence of activities associated with male cultures of honor. Thus the post-Freudian theory about the importance of coparenting is corroborated: when young boys have primary caretakers of both sexes, they are less likely as adults to engage in woman-devaluing activities and in self-aggrandizing, cruel or overly competitive male cults.

Breaking the Cycle: A Final Case Study

In a previous chapter I noted that although the early church made some concessions to the male code of honor, it was a strong force for increased female equality, decreased patriarchy, heightened levels of male servanthood and greater concern for children. This might lead us to ask whether gender relations will become more mutually supportive—even in cultures known for practicing

---

[38]Coltrane, "Micropolitics of Gender."

severe manhood rites and misogyny—if the gospel is presented in a way that neither reinforces male hegemony nor appeals to the kinds of vanity and acquisitiveness that characterize male honor codes. There may be little or no systematic research on this question, but one seasoned missionary's experience with the Masai is highly suggestive.[39]

Vincent Donovan was a Catholic priest who worked in Tanzania for seventeen years as a Holy Ghost father. Members of his order had been stationed in the Masai territory near the Serengeti plains for almost a decade by the mid-1960s. But although they had built hospitals, schools and veterinary clinics that were patronized by the Masai, not one had embraced Christianity. Many missionaries had concluded that the seminomadic Masai were so clannish and self-satisfied that it would take another century before they were willing to talk about the God of the Bible.

Donovan had two reasons for resisting this conclusion. The first was that he had come to see his order's relationship to the Masai as "dismal, time consuming, wearying, expensive, and materialistic," focused mainly on the delivery of services that were rapidly being absorbed by the newly independent government of Tanzania.[40] His second reason came from a study of the missionary methods of the early church. In particular, Donovan noted, the apostle Paul covered a great deal of territory during his missionary journeys but stayed in each place only long enough to preach the gospel and establish an embryonic church under the leadership of local Christians. Letters and other visits might follow, but essentially each new church and ethnic group, armed with the sacraments and the gifts of the Spirit, was to discern its own way to live out and spread the gospel.

With the blessing of his bishop, Donovan became an itinerant missionary to Masai *kraals* or homesteads spread over a five-thousand-square-mile area, bearing nothing but his hope of talking once a week for several successive months to each scattered community. To his surprise, when he explained to Masai leaders that he wished to talk with their people not about schools, hospitals or veterinary services but about God, because that was his original reason for coming to Tanzania, the frequent reply was "If that is why you came here, why did you wait so long to tell us about this? Who can refuse to talk about God?"[41] The sole condition was that he converse with members of entire *kraals* together, and do so early each morning before the demands of cattle herding took over the day.

---

[39]Donovan, *Christianity Rediscovered.*
[40]Ibid., p. 15.
[41]Ibid., p. 22.

While the Masai traditionally have a monotheistic concept of God, or Engai, that God is a tribal God, loving the Masai almost exclusively, and the most healthy and cattle-rich Masai best of all. Consequently Donovan learned to speak with them about Abraham and his strange call to leave his tribe so that all nations would be blessed by Jehovah, the High God so great and loving that he cannot be confined by the limits of wealth, race, clan, tribe or even family. He was quick to admit (because his Masai hearers pointed it out) that his own tribe had been all too eager to confine God to themselves and their pet causes. But he asked that together they explore and extend the kindness of the God "who has appeared to all people" (Tit 3:4) and appeared most clearly in the incarnation of his Son.

That kin-based honor codes can sink deep into a culture's psyche is shown in the fact that it was a Masai woman, not a man, who first expressed her shock to Donovan about the implications of the gospel. She concluded that it meant that they were to learn to love and cooperate with "the people of Kisangiro," a village just three miles away but whose people were of a different clan and hence by tradition "those dark, evil people out there."[42] The big hurdle for this woman and her homestead was not learning to respect Europeans or Indian traders or even other Tanzanian tribes; the challenge was right within her own tribe, with people of another clan living just three miles down the road. For a culture of honor whose manhood is certified in large part by success in stealing cattle from their neighbors, this was a startling revelation!

Seeds of Gender Reconciliation

Nevertheless, whole communities—not just individual Masai—began to make the decision to follow "the man Jesus," so many that by the time Donovan had finished a five-year missionary circuit, there were around three thousand baptized Masai in linked and indigenously led church groups. And although Donovan was careful to work largely within the confines of existing Masai customs, he could not help but note that the power of the gospel affected not just relations with other clans but relations between the sexes. In the very first Masai community he visited, the first woman ever to speak out in a gathering was an illiterate young mother. At first the male elders were startled and upset at her brashness, as women were normally never consulted about anything in public. But before long they admitted that her questions and insights were second to

---

[42]Ibid., p. 48.

none. In time they became visibly proud of her and endorsed her to explain this new message about God to others in the village.

Equally telling was Donovan's first Communion ceremony with the first group of Masai Christians, where he drank wine from a gourd, passed it to the woman beside him, and instructed her to drink from it and pass it to the man sitting next to her. How did the Masai men respond to this breaking of their taboo on eating and drinking with women? "They did accept it, but it was surely a traumatic moment for them. . . . I was not surprised some time later when a group of teenage girls told me privately that the *ilomon sidai* (the good news), that I talked about so constantly, was really good news for them."[43]

A final watershed for gender relations came during discussions regarding what Masai term would be used to describe the followers of Jesus. In the end they chose the term *Oropor L'Engai*—the brotherhood of God, *oropor* being a term previously reserved for male warriors initiated within successive seven-year time spans. In a remarkable affirmation of both common grace and the reconciling power of the gospel,

> the *oropor* of God would not span seven years, but extend from now until the end. It would, because of the message that brought it into being, cross sex lines, age lines, clan lines, tribal lines, national lines. . . . It would necessarily still be an age group brotherhood—but of the last age, the final age reaching to the kingdom. . . . In the evangelization of the Masai people, there has been no notion brought forward, with the exception perhaps of "the man Jesus" that has made them feel so certain that that which they have been treasuring and valuing for generations has not been a waste, but rather a sign of God's continuing love for them.[44]

A Convergence of Findings

We have seen in this chapter that expressions of masculinity both depend on and go beyond the survival challenges that confront traditional cultures. Harsh environments are conducive to the formation of harsh manhood rites and practices, if only because of the practical necessity for men to take physical risks that cannot sensibly be taken by women of reproductive age. And yet we have seen that this connection is not inevitable. Even in difficult environments there are cultures such as the !Kung that are able to socialize men for sacrifice and re-

---

[43]Ibid., p. 121.
[44]Ibid., pp. 93-94.

sponsibility without being excessively cruel to boys and without devaluing or marginalizing women.

We have also seen that such cultures are most likely to be ones in which fathers are regularly involved in affectionate caretaking activities with young children, a connection that seems to be just as significant in premodern cultures as the last chapter showed it to be in our own. Finally there is the case study of the Masai with which this chapter opens and closes. In it we saw that through the working of common grace and the power of the gospel, even a culture with a male honor code that devalues women and harshly socializes boys is capable of dramatic change. These are changes, moreover, that leave the dignity and autonomy of the group intact even as they promote greater justice and peace within the culture and between it and its neighbors.

At a time when the doctrine of extreme cultural relativism has undermined many people's commitment to mission activity both at home and abroad, I believe that the worldwide church is being called to recover and expand its mission focus. Certainly it should do so using the best insights of crosscultural research that are available. And it should do so not just in obedience to Jesus' command to preach the gospel to all nations but for the sake of the men, women and children whose lives and relationships can be made richer and more just by its leavening power.

PART THREE

CONTINUING

CHALLENGES

The Challenge of
Evolutionary Psychology

THE FIRST SECTION OF THIS BOOK concentrated on some "big picture" issues regarding masculinity. These included some current challenges facing men, the significance of a Christian worldview for understanding gender relations, and the ways the Hebrew and Christian Scriptures challenged—even as they partly accommodated—traditional male honor codes. In the second section I narrowed my focus to consider masculinity from the disciplinary perspectives of biology, developmental psychology and cultural anthropology, building on the worldview foundation articulated earlier. In this section I will examine some continuing cultural challenges that are particularly salient (although not exclusively so) in North America. Each has implications for the way masculinity might be shaped in the new millennium and for how Christians might participate in that process. In this chapter we consider the challenge of evolutionary psychology and in the next chapter the impact of the Industrial Revolution on gender relations in general and on men's sense of identity in particular. That chapter will focus on changes in family, church and social life that took place in the nineteenth century up to the time of the first wave of Western feminism, whose main result was the acquisition of voting rights for women. In the last chapter of this section I will take a critical look at some religious and secular men's movements that have arisen as a response to the second wave of feminism that began in the 1960s.

I begin with one of the most strongly defended *and* criticized intellectual currents in social science today: what has come to be known as the "science" of evolutionary psychology. Although there is much careful research done in the field of evolutionary biology, evolutionary theory in general and evolutionary psychology in particular set before us what amounts to an alternative faith-based cosmic drama—one that gives very different answers from Christianity's to worldview questions such as *Who are we? Where are we? What's human-kind's biggest problem?* and *What's the solution?* In trying to answer such questions in the context of a naturalistic worldview, evolutionary psychologists also biologize and trivialize certain questionable male-associated behavioral patterns. In this chapter I will describe the answers that evolutionary psychologists give to basic worldview questions and evaluate those answers according to the scientific criteria that they claim to be following and the Christian worldview that evolutionary psychology claims—in the name of science—to have replaced.

In brief, evolutionary psychology defends the view that genes largely determine not only our human physical characteristics but our behavioral tendencies as well, and that this occurs because certain behaviors—including those that differ by sex—are adaptive for survival and reproduction. However, before examining these claims in detail I need briefly to distinguish evolutionary psychology from other fields that study the relative importance of genes and environment for the human condition.

Do Genes Matter?

More than two decades ago I participated with a number of other scholars in a multidisciplinary research project based in the Central African Republic. Among the targets of our study were the Mbeka Pygmy who, like the !Kung, are a hunter-gatherer group of ancient genetic and cultural lineage. The social scientists among us were studying how their nomadic subsistence style correlated with the way they raised their children and with the strength of certain cognitive and perceptual skills, especially as compared to their sedentary agricultural neighbors, the taller African Bangandou.[1] The biologists in the group were isolating genetic markers from blood samples in order to learn, among other things, when in the distant past the Pygmy may have separated from other migrating groups of people.[2]

What geneticists have learned from such work is that popular stereotypes about race are largely meaningless. Differences visibly connected to what we call race appear to be superficial adaptations to the climates—hot or cold, dry or damp—in which various populations have lived over thousands of years. Indeed the greatest genetic variation between any existing "racial" groups is far less than that found within any group of any color. Different-looking groups

---

[1]See John W. Berry et al., *On the Edge of the Forest: Cultural Adaptation and Cognitive Development in Central Africa* (Lisse, Netherlands: Swets & Zeitlinger, 1986).
[2]Luca Cavalli-Sforza, Paolo Mennozi and Alberto Piazza, *The History and Geography of Human Genes* (Princeton, N.J.: Princeton University Press, 1994).

such as Kenyans and Icelanders are actually so similar to each other that if only one of those groups survived a worldwide catastrophe to continue reproducing, the human species would suffer a very trivial reduction in its genetic diversity.[3] And as noted in previous chapters, human beings' most important genetic legacy is their capacity to adapt to existing environments and create new ones.

How much more specific can we get about the impact of genes on human differences, minor though those differences might be compared to the biological and psychic unity of humankind? Sometimes quite a bit more, as the fields of behavioral and medical genetics teach us. Two kinds of events—the formation of twins and the formation of adoptive families—allow us to assess the relative effect of genes and environment on a number of conditions. For instance, identical twins (whose origins are in a single fertilized ovum that splits in two) have 100 percent of their genes in common, whereas fraternal twins (who develop from two separately fertilized eggs) share only 50 percent and thus are no more genetically similar than ordinary siblings. So, for example, when we find that the shared lifetime risk of developing schizophrenia is almost 50 percent for identical twins but less than 20 percent for fraternal twins, we can conclude that the disease has a strong genetic component. But because the shared risk decreases to less than 10 percent in siblings born at separate times in one family, we know that environmental differences also have some effect. The practice of adoption creates two parallel groups of relatives—biological and nonbiological—and thus gives us another opportunity to tease apart the contribution of genes and environment to individual differences. When we find that adopted individuals are more susceptible to alcoholism if one or both of their biological parents had a history of alcoholism, even if they never lived with those parents, then again we can conclude that there is genetic vulnerability to this problem.[4]

Geneticists have also uncovered information of medical and historical significance for some groups. For example, the risk of sickle-cell anemia is higher in people of African origin, although, interestingly, it turns out that one gene causing it also helps prevent another disease—malaria—that is common in mosquito-infested parts of Africa. Perhaps the most intriguing work in genetics comes from the fact that every human father passes on to his sons a nearly exact copy of the genetic information on his Y chromosome. This is because, unlike other

---

[3]Richard Lewontin, *Human Diversity* (New York: Scientific American, 1982). See also David Unander, *Shattering the Myth of Race: Genetic Realities and Biblical Truths* (Valley Forge, Penn.: Judson, 2000).

[4]In fact in 1993 molecular geneticists identified a gene on chromosome 11 that is more common among alcoholics than nonalcoholics. See David Myers, *Psychology*, 5th ed. (New York: Worth, 1998), chap. 7.

chromosomes, the Y chromosome does not undergo a reshuffling of its genes with a partner (in this case an X chromosome) when sperm are being produced. The virtually fixed nature of the Y chromosome from generation to generation was what enabled researchers to conclude that Thomas Jefferson, the third president of the United States, could have fathered the child of one of his slaves, Sally Hemmings. At the same time, the fact that genetic mutations *do* occur at a slow but constant rate through history enables population geneticists to calculate how long ago migrating groups with common ancestors separated from each other. Through examination of saliva samples submitted for genetic analysis, this kind of research is helping African American descendants of slaves to find out which part of Africa their more immediate ancestors came from.[5]

A Possible Scenario

From this brief tour of some current research trends we see that genes *are* important contributors to human differences—both indirectly, in their contribution to the remarkable adaptive flexibility of every human brain, and more directly in their contribution to specific physical and psychological problems. But can we appeal to genes as a partial explanation for more complex and common behaviors?

Centuries before humans even knew about the existence of genes they were breeding horses, dogs and other animals not just for desired physical but also behavioral traits. As a result of such "artificial selection" we have sheepdogs that herd, bloodhounds that track, pit bulls that fight and lapdogs that sit serenely in people's laps. Dogs, to be sure, are on a much tighter genetic leash than humans—which means they pretty much do what they've been bred to do. No amount of environmental engineering will make a lapdog behave like a bloodhound. But a Vietnamese baby adopted into an American setting will grow up behaving like other Americans. The legacy of a large cerebral cortex puts humans on a much looser genetic leash, with the result that, more than any other species, we are created for behavioral flexibility—for passing on what we have produced culturally, not just what we have been programmed to do genetically.

Nevertheless, it's possible that over thousands of years certain adaptive psychological tendencies—just like certain skin tones and disease resistances—were genetically strengthened in various human groups by the "breeding forces" of their environments. This is the theory of natural selection advanced by Charles

---

[5]L.Luca Cavalli-Sforza, *Genes, People and Languages,* trans. Mark Seielstad (New York: North Point Press, 2000).

Darwin in the mid-nineteenth century. According to this concept, in any species that lives in a given ecological niche those members who happen to have the genes (by mutation and/or inheritance from parents) that allow them to cope more successfully with their environmental challenges are the ones most likely to survive and reproduce. Thus it's possible that, over the centuries, certain genes related to spatial ability have accumulated in the Pygmy as a group, since individual Pygmies without such genes were less likely to survive the demands of a nomadic lifestyle and pass on those genes to following generations.[6]

Micro- and Macroevolution

The above scenario is, of course, about *micro-* rather than *macro*evolution— that is, the possibility of small, environmentally driven (and not even necessarily permanent) genetic changes within species. It is not about the claim that over time new species emerge from older ones, or the even larger claim that all species are descended from a common ancestor, or that life originally emerged from nonliving matter. These are claims about which there is continuing debate, although Christians are united in rejecting the completely naturalistic view of the universe embraced by many evolutionists.[7] But as Catholic biochemist Michael Behe has observed, among biologists of all religious stripes microevolution "is now about as controversial as an athlete's assertion that he or she can jump over a four-foot ditch."[8] Darwin's notion that relatively tiny changes can occur in nature is supported by studies as diverse as laboratory experiments with the fruit fly *Drosophila* and field observations of generations of finches in the Galápagos Islands, not to mention all those practical experiments with plant and dog breeding that humans have been doing for centuries.

Such variation over time does not happen equally often in all species: fruit flies undergo trait mutations more easily than dogs, and dogs more so than humans. But genetic changes do take place at all levels of species complexity.[9] In-

---

[6]For a particularly nuanced treatment of the interaction of cultural and biological evolution, see Marshall H. Segall, Pierre R. Dasen, John W. Berry and Ype H. Poortinga, *Human Behavior in Global Perspective* (New York: Pergamon, 1990), especially chap. 1.

[7]For a summary of these debates, see Nancy Pearcey, "We're Not in Kansas Anymore," *Christianity Today* 44, no. 5 (2000): 42-49, and also Cornelius Hunter, *Darwin's God: Evolution and the Problem of Evil* (Grand Rapids, Mich.: Brazos, 2001).

[8]Michael J. Behe, *Darwin's Black Box: The Biochemical Challenge to Evolution* (New York: Simon & Schuster, 1996), p. 15.

[9]Cornelius Hunter notes that "viruses and bacteria can change significantly (although they are still viruses and bacteria), but in multicellular organisms [genetic] mutations are almost universally not beneficial, and there is a resistance to change" (*Darwin's God,* p. 57).

deed it is the record of such changes that now allows the American descendants of slaves to trace their geographic roots in Africa.

Assumptions of Evolutionary Psychology

How do these relatively cautious claims about genes differ from the claims of evolutionary psychology, and particularly that part of it claiming to explain motivational and behavioral differences between men and women? First formalized a quarter of a century ago under the rubric "sociobiology,"[10] the field now called evolutionary psychology rests on certain controversial assumptions, most of which concern the structure of the human brain. Although evo-psychologists (as I will call them) do not deny that human beings have *somewhat* greater latitude for adaptive learning than other species, they insist that past environmental challenges have produced certain uniform "design features" in human brains everywhere. Some of these are common to male and female brains, but (more controversially) others are said to be sex-specific. We look first at behaviors said to be selected for humans regardless of sex.

At the dawn of human history, so this story goes, human beings faced certain common challenges: how to find food and shelter, how to avoid or overcome predators, how to get copies of their genes into the next generation. Over time, the genes that gave their carriers the greatest edge in meeting these challenges gradually spread through the species to become universal. Thus, according to evolutionary psychologists, little can be learned by studying behavioral variation, whether intra- or crossculturally. By meeting survival challenges of their early "environment of evolutionary adaptation," human brains all ended up pretty much the same, with only a light dusting of flexibility and variability. The behavioral tendencies said to have endured from this common genetic legacy are deemed more important to describe and explain.

To evo-psychologists the mature brain is thus seen less as a general-purpose, flexible problem-solving organ than a collection of fixed "modules" or "programs" that push all humans to behave in similar ways, even though they are largely unaware of this programming.[11] On this account "virtually every human action or feeling, including depression, homosexuality, religion, and consciousness, was put directly into our brains by natural selection. . . . Evolution be-

---

[10]See Edward O. Wilson, *Sociobiology: The New Synthesis* (Cambridge, Mass.: Harvard University Press, 1975), and *On Human Nature* (Cambridge, Mass.: Harvard University Press, 1978).
[11]Leda Cosmides, John Tooby and John Barkow, *The Adapted Mind: Evolutionary Psychology and the Generation of Culture* (New York: Oxford University Press, 1992).

comes the key—the only key—that can unlock our humanity."[12] It not just basic physiological and perceptual processes that have been hard-wired by natural selection but just about everything else too. For evo-psychologists, humans are on a tighter genetic leash than most of them would like to believe.[13]

Thus depression is said to be a trait favored by natural selection because it enabled our ancestors to solve problems by withdrawing from threatening situations and thereby surviving to reproduce. Homosexuality is adaptive because according to the concepts of "kin selection" and "kin altruism," even if gay people do not have children of their own, they share a quarter of their genes with their nieces and nephews and by helping them can keep copies of those genes circulating. Religion is adaptive because its teachings about loving our neighbor point us beyond the narrow tribalism of kin altruism to a wider sense of sharing, or "reciprocal altruism," that enhances the reproductive chances of all who practice it. All human inclinations, if examined closely enough, are simply gene-driven ways of enabling their bearers to survive long enough get those genes copied.[14]

A further assumption of evolutionary psychology is that the specialized, modular brain that humans acquired in their primal environment has not changed appreciably. It took many thousands of years to develop, and given the slow rate at which natural selection and mutation proceed, it is presumed to be with us still. Thus no matter how odd some human behaviors may seem today, they are said to make sense in terms of that primal setting. The world has changed faster than our genes are able to, so some behaviors have become maladaptive—for example, eating as much high-fat food as we can get our hands on, or having very large families. Yet the urge to engage in those behaviors endures. On this account, in our innermost genetic beings we are all Pleistocene hunter-gatherers.

Is This Science?

Perhaps now you can see why earlier I used quotation marks when I called evolutionary psychology a science. In the words of Ian Tattersall, a curator at the American Museum of Natural History, "it provides a perfect foil for reductionist story-telling, since with enough imagination almost any characteristic of an organism can be identified as an 'adaptation' with a distinctive role to play in the evo-

---

[12]Jerry A. Coyne, "Of Vice and Men," *The New Republic*, no. 4,416 (April 3, 2000): 27-34, quotation from p. 27.

[13]This statement possibly excludes evo-psychologists themselves, since they are brilliant and insightful enough to have discovered evolutionary psychology.

[14]See Robert Wright, *The Moral Animal: Evolutionary Psychology and Everyday Life* (New York: Vintage, 1994), and *Nonzero: The Logic of Human Destiny* (New York: Pantheon, 1999).

lutionary scenario."[15] Because we cannot get into a time machine to gather data from the Pleistocene era, and because (as another critic has pointed out) "behavior leaves no fossils,"[16] there is no way to confirm or disconfirm the basic tenets of the theory. As a result, it is possible to explain apparently quite incompatible behaviors using ad hoc evo-psychological concepts. Why are mothers willing die for their children? Of course: to maximize reproductive fitness (by protecting the presumably good genes they've passed on). Well then, why do some mothers kill their children? Of course: to maximize reproductive fitness (by getting rid of the presumably bad genes they've passed on). Why do adults invest more resources in children the more closely they are related to them biologically? Of course: the closer the relationship, the greater the number of one's own genes that are shared! Well then, why would people ever adopt biologically unrelated children? Of course: because of the more generic gene for reciprocal altruism! Auxiliary concepts are multiplied to explain away whatever data are embarrassing to the main theory. Thus evolutionary psychology becomes "simply a theory of everything."[17]

It's not that theorizing—even visionary, faith-based theorizing—is inimical to scientific work. It is vital to good science, as I tried to show in my earlier chapter describing and examining the implications of a Christian worldview. But as philosopher of science Karl Popper noted, any theory that *routinely* explains away contradictory data is not scientific at all. As Popper would put it, a theory that explains everything explains nothing.[18] Ironically, although evo-psychologists believe they are being "scientific" in a way that classical Freudians are not, their theories are just as reductionistic and resistant to empirical challenge. In the words of University of Chicago biologist Jerry Coyne (who thinks evolutionary psychology is far closer to phrenology than to physics), "Now that Darwin is ascendant, [you can] blame your genes, not your mother."[19] An interesting cocktail-party game perhaps, but it should not be mistaken for science.

Sexual Selection and Games People Play

But thus far the evo-psychological scenario, though highly reductionistic and

---

[15]Ian Tattersall, "Whatever Turns You On," *New York Times Book Review,* June 11, 2000, p. 35.
[16]Ruth Hubbard, "The Political Nature of Human Nature," in *Questions of Gender: Perspectives and Paradoxes,* ed. Dina L. Anslemi and Anne L. Law (Boston: McGraw-Hill, 1998), pp. 146-53, quotation from p. 149.
[17]Andrew Ferguson, "Evolutionary Psychology and Its True Believers," *Weekly Standard* 6, no. 26 (2001): 31-39, quotation from p. 33.
[18]Karl Popper, *The Logic of Scientific Discovery* (New York: Basic Books, 1959).
[19]Coyne, "Of Vice and Men," p. 27.

dubiously scientific, is still pretty generically human. It holds that natural selection for certain brain-mapped behaviors happened because of early environmental challenges common to everyone: how to obtain adequate food and shelter and stay safe from predators. However, when it comes to explaining how our ancestors adapted to the actual business of reproduction, evo-psychologists have written very different scripts for men and women. At this point *natural* selection is augmented by what Darwin called *sexual* selection. This is the idea that while women and men may share the same survival interests—and hence the same behavioral tendencies—with regard to routine things like food and shelter, when it comes to reproduction they are programmed for quite different values and behaviors.

The basic idea behind sexual selection is this: if all motives and actions are ultimately in the service of getting one's own genes copied as often and as reliably as possible, then men and women have by necessity evolved markedly different, genetically hard-wired "reproductive strategies" to ensure that this happens. In terms of sheer biology, men can generate many more offspring than women, who are infertile during each nine-month pregnancy (and often after birth if they are nursing) and whose supply of eggs runs dry at an earlier age than men's sperm-producing capacity does. As explained by evo-psychologist Stephen Pinker, "A prehistoric man who slept with fifty women could have sired fifty children, and would have been more likely to leave descendants who inherited his [promiscuous] tastes. A woman who slept with fifty men would have no more descendants that a woman who slept with one."[20] If this is so, then human males are said to have two possible reproductive strategies, while females really only have one.

On the evo-psychological account, females need (and thus *want*, albeit unconsciously) to make sure that the limited number of offspring they can gestate during their fertile years are brought to maturity so that they can continue to pass on copies of their genes. And so women are sensibly choosy about which males they mate with. They look for evidence of a good genetic pedigree in the form of strength to defeat rival males for their affections (the "deer strategy") or in the form of impressive body or other resource markers (the "peacock strategy"). It is such males—or so women's genes are said to reason on their behalf—who will be most likely to pass on copies of well-selected genes, raising the probability that their offspring will themselves survive to reproduce.[21]

---

[20]Stephen Pinker, "Boys Will Be Boys," *New Yorker,* February 9, 1998, p. 21.
[21]Geoffrey Miller, *The Mating Mind: How Sexual Choice Shaped the Evolution of Human Nature* (New York: Doubleday, 2000).

On this account, a woman gains nothing by being endlessly promiscuous. She can get pregnant only a limited number of times, and so as a result of the forces of sexual selection she is inclined to focus on mating with the one, perfect "alpha male"—younger or older, it matters not, as long as he has genetic and material resources. Hopefully he will stay around long enough to help raise any children she has by him, but this is an iffy proposition, as we will see shortly.

A man, by contrast, has two possibilities for multiplying copies of his genes. On the one hand, he can aim for *quantity* of offspring—impregnating as many young, fertile females as possible but not staying around to help raise any of the resulting children. The (again unconscious) calculation is that by virtue of the sheer numbers conceived, enough will survive to adulthood to keep passing on copies of the father's genes, even if some die in infancy or childhood for lack of dual-parent protection. Alternately, he can embrace the *quality* strategy: he can stick with one female partner, because their jointly generated offspring, though fewer in number than if he were promiscuous, are more likely to survive and reproduce with their father's long-term care and protection added to their mother's. These contrasting male scripts have been cutely labeled the "cad strategy" and the "dad strategy."[22]

Now why would any red-blooded male whose sole purpose in life is to get his genes copied as often as possible ever settle for the dad strategy when being a cad seems to deliver the best of all worlds: sexual variety and lots of offspring without any long-term responsibility? Here is where the plasticity of evolutionary psychology allows it to be invoked for quite contrasting ideological agendas.[23] If you wish to support monogamous, permanent unions as a moral (and realistic) ideal, you can fantasize as follows: Human females' sexual receptivity is not narrowly limited to seasonal periods of "heat" or estrus, as is the case with other mammals. Furthermore, their fertile period is not registered in externally obvious body changes (again, unlike other mammals). Therefore since a man can never be sure which of his sexual acts will yield him offspring, and since it would be a genetic disaster to end up raising the children of other men, it's generally a better reproductive strategy to "pair bond"—that is, to stick by one woman, copulate with her regularly and keep her away from other men. Not only is this compromise a man's best guarantee of "paternity certainty," but it will probably help him live longer, since other males would not take kindly to his attempts to get his gametes into females *they* are trying to impregnate.

---

[22]Patricia Draper and Henry Harpending, "Father Absence and Reproductive Strategy: An Evolutionary Perspective," *Journal of Anthropological Research* 38, no. 3 (1982): 255-73.
[23]For a further discussion of this ideological plasticity, see Ferguson, "Evolutionary Psychology and Its True Believers."

According to this more morally traditionalist or "softcore" reading of evolutionary psychology, pair bonding is good for children too. Because the time needed for human infants to reach self-sufficiency is so much longer than in other species, it is more likely to be successful with two highly invested caretakers than with just one. Thus men's genes for pair bonding may trump (if barely) their genes for bed-hopping, provided that the pair-bonding tendency is reinforced by cultural incentives and sanctions.[24] This "softcore" version of evolutionary psychology already biologizes a lot of questionable stereotypes, such as men's insatiable sex drive and their jealous need to guard access to their mates. But the more widely disseminated "hardcore" version goes even further.

Of Hoggamus and Hogwash

If you are a male who favors sexual freedom and material acquisition, the "hardcore" version of evolutionary psychology can help you clothe an age-old double standard in the mantle of science. In this version polygamy, not pair bonding, is men's basic nature. Colin McGinn offers this ironic summary:

> Males will fight, seek resources and posture in order to gain access to females, and the tougher and richer the male, the more copulatory success he will enjoy. . . . It is the old, old story: men look for youth and beauty in their mates, while women seek men who will put a roof over their heads, the fancier the better, even if that means sharing their husband with another woman.[25]

Or, as expressed in a bit of doggerel by nineteenth-century scholar William James, "Hoggamus, higgamus, men are polygamous; Higgamus, hoggamus, women monogamous."[26]

New York Times science writer Natalie Angier rephrased this anticipation of hardcore evo-psychology as follows: "Higgamous, hoggamus, Pygmalionus, *Playboy* magazine eternitas. Amen"—indicating that she sees the enterprise more as a faith-based ideology and an excuse for male sexual license than an example of cutting-edge science.[27] Evo-psychologists, in turn, regard feminism,

---

[24]See for example David Popenoe, *Life Without Father* (New York: Free Press, 1996), chap. 6, and Don S. Browning, Bonnie J. Miller-McLemore, Pamela D. Couture, K. Brynolf Lyon and Rombert M. Franklin, *From Culture Wars to Common Ground: Religion and the American Family Debate* (Louisville, Ky.: Westminster John Knox, 1997), chap. 4.

[25]Colin McGinn, "Some Guys Have All the Luck: How the Dominant Males Rule the Reproductive Roost," *New York Times Book Review,* January 9, 2000, p. 12.

[26]As quoted in Natalie Angier, *Women: An Intimate Geography* (Boston: Houghton Mifflin, 1999), p. 324. (I am also indebted to her for the heading of this section of the chapter!)

[27]Ibid., p. 326.

with its claim that gender stereotypes are the product more of nurture than of nature, as a misguided movement that underestimates the biological strength of men's motivation to be philanderers and women's to be gold diggers. So it's not surprising that feminist critics of both sexes have gone over hardcore evolution-ary psychology with a fine-toothed critical comb and found it wanting. Angier agrees (as do I) that humans are "not above the rude little prods and jests of natural selection." But she concludes that hardcore evo-psychology, "as it has been disseminated across mainstream consciousness, is a cranky and despotic Cyclops, its single eye glaring through an overwhelmingly masculinist lens. I say 'masculinist' rather than 'male' because the view of male behavior promulgated by hardcore evolutionary psychologists is as narrow and inflexible as their view of womanhood is."[28]

Perhaps the most egregious example of evo-psychology's endorsement of negative male stereotypes appeared in the year 2000 book *A Natural History of Rape,* by two American academics, Randy Thornhill and Craig Palmer.[29] Many social scientists believe that rape is driven less by sexual arousal than by men's culturally learned desire to subjugate women.[30] By contrast, Thornhill and Palm-er argue that rape tendencies have been favored by sexual selection to give so-cially unsuccessful males a chance to beget offspring and also to give males who do have mates an extra chance to get their genes copied. Such tendencies might be activated when men are unable to attract women by the usual evolutionary routes of looks, wealth or status. Or it might happen when men's—*any* men's—genes inform them that the reproductive benefits of rape might outweigh the risks—for example, when a woman is alone and unprotected, or when the man has such a clear physical advantage that he cannot be injured by the woman in question.

Thornhill and Palmer hasten to add that they do not by their analysis intend to commit the naturalistic fallacy: men's biological priming for rape doesn't mean such behavior is justified. But the obvious question is, why on earth not? Once you have reduced all behavioral tendencies to inexorable genetic mech-anisms, then humans are no more responsible for their behavior than my local ATM machine is when it fails to give me the money I'm trying to withdraw from

---

[28]Ibid., p. 325.

[29]Randy Thornhill and Craig T. Palmer, *A Natural History of Rape: Biological Bases of Sexual Coercion* (Cambridge, Mass.: M.I.T. Press, 2000).

[30]Other more radical feminists claim—much like evo-psychologists—that men in general are programmed to rape. For discussions of the range of positions, see Susan Brownmiller, *Against Our Will: Men, Women and Rape* (New York: Simon & Schuster, 1975); Susan Griffin, *Rape: The Power of Consciousness* (San Francisco: Harper & Row, 1979); Susan Schecter, *Women and Male Violence* (Boston: South End, 1982); Margaret T. Gordon and Stephanie Riger, *The Female Fear: The Social Cost of Rape* (Urbana: University of Illinois Press, 1989).

my account. You cannot get ethics from mechanics, so the obvious evolutionary default setting is simply that might makes right.

Even if we ignore this ethical contradiction, the authors' ideas for rape prevention border on the absurd. Women, they write, should stay away from secluded places, keep their eyes averted and not expose too much skin. (Would they, one wonders, have prescribed similar precautions to African American men in order to avoid being lynched during the era of the Jim Crow laws?) When women do get raped, Thornhill and Palmer continue, they can be comforted by knowing that their trauma and depression are nature's way of making them withdraw temporarily to lick their wounds. And men? Well, if we just explain to them the evolutionary roots of their impulses, then they may be able to avoid behaving in an adaptive fashion that is harmful to others. To which suggestion mainstream biologist Coyne replies, "Does anyone imagine that young men will be *less* inclined to rape when they are told it is in their genes?"[31]

Scientific Rationality or Rationalization?

Thornhill and Palmer routinely assume that anyone who resists their conclusions is a mindless ideologue or an obscurantist bent on impeding rigorous scientific inquiry. But among evo-psychologists, respect for scientific rigor is often more apparent than real. For example, Thornhill and Palmer claim that women of reproductive age are overly represented among rape victims, just as one might expect if rape is a strategy for getting more of one's genes copied. Yet their own data, when examined closely, indicate that over half of the victims are either prepubertal or postmenopausal women. Moreover, if the goal of rape is to increase the probability of offspring for individual males, how are we to explain gang rapes or wartime soldiers' bordellos? In terms of hardcore evo-psychology, such group behaviors are maladaptive, because competition between multiple rapists lowers each individual's chance to fertilize a possibly waiting egg. How are we to explain the substantial proportion of rapes accompanied by murder, or at least by egregious violence that would lower chances of a viable pregnancy? How are we to explain homosexual rape in prisons and elsewhere?

Selective use of evidence and ignoring contrary data are the stock in trade of many evolutionary psychologists, not just the authors of *A Natural History of Rape*. For example, University of Texas psychologist David Buss makes much of the fact that his surveys in thirty-seven countries show men consistently rating

---

[31]Coyne, "Of Vice and Men," p. 33.

youth and beauty as important traits in a sexual partner, while women give greater weight to ambition and wealth. This apparently explains why men have more extramarital affairs than women, because, Buss tells us, asking a man not to lust after attractive young women is like asking a carnivore not to eat meat.[32] But data collected by Annette Lawson of the Berkeley Institute of Human Development show that since women have entered the waged workforce in large numbers, the number of extramarital dalliances by young women now slightly exceeds the number reported by men. This suggests that the frequency of such behavior—however we might judge it morally—depends less on evolutionary selection of sex-specific motivations than on sheer opportunity and changing gender-role norms.[33]

Even Buss's own data undermine his argument. In his crosscultural surveys of mate preference, when asked what qualities are *most* important, both sexes on average ranked love, dependability, emotional stability and a pleasant personality as the highest four. Only in the fifth ranking did predicted evo-psychological differences emerge, in a modest way, between the sexes.

Moreover, there is a large social-psychological literature affirming that men and women generally marry people like themselves—people who are close in education, economic status, religion, politics, age and even appearance. They marry people they feel comfortable with; empirically it is less the case that "opposites attract" than that "birds of a feather flock together."[34] That powerful older men marry gorgeous younger women more than the opposite scenario is undeniably true. But as with the appeal to differential rates of infidelity, this fact is uninterpretable as long as opportunity remains unequal between the sexes. As Angier wryly comments, "If some women continue to worry that they need a man's money because the playing field remains about as level as Mars—or Venus, if you prefer—then we can't conclude anything about innate preferences."[35]

The significance of differing opportunities for men and women has been further examined by two social psychologists, Alice Eagly and Wendy Wood. These scholars took the thirty-seven cultures of Buss's study and rank-ordered them according to two indices of gender equality devised by the United Nations Development Program. One is the Gender-Related Development Index, which rates nations on the degree to which their female citizens approximate male citizens' life span, education and basic income. The other is the Gender Empow-

---

[32]David Buss, *The Evolution of Desire* (New York: BasicBooks, 1994).
[33]As reported in John Gottman and Nan Silver, *The Seven Principles for Making Marriage Work* (New York: Three Rivers, 1999), p. 16.
[34]Myers, *Psychology,* chap. 18.
[35]Angier, *Women,* p. 331.

erment Measure, which rates nations on the degree to which women, in comparison to men, have entered the public arena as local and national politicians and as professionals and managers.[36] Using these two measures, they found that as gender equality in Buss's thirty-seven nation list increased, the tendency for either sex to choose mates according to the so-called sex-selection criteria of evolutionary psychology *decreased.*

Eagly and Wood concluded from this reanalysis that sex differences in mate selection criteria—differences that Buss and other evo-psychologists claim are "hard-wired" in all humans by evolution—are more likely the result of the historically constructed sexual division of labor, which has kept women dependent on men's income and men dependent on women's domestic skills. As this wall of separation between men's and women's spheres breaks down (a process nicely traced in the two UN measures used by Eagly and Wood), both sexes begin to use more generically human criteria—such as love, dependability and a pleasing personality—to judge potential mates.[37]

There are other contradictions in hardcore evolutionary psychology. For example, if male promiscuity is such an adaptive reproductive strategy, why do sexually transmitted diseases persist, mutate and multiply? If older, resource-rich males are so naturally attractive to young, fertile women, why do men routinely fret about going bald? There is no evidence that women admire, rather than merely tolerate, a receding hairline. "Yet," observes Angier, "the legend of the sexy older man persists—particularly among older men."[38] She summarizes the methodological issues quite trenchantly: Hardcore evo-psychologists "declare ringing confirmation for their theories in the face of feeble data. They suffer amusing contradictions of their data. They pick and choose, one from column A, one from column B, and good food, good meat, holy Darwin, let's eat!"[39]

Evolutionary Psychology as Worldview

In view of its dubiously scientific status, why does evo-psychology—as measured by sales of its proponents' books—have such wide appeal? To a great ex-

---

[36]For a further explanation of these measures, see *Human Development Report of the United Nations Development Program* (New York: Oxford University Press, 1995). See also Mary Stewart Van Leeuwen, "Faith, Feminism and Family in an Age of Globalization," in *Religion and the Powers of the Common Life*, ed. Max Stackhouse and Peter Paris (Harrisburg, Penn.: Trinity Press International, 2000), pp. 184-230.

[37]Alice H. Eagly and Wendy Wood, "The Origins of Sex Differences in Human Behavior: Evolved Dispositions Versus Social Roles," *American Psychologist* 54, no. 6 (1999): 408-23.

[38]Angier, *Women,* p. 332.

[39]Ibid., p. 326.

tent its popularity, like that of psychoanalysis or behaviorism in previous
decades, rests on the naive hope of a comprehensive "scientific" explanation for
everything humans do. "Evolutionary psychology," writes Coyne, "satisfies the
post-ideological hunger for a totalistic explanation of human behavior, for a theory that will remove many of the ambiguities and uncertainties of emotional and
moral life."[40] That it tries to reduce religious faith to just another reproductive
strategy, while itself being a profoundly faith-based, totalizing worldview, has
not been lost on its many critics. One group of scientists, referring to the academic gathering place of several famous evo-psychologists, jokingly refers to
the movement as "the Santa Barbara Church."[41]

Pointing out the faith-based nature of their theory is lost on most evo-psychologists, who continue to see themselves as cutting-edge representatives of
hard science.[42] But there are telling exceptions. Evolutionary biologist Richard
Lewontin has admitted that his and his colleagues' "willingness to accept scientific claims that are against common sense is the key to understanding the real
struggle—that between science and the supernatural":

> We take the side of [evolutionary] science . . . *in spite of* [its] tolerance of unsub-
> stantiated just-so stories, because we have a prior commitment to materialism. It is
> not that the methods and institutions of science somehow compel us to accept a
> material explanation of the phenomenal world, but on the contrary, that we are
> forced by our *a priori* adherence to material causes to create . . . a set of concepts
> that produce material explanations, no matter how counterintuitive, no matter how
> mystifying to the uninitiated. Moreover, that materialism is absolute, for we cannot
> allow a Divine Foot in the door.[43]

So there you have it. Evo-psychology, like its doctrinaire psychoanalytic and
behaviorist forerunners, is the latest academic attempt to have one's cake and
eat it: to use the language of science while bending the rules for scientific evidence, while at the same time ruling religious explanations for *anything* out of
order. It is the latest incarnation of repeated efforts to dismiss God not just on-

---

[40]Coyne, "Of Vice and Men," p. 27.

[41]Erica Goode, "Human Nature: Born or Made? Evolutionary Theorists Provoke an Uproar," *New York Times,* March 14, 2000, pp. F-1, F-9, quotation from p. F-9.

[42]Neuroscientist Robert Sapolsky, borrowing a page from Freud, calls this "physics envy": "the disease among scientists where the behavioral biologists fear their discipline lacks the rigor of physiology, the physiologists wish for the techniques of the biochemists, the biochemists covet the clarity of the answers revealed by molecular biologists, all the way down until you get to the physicists, who confer only with God." See Robert M. Sapolsky, *The Trouble with Testosterone, and Other Essays on the Biology of the Human Predicament* (New York: Touchstone, 1997), p. 152.

[43]In *New York Review of Books,* January 9, 1997, as quoted by Richard John Neuhaus, "The Public Square," *First Things,* no. 90 (February 1999): 79-80 (Lewontin's italics).

tologically but ethically. Fortunately for all of us, many evo-psychologists do continue to distinguish between the might-makes-right implications of their materialist worldview and the higher morals to which they agree we should all aspire. But since that materialist worldview provides no basis for morality, this simply means that as human beings they are better than their theories. It does not make them more scientific or intellectually consistent. Nor does it guarantee that their intellectual descendants will not slide back to a more consistent might-makes-right stance, also as regards gender relations. After all, boys will be boys, will they not?[44]

Can Anything Good Come out of This?

If evolutionary psychology is less a science and more a materialist and libertarian ideology bent on excluding any appeal to revealed truth, does that mean nothing in it is redeemable? After all, classical psychoanalysis and behaviorism were equally antireligious worldviews, yet the former taught us something about the role of the unconscious and the irrational in human functioning, and the latter something about the role of environmental constraints and incentives in shaping behavior. Is there an analogous kernel of wheat amid the considerable chaff that I have documented in evolutionary psychology? I believe the answer to that question is a cautious yes.

Historically, there has been a recurring pull toward gnosticism among Christians—that is, a tendency to regard the material world as antithetical to an ideally disembodied spiritual existence. In its extreme form, this attitude downplays both the created goodness of the body and the degree to which that goodness is compromised by sin. That is why gnostic sexual ethics vacillate between asceticism and license: if the body is nothing but a trap for the spirit, then it should be either disciplined into complete submission or, conversely, allowed to do whatever its whims dictate.[45] Against such dualism, evolutionary psychology reminds us that biology does affect our behavioral impulses and limit our freedom of action. We do not have to endorse its genetic reductionism in order to acknowledge it as a salutary corrective not just to gnostic tendencies among Christians but to other historically antibiological

---

[44]For example Stephen Goldberg, *The Inevitability of Patriarchy* (New York: Simon & Schuster, 1973)

[45]See for example Hans Jonas, *The Gnostic Religion: The Message of an Alien God and the Beginnings of Christianity,* 2nd ed. (Boston: Beacon, 1963), and for an account of its lingering influence in contemporary Christianity, Harold Bloom, *The American Religion: The Emergence of the Post-Christian Nation* (New York: Riverhead, 2000).

tendencies in psychology. These include behaviorism and (oppositely) the
kind of humanistic psychology that questions any limits—biological *or* environmental—on human freedom of action.[46]

However, in contrast to the biblical worldview and theologies that have been
built on it, evolutionary psychology has no basis for sorting out what is created
from what is fallen in human behavior. Thomas Aquinas, in his *Summa Contra
Gentiles,* was willing to concede that men's care for their wives and children has
a "natural" basis in their desire for paternal certainty and their desire, "in common with other animals and with plants . . . to leave behind them an image of
themselves."[47] He also realized that these "natural" ends could be very efficiently
achieved in the practice of polygamy, which lets men—or at least some men—
use their power to take multiple wives and monitor them closely to make sure
that they bear no other men's children. At first glance this seems very much like
a medieval anticipation of evolutionary psychology. However, Aquinas rejects
not only polygamy but also male-initiated divorce as practices unjust to women.
Polygamy pits cowives against each other for their husband's favor, thus allowing them to be "treated as servants" and undermining the ethical norm of marital
friendship between spouses. As for the man who wants to divorce an older wife
for a younger, more fertile one, Aquinas asserts that this too "does her an injury,
contrary to natural equity."[48]

Ultimately Aquinas appeals to Christ's self-sacrificing action as the pattern for
husbands and fathers. As practical theologian Don Browning has noted,

> This means that the husband is to imitate Christ both in the husband's unbreakable
> commitment to the family but also in his capacity for sacrificial love or charity. . . .
> The purpose of this sacrificial love is to endure in the relationship and restore it to
> the equity of friendship. Friendship with one's spouse, friendship with the neigh-
> bor, and finally friendship with God—these are the purposes of Christ's passion.[49]

These standards of marital exclusiveness, equity and friendship rest in turn
on creation norms summarized in Genesis 2:24: "Therefore a man leaves his father and his mother and cleaves to his wife, and they become one flesh." Sociologist David Fraser notes that this verse holds in tension three essential aspects
of marriage: public wedlock ("leaving"), sexual union ("one flesh") and a love

---

[46]For further discussion of these issues, see Mary Stewart Van Leeuwen, "Scuttling the Schizo-
phrenic Student Mind: On the Unity of Faith and Learning in Psychology," in *Essays on
Church-Related Higher Education,* ed. Arlen Miggliazzo (Omaha, Neb.: Creighton University
Press, forthcoming), and also Don S. Browning, *Religious Thought and the Modern Psycholo-
gies* (Philadelphia: Fortress, 1987).
[47]Quoted in Browning et al., *From Culture Wars to Common Ground,* p. 117.
[48]Ibid, pp. 119, 122.
[49]Ibid., p. 123.

ethic of mutual regard ("cleaving"). Yet Fraser significantly notes that "in this passage the couple is complete without children."[50]

Thus in the biblical worldview pair bonding is not simply a way to get one's genes copied—though children are indeed part of God's promised blessing in creation. It is based on the deeper recognition that women and men are both created in the image of God, derive equal dignity and respect from that image, and are called to be God's earthly regents—not separately, nor in genetic competition with each other, but in cooperation with each other. That God includes among their assigned tasks the command to "be fruitful and multiply" in no way supports the selfish-gene reductionism of evolutionary psychology. Fecundity is an aspect—and a blessing—of the image of God in humans. But the image is much more than fecundity, and the pursuit of fecundity—if it is to be a blessing to all who are involved—must respect God's original intentions for life together.

Thus in the words of Browning, as Christians consider an ethic of human sexuality for the twenty-first century, they "should use the disciplines of biology last, not first. They should begin with the scriptures of the communities of faith that form them, with the Genesis ordinances about male and female leaving their families of origin and becoming one flesh."[51] Careful genetic research—such as the kind summarized at the beginning of this chapter—may eventually help us understand some of the challenges our bodies pose in realizing these ideals. But evolutionary psychology, inasmuch as it aims to replace those ideals with a thoroughly materialist worldview, is not the foundation on which to build a sexual ethic, either for men or for women. It is the biblical worldview to which evolutionary psychology must be held accountable, and not vice versa.

---

[50]David A. Fraser, "Focus on the 'Biblical Family': Sociological and Normative Considerations," in *The Gospel with Extra Salt*, ed. Joseph B. Modica (Valley Forge, Penn.: Judson, 2000), pp. 1-29, quotation from p. 18.

[51]Browning et al., *From Culture wars to Common Ground*, p. 125.

Men, Religion and the
Distortion of the Cultural Mandate

I N THE YEAR 1896, OF A TOTAL U.S. ADULT male population of nineteen million, close to six million males belonged to what were called fraternal orders or lodges. Modeled on, yet different from, earlier British men's lodges (whose main aims were sociability and mutual aid), they included groups with members in the hundreds of thousands, such as the Odd Fellows, the Freemasons, the Knights of Pythias and the Red Men, in addition to hundreds of smaller orders. While incidentally providing a social outlet and sometimes low-cost insurance for members, the American lodges were attractive primarily for the graded hierarchy of quasi-religious, secret rituals they enabled men to take part in.

Many of these rituals were devised by Protestant ministers who were themselves lodge members. Catholics and evangelicals opposed lodges on account of their secrecy and because they believed that their contrived rituals—loosely based on everything from Greek mythology to American Indian lore—offered an emotionally charged but bogus conversion experience. Charles Finney, the well-known nineteenth-century evangelical revivalist, was a convert from Masonic ritualism, in which he had previously attained the "sublime degree" of Master Mason. In 1860 Jonathan Blanchard, a Congregationalist minister, founded Wheaton College in Illinois in part as an antilodge citadel. Blanchard was also a leader in the National Christian Association, a group that had earlier worked for the eradication of slavery. After the Civil War the NCA opposed the resurgence of lodge activity, which it saw as a potentially undemocratic institution that divided men's religious loyalties and reduced male presence and leadership in the churches.[1]

---

[1]Mark C. Carnes, *Secret Ritual and Manhood in Victorian America* (New Haven, Conn.: Yale University Press, 1989), prologue and chap. 3.

The NCA's concerns did not lack empirical merit. Known by lodge historians as the "Golden Age of Fraternity" in the United States, the last third of the nineteenth century also saw close to a tripling of the number of Protestant church members, who by 1890 made up 45 percent of the nation's population. But fully two-thirds of American Protestants were women.[2] At the same time, one in four adult men—and a majority among white-collar and professional city dwellers—belonged to one or more fraternal societies. Thus, according to historian David Hackett, it is not an exaggeration to say that "among the urban, middle-class . . . the women were in the churches and the men were in the lodges."[3] And the lodges were unquestionably male enclaves. Although some grudgingly tolerated the introduction of ladies' auxiliaries beginning in the 1860s, the status of women members was always linked to that of their husbands or fathers in the more wealthy and numerous men's lodges. Women were not privy to the rituals and secrets of the male lodges, and the latter appear to have valued the women's auxiliaries mainly as a way of warding off antilodge sentiment from the broader public.[4]

A century later most fraternal orders have vanished, having begun steep membership declines during the Great Depression, and today the American public knows them mostly as convenient means for renting meeting halls. They are occasionally resurrected for entertainment—for example, to give unwitting help to a time-traveler in the movie *Peggy Sue Got Married,* or to make the clueless Ralph Kramden of *The Honeymooners* (who belonged to the Loyal Order of Raccoons) seem even more out of step with his times.

But in the past three decades men's movements—albeit looser, smaller, less secretive and more varied in their missions—have begun to dot the North American landscape again. Some, like the Promise Keepers and the Million Man March, have clear confessional connections to conservative Christianity or Islam. Some, like the Mythopoetic Men's Movement, are more vaguely spiritual in their aims and content. Others, such as the National Organization for Men Against Sexism, exist as species of men's auxiliaries to one or other expression of sec-

---

[2]This gender disproportion in the churches was not new, and it is also the case that in colonial times, when church membership was required, it is possible that many men (and women) were "formal" rather than "convinced" church members. Also, definitions of church membership were undoubtedly variable in the nineteenth century, sometimes referring to baptized members, sometimes to confirmed members and sometimes to adherents. The point in this section is not so much the history of gender disparity in apparent church membership in America but the tremendous attraction of lodges for men during this period, and the reasons for that attraction. My thanks to Charles Lippy of the University of Tennessee history department for reminding me of the above qualifiers.

[3]David G. Hackett, "Gender and Religion in American Culture, 1870-1930," *Religion and American Culture* 5, no. 2 (1995): 127-57, quotation from p. 132.

[4]Carnes, *Secret Ritual and Manhood in Victorian America,* pp. 81-89.

ond-wave feminism—liberal, radical, Marxist or socialist. And still others, like the Men's Rights Movement, challenge the very notion that women as a group suffer more injustice than men do.

What are the connections between religious men's movements of the nineteenth century and those of today? And what can Christians learn from both periods in deciding what expressions of masculinity they will encourage in the twenty-first century? These are the questions addressed by this and the following chapter, drawing on selected case studies of Christian and other men's movements that have come and gone over more than a century of vast social change.[5]

Sharing the Cultural Mandate in Preindustrial Times

To begin answering them, I should note it is no accident that the so-called Golden Age of Fraternity coincided with the increasing impact of the Industrial Revolution on America. In the second half of the nineteenth century, with a growing and relatively prosperous population, the United States quickly adopted new technologies such as the telegraph and the steam engine to meet the challenge of large distances between population centers. "Yankee ingenuity" led to the invention and eventually mass production of machines as varied as the reaper, the sewing machine, the Colt revolver and the water-powered loom. These technological advances held the promise of a higher material standard of living for the entire nation, but at the same time led to tremendous changes in relationships between parents and children, between women and men, and between families and the churches they belonged to.[6]

Prior to the Industrial Revolution, family and social life were quite organically unified. Once settled, most communities remained small and stable, so that peo-

---

[5]For reasons of space, these chapters will not do detailed coverage of today's politically oriented men's movements, for surveys of which the reader should see Kenneth Clatterbaugh, *Contemporary Perspectives on Masculinity: Men, Women and Politics in Modern Society*, 2nd ed. (Boulder, Colo.: Westview, 1997), or Michael A. Messner, *Politics of Masculinities: Men in Movements* (Thousand Oaks, Calif.: Sage, 1997). Space also precludes detailed analysis of the relationship between religion and sport that began in the nineteenth century, for a good treatment of which see Tony Ladd and James A. Mathisen, *Muscular Christianity: Evangelical Protestants and the Development of American Sport* (Grand Rapids, Mich.: Baker, 1999).

[6]See for example Peter G. Filene, *Him/Her/Self: Sex Roles in Modern America*, 2nd ed. (Baltimore: Johns Hopkins University Press, 1986); Carl Degler, *At Odds: Women and the Family in America from the Revolution to the Present* (New York: Oxford University Press, 1980); Margaret L. Bendroth, *Fundamentalism and Gender: 1875 to the Present* (New Haven, Conn.: Yale University Press, 1993); Barbara Leslie Epstein, *The Politics of Domesicity: Women, Evangelism and Temperance in Nineteenth Century America* (Middletown, Conn.: Wesleyan University Press, 1981); and Gail Bederman, *Manlinesss and Civilization: A Cultural History of Gender and Race in the United States, 1880-1917* (Chicago: University of Chicago Press, 1996).

ple lived, worked, worshiped and grew old in a network of family, friends and acquaintances that changed only slowly. Family businesses—either subsistence farms or small shops—were the norm; each household was a locus of economic production in which all family members except the very youngest took part. As summarized by sociologist David Popenoe, colonial nuclear families and those of the early U.S. republic were "highly multifunctional and relatively self-suffi-cient, serving as workshop and business, school, vocational institute, church, welfare institution, and even house of correction, as well as the seat of all do-mestic activities."[7] In addition, families were embedded in wider church and civ-ic networks and thus did not function in complete isolation.

Gender roles did exist; indeed the labor-intensive nature of colonial life—and women's vulnerability to frequent pregnancies—made it only sensible for men to do the heaviest work. But there were flexibility and seasonal overlap in men's and women's activities, with the result that both parts of the cultural mandate—to be fruitful and multiply, and to subdue the earth—were undertaken more or less equally by both sexes. Workplace, dwelling space and childrearing space largely coincided for both fathers and mothers, who had strong ties to their chil-dren because most farms and businesses were handed on from one generation to the next. And although family subsistence demanded hard physical work, it had a seasonal cycle, which meant that during the more leisurely winters family bonds—for good or ill—became even closer.[8]

Colonial families were patriarchal to a degree that few people would coun-tenance today. For example, the nuclear family ceased to exist as a legal entity if its father (but not if its mother) died. Divorce, though rarer than today, rou-tinely resulted in child custody's being assigned to the father. And because women were considered morally weaker than men, childrearing advice was ad-dressed almost exclusively to fathers, who were also expected to lead the family in prayer, Bible study and the singing of psalms.[9] But whatever we think of the authority structure of preindustrial families, they had this advantage: children of both sexes had adults of both sexes consistently present in their lives. As histo-rian Mark Carnes notes, this meant that "boys and young men in the colonial era . . . at an early age dressed like men [and] worked with their fathers and other adult men at tasks related to their adult life."[10]

Relationships between colonial fathers and sons were no doubt emotionally

[7]David Popenoe, *Life Without Father* (New York: Free Press, 1996), p. 87.
[8]Carnes, *Secret Ritual and Manhood in Victorian America*, chap. 4.
[9]Ibid., chap. 4. See also Robert L. Griswold, *Fatherhood in America: A History* (New York: Ba-sicBooks, 1993), chaps. 2-3.
[10]Carnes, *Secret Ritual and Manhood in Victorian America*, p. 113.

ambivalent. Fathers could decide when to set sons up with their own shops or farms, thus also determining when they could marry. They not infrequently delayed this decision to keep sons' labor available for their own household, causing resentment in young men chafing for independent adult status. However, years of side-by-side labor with fathers at least meant that boys, like their sisters, picked up adult roles experientially, through daily contact with a same-sex role model. They were thus less likely to grow up with a fragile male identity and to practice the resulting overcompensations that, as we have already seen, can occur when boys are raised in more father-distant cultures.

Dividing the Cultural Mandate in the Industrial Era

It would be hard to exaggerate how much this state of affairs changed as the Industrial Revolution gathered momentum. Subsistence farming gave way to more mechanized commercial agriculture. With steadily cheaper consumer goods available, adult women were less occupied with traditional tasks such as spinning, weaving, soap making and poultry raising, so they gradually went from being coproducers to being mainly purchasers and consumers of household goods. Some men, attracted by the possibilities of the expanding American economy, exchanged the family shop or farm with its seasonal rhythms of hard work and leisure for year-round waged labor in factories or offices. Increasingly away from home for most days of the week, they began to lose their traditional concerns for nurturing family and faith, finding it easier to turn these tasks over to their more homebound wives.

Men's increasing withdrawal from the domestic sphere and women's increasing specialization in it—often seen by later evangelicals as "biblical" and "natural"—were at first rightly recognized as causes for concern. "Paternal neglect at the present time is one of the most abundant sources of domestic sorrow," wrote the Rev. John S. C. Abbott in the mid-nineteenth century. "The father . . . eager in the pursuit of business, toils early and late, and finds no time to fulfill duties to his children."[11] But as capitalism and commerce expanded, this extreme division of labor was more and more portrayed as both natural and sacred. Women were to become "angels of the home" and men "captains of industry," even though in practice this bifurcation of gender roles was a luxury beyond the reach of many poor urban families—not to mention those still work-

---

[11]John S. C. Abbott, "Paternal Neglect," *Parent's Magazine* 2 (March 1842): 148; quoted in Carnes, *Secret Ritual and Manhood in Victorian America,* p. 111.

ing on family farms—whose survival required the economic activity of all family members.[12]

Thus was born the nineteenth-century "doctrine of separate spheres," according to which masculinity entailed rationality, competition and profit in public arenas such as the marketplace, the academy and the political forum, while femininity was associated with domesticity, sacrifice, tender emotion and piety.[13] During this period, in the words of historian Gail Bederman, "middle class Americans used gender to wed morality to productivity—literally."[14] No longer economic partners with men, women were to be full-time nurturers of children and providers of emotional respite to their husbands from the ruthless public world of profit and competition. Aided by child-focused books such as Horace Bushnell's 1847 volume *Christian Nurture*,[15] motherhood came to be seen as a sacred calling for which women were morally equipped in a way men were not. This, we should note, was a reversal of the colonial-era notion that women were men's moral and spiritual inferiors in matters of childrearing. In effect, the cultural mandate was now to be divided by gender and location: women were to specialize in being fruitful at home, while men subdued the earth elsewhere. Thus "pious women would keep their sons and husbands moral; productive men would work to become successful entrepreneurs . . . and together they would forge godly homes, the epitome of Christian progress."[16]

At the same time that pious language was being co-opted to justify women's confinement to domesticity, religious symbolism was being used to affirm men's place in the public sphere. It is no accident that banks were often called "temples of commerce" and universities "cathedrals of learning," and that many of them were architecturally designed to look like churches. Yet thanks to the growing worship of technological and economic progress, the public square was actually stripped of much Christian influence because religious faith, increasingly regarded as emotional, subjective and unscientific (albeit useful for

---

[12]See for example Jacqueline Jones, *Labor of Love, Labor of Sorrow: Black Women, Work and the Family, from Slavery to the Present* (New York: Basic Books, 1985).

[13]Perhaps I should say that the doctrine of separate spheres was "reborn," since, as I have noted in previous chapters, it has been a feature of cultures of honor at various times in history. For a historical overview see Jean Bethke Elshtain, *Public Man, Private Woman: Women in Social and Political Thought* (Princeton, N.J.: Princeton University Press, 1981).

[14]Gail Bederman, "'The Women Have Had Charge of the Church Work Long Enough': The Men and Religion Forward Movement of 1911-1912 and the Masculinization of Middle-Class Protestantism," *American Quarterly* 41, no. 3 (1989): 432-65; quotation from p. 436.

[15]Horace Bushnell, *Christian Nurture*, introduction by Luther A. Weigle (New Haven, Conn.: Yale University Press, 1947). See also Margaret Bendroth, "Horace Bushnell's *Christian Nurture*," in *The Child in Christian Thought and Practice*, ed. Marcia J. Bunge (Grand Rapids, Mich.: Eerdmans, 2000), pp. 348-62.

[16]Bederman, "Women Have Had Charge," p. 436.

promoting morality), was now to be confined to private life.[17] The artificial separation of public "facts" from personal "values" was more and more taken for granted.

Mixed Messages for Young Men

Notice what has happened here. Under the doctrine of separate spheres, women were relegated to domesticity because they were said to be unsuited for public-domain rationality and economic achievement. Religion was largely removed from the public domain because it too was seen as representing self-denial, emotionality and a world of faith rather than facts. The result, not surprisingly, is that religion came to be seen as a feminine, not a masculine, pursuit. Throughout the last half of the nineteenth century, white Protestant churches more and more became enclaves for women's activities, and the masculinity of churchgoing men in general, and pastors in particular, came to be somewhat culturally suspect.

We should note that among socially less powerful groups, such as blacks and Catholics, this was less the case. African American men formed a group known as the Prince Hall Masons whose members provided vital leadership to the black church, and Catholics promoted the Knights of Columbus as a church-based men's society whose mission was to strengthen American Catholicism both numerically and financially.[18]

Moreover, the compartmentalization of "masculine" public from "feminine" domestic and religious activity was never complete even in the Protestant middle class. Christian postmillennialists of both sexes—many of whom first became activists fighting against slavery—worked to open up higher education to girls and argued that the franchise should similarly be extended to women.[19] Because their postmillennial theology emphasized "making the good of society better" as a way of hastening the coming of God's kingdom, they also encouraged the development of sport among Christians of both sexes as the "muscular Christianity" movement spread from England to the United States in the mid-nineteenth century.[20]

---

[17]See Richard John Neuhaus, *The Naked Public Square,* 2nd ed. (Grand Rapids, Mich.: Eerdmans, 1984).
[18]Hackett, "Gender and Religion in American Culture."
[19]See for example Nancy Cott, *The Grounding of Modern Feminism* (New Haven, Conn.: Yale University Press, 1987), and Aileen S. Kraditor, ed., *Up from the Pedestal: Selected Writings in the History of American Feminism* (New York: Quadrangle, 1968).
[20]Ladd and Mathisen, *Muscular Christianity,* chap. 1.

Other so-called domestic feminists challenged the doctrine of separate spheres less directly. They argued that women's supposedly greater natural concern for morality and for family welfare meant that they had a calling to clean up public life by participating in evangelistic and temperance organizations, campaigns to extend and improve public schooling, and programs to promote sexual purity. (One of their slogans was "Votes for Women and Chastity for Men.") They insisted that working for such reforms made women more devoted wives and mothers, even though it involved activity that sometimes took them away from their families.[21]

Nevertheless, focused childrearing was idealized in theory as women's primary vocation. And it was made possible for many families in practice by the availability of cheaper consumer goods and the fact that the average number of children born to white women in the United States dropped from seven to about half that number over the course of the nineteenth century.[22] Carnes points out that middle-class women were not simply passive victims of this "cult of true womanhood. As noted in the previous paragraph, vocal minorities among them did challenge it. But women in general were the coauthors of "a bifurcated gender system that elevated their status even as it circumscribed their actions at home. Though they remained the legal and social inferiors of men, women acquired new status as moral guardians of the young."[23]

In light of earlier chapters you can probably understand the kind of gender asymmetry in childrearing that resulted from all this. Homes were to be "havens in a heartless world" presided over by wives and mothers, who were to remind their husbands and children that the Christian virtues of temperance, compassion and self-effacement were more important than the marketplace values of unbridled competition and profit. But middle-class fathers were no longer at home day by day to model these virtues to their sons; instead they functioned in the outside "domain of masculine aggression and turpitude . . . devoid of salutary feminine influences."[24] Boys were thus raised in a world of so-called feminine sentiment—and not just at home but at school, since by 1890 nearly two-thirds of public school teachers in the United States were unmarried women.

Barred from formal political and economic activity, middle-class mothers threw much energy into keeping their sons moral, even into their adult working

---

[21]For accounts of domestic feminism see for example Epstein, *Politics of Domesticity,* and William Leach, *True Love and Perfect Union: The Feminist Reform of Sex and Society,* 2nd ed. (Middletown, Conn.: Wesleyan University Press, 1989).

[22]Carnes, *Secret Ritual and Manhood in Victorian America,* p. 112.

[23]Ibid., p. 111. See also Degler, *At Odds.*

[24]Carnes, *Secret Ritual and Manhood in Victorian America,* p. 113.

life. Women's magazines abounded with stories of sons who left home to work in the cities and soon became utterly debauched. To guard against this, mothers—already the most potent force in their children's lives—managed so successfully to keep sons living at home that by the 1870s most did so right up until their late twenties or early thirties, when they were financially stable enough to support a wife in an independent household.[25] And to which set of virtues were young men to give their allegiance: the fruits of the Spirit such as kindness, generosity and self-control, as enjoined for so many years by their mothers, or the values of the marketplace that they had to embrace to make a living and save enough to get married? Carnes notes that under the rigidly gendered doctrine of separate spheres, unless a young man became a minister or schoolteacher (both "feminine" jobs associated with nurturing activities and offering low pay and status), a middle-class boy's "presumed destiny as a man was at odds with the lessons and sensibilities he had learned at his mother's knee. He could fulfill his duty to his mother only by sacrificing his status as a man."[26]

Fraternal Lodges Revisited

It should surprise no one to learn that men's lodges in nineteenth-century America served much the same psychological function that harsh initiation rites do in preindustrial cultures characterized by low father involvement. Lodge rituals—though generally not with the conscious knowledge of their creators—worked to sever young men's ambivalent emotional ties to women and reattach them to adult males. What is noteworthy is the way that religious language was co-opted to accomplish this. In general, middle-class mothers embraced the theologically liberal notion that children's innate goodness could be drawn out by gentle, unwavering maternal guidance. In a surprisingly consistent way—given that they drew on sources as varied as Druid mythology, Arthurian legends, Old Testament stories and Indian lore—lodge rituals repudiated both this optimistic view of human nature and the "feminine" environment that nurtured it. Initiates were treated as inherently sinful and made to embark on a symbolic but harsh pilgrimage for religious truth. This culminated in a dramatic conversion experience, often symbolized as death or near-death, and a rebirth into fellowship with, and acceptance by, a patriarchal god and his male representatives.

Thus the 1880 Odd Fellows' "Patriarchal degree" required the aspiring young

---

[25]Ibid.
[26]Ibid., p. 116.

candidate, wearing sandals and shepherd's attire, to symbolically cross a desert to meet a group of Old Testament patriarchs. The latter seized and bound him and identified him as Isaac, the son of Abraham, toward whom he then had to "travel" blindfolded across a symbolic Wilderness of Paran. Father and son then "journeyed" together to Mount Moriah, where the older Abraham figure prepared to sacrifice his "son" on an altar. But just as he lifted a knife to the candidate's throat, a muffled gong sounded, and "Abraham" announced that God had decided "Isaac" should not be sacrificed but should rather become an accepted member of the patriarchal group.[27] In this way "father" and "son" could now become brothers.

It requires only a modicum of Sunday school literacy to recognize that this ritual took certain liberties with the Genesis account of Abraham and his family. It was Hagar's son Ishmael, not Isaac, who was cast into the Wilderness of Paran, but the Odd Fellows chose to fuse the story of Ishmael's banishment with Abraham's sacrifice of Isaac. Carnes believes that the conflation of these two accounts was no accident:

> The ritual resolved psychological tensions by reassuring the initiate that his father, though distant and imposing, had always loved him. . . . Rituals such as the Patriarchal degree acted out anxieties that young middle-class men may have felt about their fathers and about the unfathomable emotional distance they had to travel to acquire the attributes of manhood. By emphasizing a surrogate father's benevolence and love, the ritual made it easier to identify with the male role; and by accepting the initiate into the family of patriarchs, the ritual made it possible to approach manhood with greater self-assurance.[28]

Thus, Carnes concludes, the candidate's ritual "religious" journey, beginning with recognition of his unworthiness, through wrenching conversion to acceptance by older males, served to catalyze a deeper emotional journey. Middle-class males often reached adulthood feeling less than adequately masculine after two decades of heavy female influence in home, church and school. Lodge rituals let them act out an alternative script, one that symbolically erased a feminized childhood and reconciled them with distant and little-known fathers. Since it was not their own fathers who initiated them, we might wonder what led older lodge members to expend so much time and effort on these activities. Carnes suggests that they "surely must have enjoyed the symbolic veneration accorded patriarchs" but that they also used the rituals as "a replacement for emotional ties to their own children: the gender bifurcation of middle-class life

---

[27]Ibid., pp. 121-22.
[28]Ibid., pp. 122-23.

had produced fathers without attentive children, as well as children without effective fathers."[29]

"Women Have Had Charge of the Church Work Long Enough"

I have noted that American evangelicals strenuously opposed fraternal lodges because they required secret oaths, created a sub-Christian "conversion" experience and diverted men's energies from church life. But ironically, evangelicals also helped to maintain the doctrine of separate spheres and the extreme feminization of the church resulting from it. Rather than aiming for a more equitable gender balance in church attendance and activities, the revivalist descendants of Charles Finney worked on reaching young men by appealing to the newly popular language of sport in revival meetings and by developing athletic programs in organizations such as the YMCA, which began in the United States in 1858.

Begun as an evangelistic and social service agency for urban dwellers with little regard to age or sex, the YMCA soon narrowed its focus to "muscular Christian" messages and activities with the aim of reaching mainly young middle-class males. The earlier postmillennial focus on "making the good of society better" was replaced by a premillennial theology stressing that the world will slowly get worse until Christ's return. On the premillennial account, Christians are called to concentrate on "making the bad of society good"—that is, saving souls more than spending time on social reform. Muscular Christian sports activities, along with testimonies by famous athletes at YMCA meetings and elsewhere, became means to this greater end, with young men as the preferred target audience. Such activities did succeed in providing a Christian alternative to lodge membership; but rather than directing young men back to churches to make them more heterogeneous, they functioned for many as substitute churches.[30]

Toward the end of the nineteenth century, male church leaders confronted this inconsistency not (as one might hope) by mounting a theological challenge to the gendered splitting of the cultural mandate, the compartmentalization of public from domestic and religious life, and the idolatry of reason and material progress. Instead, to attract men back to the churches, they began grassroots movements that infused Christianity with the emerging language of corporate business principles. Why did these movements arise when they did, and what

---

[29]Ibid., p. 123.
[30]Ladd and Mathisen, *Muscular Christianity,* chap. 1.

were some of their effects on gender relations in Christian circles?

Around 1880 the contrived division of labor between feminine domesticity and masculine productivity began to falter as the American economy was increasingly organized around large corporations. Fewer and fewer men earned a living from farms or small businesses; instead many worked within a hierarchical structure in offices and manufacturing establishments. Although they were still breadwinners for their families, their culturally required self-image of masculine independence—already fragile from an overly feminized upbringing—seemed to be weakening further in the web of corporate bureaucracy. In addition, the early-nineteenth-century emphasis on thrift, buttressed by the Protestant ethic of self-denial, gave way to an ethos of consumerism and enjoyment of leisure, and so domestic feminine piety, with its continuing emphasis on sacrifice and self-control, began to seem culturally dated. Church leaders worried that as men became anonymous workers in large corporations, they were losing the traits of honesty and dependability that had been essential features of earlier, family-run small businesses.

The male-centered revivals of the early 1900s represented a frank attempt to inject a counterdose of masculinity, suitably redefined for a corporate age, into a church life now perceived to be overly feminized. For example, J. Wilbur Chapman's 1909 Boston Crusade and the Men and Religion Forward Movement of 1911-1912 were among the first to make use of corporate organizing and advertising techniques. Chapman's campaign slogan, "The King's Business," appeared on thousands of lapel pins and meeting tickets, and his noon-hour meetings in Tremont Temple repeatedly stressed the theme that "a man can succeed in business and be a Christian."[31] At many of the meetings women were relegated to the gallery, and their voices were regularly pitted against the men's to see who could sing the loudest. The result, according to church historian Margaret Bendroth, "was an audible as well as visible denial of religious feminization."[32]

A similar combination of commercial, religious and "masculine" themes characterized the extensive Men and Religion Forward Movement (M&RFM) of 1911-1912. Using newly available hydroelectricity, lighted billboards directed men to churches and other large gathering places in American and Canadian cities, where meetings were underwritten in part by business titans such as John D. Rockefeller and J. Pierpont Morgan. Draped with banners bearing the move-

---

[31]Quoted in Margaret L. Bendroth, "Men, Masculinity and Urban Revivalism: J. Wilbur Chapman's Boston Crusade, 1909," *Journal of Presbyterian History* 75, no. 14 (1997): 235-46.
[32]Ibid., p. 244. See also Mary Stewart Van Leeuwen, "Weeping Warriors," *Books & Culture* 3, no. 6 (1997): 9-11.

ment's slogan—"More Men for Religion, More Religion for Men"—these spaces were, with few exceptions, off-limits to women. This made the M&RFM the only large religious revival in American history (until the emergence of the Promise Keepers movement eighty years later) that explicitly excluded females.[33] According to the M&RFM's recasting, church work—including Bible study, evangelism, missions and social service—was highly amenable to modern corporate techniques, and thus the province of assertively businesslike men. As one of the movement's organizers put it, "The women have had charge of the church work long enough."[34]

Separate Spheres Become Even More Separate

The Chapman Crusade had retained some vestiges of Victorian family sentimentalism, particularly in its portrayal of devoted and prayerful mothers as a way of softening up young men for an altar call. But the M&RFM leaders studiously avoided emotional appeals and references to home life in order to show that religion was no longer part of the feminized domestic sphere and that religious men could be powerful, logical and self-controlled. One much-reprinted description of the movement went as follows:

> There is one thing that should be clearly understood: there will not be a trace of emotionalism or sensationalism in this entire campaign. The gospel of Jesus of Nazareth—and its practical application to our daily life—is presented calmly, sanely, logically, so that it will convince the average man, who is a man of sane, logical common sense. Women have no part in this movement, the reason being that . . . the manly gospel of Christ should be presented to men by men.[35]

The campaigns of the early 1900s to "masculinize" church operations and outreach succeeded to a degree, but at a price. By the mid-1920s men were joining Protestant churches in greater numbers, drawn by the language of corporate business and by church sponsorship of men's clubs, sports teams and Boy Scout troops. At the same time, longstanding and very effective women's mission organizations were being absorbed by male-run church bureaucracies, and women's opportunities for teaching and evangelism—short of going to a far-off mission field—were being steadily reduced.[36] Having embraced a doctrine of

---

[33]Bederman, "Men and Religion Forward Movement," p. 434.
[34]Ibid., p. 432.
[35]Henry Rood, "Men and Religion," *The Independent* 71 (1911): 1364, quoted in Bederman, "Men and Religion Forward Movement," p. 441.
[36]Bendroth, *Fundamentalism and Gender,* chap. 3.

separate spheres that included a "natural" place for them in church leadership (albeit under male oversight), women were now told their arena of influence should be even more narrowly confined to domesticity. At the same time, men's role in families as largely absentee landlords was affirmed in popular Christian writing ranging from liberal mainline to conservative fundamentalist circles. The responsible Christian father was "often physically absent from home . . . [but] expressed his love through discipline and sacrifice. Like God the Father, he exercised daily care for his children only indirectly, by the threat of punishment and the presence of material provision."[37]

As fundamentalist premillennialism slowly gathered strength in the pre- and post-World War II era, it marginalized women even further from Christian work other than that with young children. The movement's periodicals, featuring titles like *Bible Champion, Watchman* and *The Sword of the Lord,* were characterized by masculine rhetoric in which evangelism and the defense of scriptural inerrancy were often treated in starkly athletic and militaristic terms. Stereotypically feminine traits such as gentleness, compromise and tact were taken as evidence that women were unfit for the rigors of combat against unbelief and the incursions of modernist theology. In this way the boundary between domestic feminine and public masculine spheres (the latter now clearly including the church) was raised almost to the status of a biblical absolute.[38]

▌ *Failure to Reintegrate the Cultural Mandate*

In evaluating the doctrine of separate spheres, I should first note that it was probably not a deliberate patriarchal plot aimed at keeping women downtrodden socially and economically. As originally conceived it was, for the most part, a well-intentioned response to the challenges of the Industrial Revolution and was largely supported by women themselves. It is certainly true that not all women benefited from it: prior to the rise of trade unions, many working-class people of both sexes had no alternative but to spend their lives doing heavy and ill-paid work in factories, mills and mines. But for others the doctrine of separate spheres meant relief from the heavy labor of the preindustrial household and protection from having to work in the often-dangerous settings of emerging industries. Moreover, it redefined marriage as a primarily companionate endeavor and gave women, perhaps for the first time in history, an arena in

---

[37]Ibid., p. 104.
[38]Ibid., chap. 3.

which it was assumed that they were men's moral superiors. But like all social experiments, the doctrine of separate spheres was vulnerable to the law of unintended consequences, and eventually its overdrawn division of the cultural mandate helped produce the first and second waves of feminism.

In an earlier chapter I pointed out that the creation story does not have God saying to the first female "Be fruitful and multiply" and to the first male "Subdue the earth." Both parts of the cultural mandate—generativity and accountable dominion—are given to both members of the original pair. Made jointly in the image of God, woman and man are commanded to unfold the good potential of creation in all areas of life. Together they are to work out God's vision of *shalom* in ways that are sensitive to different settings and times in history and to the life cycle of male and female human beings. Generativity and accountable dominion together constitute a human—not a gendered—mandate.

This does not preclude the possibility that some division of labor between men and women may be a just and satisfying way to organize a given family or culture during a specific, limited period of time. But it does mean that any construction of gender relations involving an exaggerated or inflexible separation of the cultural mandate by sex will eventually run into trouble and resistance, because far from being biblically normative, it is creationally distorted and therefore potentially unjust toward women *and* men. As practiced in the nineteenth century, the doctrine of separate spheres was unjust toward women in making them economic dependents rather than coproducers in their families and giving them no voice in politics, commerce or higher education. It was these issues, in the main, that prompted the first wave of feminism in the late nineteenth and early twentieth centuries and the second wave of feminism that began in the mid-1960s.

But in this chapter we have learned the less well-known lesson that the doctrine of separate spheres was unfair to men too. By placing the lifelong burden of their family's economic well-being on them, and eventually making breadwinning almost the sole criterion for adequate masculinity, it made the specter of financial failure a terrifying one for men. "When a man had a job," American historian Peter Filene observed about the early decades of the twentieth century, "just as surely the job had him. . . . [It] was like a bank containing [the family's] life savings, both economic and psychological." So not surprisingly, during the Great Depression "when jobs failed and savings vanished, men were left holding onto emptiness. . . . Some went insane; some committed suicide, and some deserted their families and joined the tramps who wandered."[39]

Men's vulnerability to such identity crises was increased by the fact that the

---

[39]Filene, *Him/Her/Self,* p. 155.

doctrine of separate spheres had failed them long before they joined the waged workforce in adulthood. By depriving boys of regular contact with fathers and other adult male role models, the public-domestic dichotomy produced gender identity conflict in many young men and the temptation to embrace dubious means for resolving it in the time-consuming (and not inexpensive) rituals of fraternal lodges. But the evangelical groups who opposed lodge membership were generally no better than others at reintegrating domestic, public and religious arenas across gender. They instead read the doctrine of separate spheres—along with male dominance in family, church and society—back into Scripture as unchanging absolutes, replacing the overbalance of feminine influence in the church with even more complete male control. As the fundamentalist movement grew in the first half of the twentieth century, this construction of gender relations hardened further, especially since a premillennial reading of Scripture encouraged cultural isolation from—rather than biblically based reform of—larger cultural institutions.

Anticipating the Second Wave of Feminism

However, cracks in the separatist mentality of fundamentalism began to appear after World War II. The term *neo-evangelical*—often associated with the founding of Fuller Seminary in 1947—emerged to describe a strand of postwar fundamentalism that worked to bring the movement out of its intellectual isolation and broaden its evangelistic appeal.[40] That cautious reengagement with culture was in no way fueled by a desire to question existing gender relations, since the larger culture of the 1950s was if anything even more devoted to the doctrine of separate spheres as a way of renormalizing society after the upheavals of World War II. But by rightly, if belatedly, reclaiming the public square as a forum for Christian reflection and action, the new evangelicals opened their doors a crack to the possibility of interaction with the second wave of feminism when it emerged in the 1960s, and to the newer men's movements that followed. An evaluation of how these relationships have developed and proceeded will be the focus of the next chapter.

---

[40]Bendroth, *Gender and Fundamentalism,* p. 5.

Men, Religion and Contemporary Feminism

WHEN I WAS A COLLEGE SOPHOMORE in the early 1960s, a couple of years before the terms feminism and women's liberation started to become common coinage on campuses, the women's society at my Canadian university did a very bold thing. They invited an American writer named Eve Merriam to come and lecture on the topic of expanding women's roles. Days before the event took place, men from the university's engineering society (few of whom had ever darkened the door of a church during their student years or showed any evidence of being Bible proof-texters) painted a large sign on a wooden hoarding in the center of campus. It read "Eve Merriam, go home!" and was followed by a passage from Ephesians 5:22-23: "Wives, be subject to your husbands as you are to the Lord. For the husband is the head of the wife just as Christ is the head of the church" (RSV).

I remember Eve Merriam mainly because I was the person appointed to pick her up at the train station when she arrived—a small, salt-and-pepper-haired woman with a gracious manner and a sharp wit. I recall as we drove through campus that I pointed out the engineers' sign to her—with some trepidation, wondering if it would intimidate or offend her. Instead she was delighted by the unintended publicity for her lecture and said she wished she had a camera to take a picture of it. Her actual talk (during which the engineers were stonily polite—remember, this was the *early* sixties) would now be classified as liberal feminist and rather uncontroversial. It championed the widening of women's roles in North American society without assuming that any of its institutions, or the men who controlled them, should be fundamentally changed or overturned in the process.

I remember Merriam's policy of telling audiences her age before she began lecturing (she was fifty-seven at the time) in order to subvert women's pursuit of youth and sex appeal as primary personal goals. She reported that in many venues she heard gasps of horror that a mature woman would commit such an egregious faux pas.[1]

Rebalancing the Canoe

Now, in an era when even the most conservative North Americans function in many ways as liberal feminists—though they may carefully avoid using the label—it is difficult to recapture the strong emotions with which the second wave of feminism was greeted in the 1960s. Regrettably, for some men and women it signaled little more than the end of the sexual double standard. Aided by easier access to abortion and birth control, sex was now to be completely uncoupled from marriage and childbearing, allowing women and men to be equally calculating and casual about their liaisons. Many men, particularly those in positions of power, treated the more political aspects of "women's lib" as a passing joke. Like toddlers throwing tantrums, women might fuss and shout for an expansion of their roles, but eventually they would run out of steam and go back to their cribs, or be placed there—gently but firmly—by male protectors who knew what was best for them and for society as a whole.

Ironically, this attitude was common not only among political conservatives but among leftist men who failed to see any connection between racial injustice (which they deplored) and the need for more equitable gender relations. Hence the notorious and much-publicized 1966 pronouncement by Stokely Carmichael, of the Student Non-Violent Coordinating Committee, to the effect that "the only position for women in S.N.C.C. is prone."[2] For men who voiced even hesitant support for any of the planks in the emerging feminist platform, a new label, "pussy-whipped," was invented, calculated to pinch the vulnerable nerve of masculine insecurity and so pull them firmly back to support of the male-dominated status quo.

But despite such attempts at intimidation, second-wave feminism persisted and expanded until it became a movement almost as multidenominational as the church. The white, liberal, middle-class women who began the movement in the 1960s soon had to share the spotlight with Marxist, radical, socialist, post-

---

[1]Merriam's views were later published in Eve Merriam, *After Nora Slammed the Door: American Women and the 1960's: the Unfinished Revolution* (Cleveland, Ohio: World, 1964). The title refers to the lead character in Henrik Ibsen's nineteenth-century feminist-leaning play *A Doll's House.*

[2]"Know Your Enemy: A Sampling of Sexist Quotes," in *Sisterhood Is Powerful: An Anthology of Writings from the Women's Liberation Movement,* ed. Robin Morgan (New York: Vintage, 1970), p. 37.

modern, multicultural and eco-feminists.[3] Aided first by a trickle, then by an av-
alanche of women's studies courses, books and other media supports, second-
wave feminists made it collectively clear that their movement was much more
than a passing infantile tantrum. In the United States, liberal feminists successfully pushed for legislation such as the Equal Employment Opportunity and the
Title IX Educational Amendment Acts of 1972, the Equal Credit Opportunity Act
of 1974 and the Pregnancy Disability Act of 1978. Marxist feminists challenged
the misogyny and closed-shop practices of male-dominated labor unions. Radical feminists opened shelters for abused women and eventually convinced leg-
islators to fund them with public tax money. To pursue a metaphor introduced
in earlier chapters, women were rocking the canoe of gender relations so vigorously that men finally realized they would have to make serious adjustments
in their own seating positions.

As with feminism itself, there was no single, agreed-upon answer as to what
those adjustments should be but rather a mix of responses influenced by political, racial, religious and other agendas. In North America and elsewhere the resulting men's movements have never grown as large or influential as the
combined expressions of feminism, for a variety of reasons that we will consider
presently. But like the nineteenth-century men's lodges and the early-twentieth-
century men's revivals, they are visible attempts to reappropriate old forms of
masculinity or to construct new ones in light of changing social conditions.

In this chapter, as in the last, I am particularly interested in how religion has
interacted with men's movements. But first we will take a look at the broader,
more secular landscape of men's organizations that have developed in response
to the second wave of feminism.[4] Like many sociological classifications, what
follows is a series of "ideal types" that may fail to account for smaller groups
and for men who don't fit comfortably under any one label. But the categories—
liberal and radical profeminists, socialist feminists and special interest groups,
mythopoetic and men's rights groups—give us a rough mapping of the movement landscape, which itself continues to shift.[5]

---

[3]For a more detailed account of the various streams of second-wave feminism, see Rosemarie
Putnam Tong, *Feminist Thought: A More Comprehensive Introduction* (Boulder, Colo.: Westview, 1998).

[4]The following sources are particularly useful: Kenneth Clatterbaugh, *Contemporary Perspectives on Masculinity: Men, Women and Politics in Modern Society*, 2nd ed. (Boulder, Colo.:
Westview Press, 1997); Michael A. Messner, *Politics of Masculinities: Men in Movements*
(Thousands Oaks, Calif.: Sage, 1997); Michael S. Kimmel, ed. *The Politics of Manhood: Profeminist Men Respond to the Mythopoetic Men's Movement (and the Mythopoetic Leaders Answer)* (Philadelphia: Temple University Press, 1995); and Kay Leigh Hagen, ed., *Women
Respond to the Men's Movement* (New York: HarperCollins, 1992).

[5]Here I mainly follow the typology used by Clatterbaugh in *Contemporary Perspectives on Masculinity,* with some help from Messner's *Politics of Masculinities.*

Remapping
Masculinity

If you asked North Americans in the 1990s what they understood by "the men's movement," most would have mentioned (perhaps with veiled snickers) something about men going on weekend retreats in the woods which featured drumming, poetry, folktales and male initiation rituals. Some would have connected these events with the name of Robert Bly, the sometime poet laureate of the United States whose 1990 book *Iron John*—the first book about men to become a year-long national bestseller—helped popularize this so-called mythopoetic men's movement.[6] But despite some intriguing similarities to nineteenth-century men's lodges, this was not the first or only organized men's response to second-wave feminism. As early as 1970, women's liberation gatherings, such as the one held during my graduate student days at Northwestern University, included workshops on "the men's liberation movement" that resulted in published collections of articles a few years later.[7]

The men's liberation movement was supportive of feminism, and being heavily populated by social scientists, it regarded much of the masculine ideal as a damaging social construction, not a biological or metaphysical given. But damaging to whom? In response to that question, two rather different answers emerged. The first, fashioned by liberal profeminist men who wrote the first textbooks of the men's movement, claimed that masculinity was a set of limitations imposed on men, just as femininity was a set of limitations imposed on men, and that its effects, even if different, were equally damaging. Thus the Berkeley Men's Center Manifesto of 1973 challenged restrictive masculine roles and urged men "to take back our full humanity. We no longer want to strain and compete to live up to an impossible, oppressive masculine image—strong, silent, cool, handsome, unemotional, successful, master of women, leader of men, wealthy, brilliant, athletic. . . . We are oppressed by conditioning which makes us only half-human."[8]

But this appeal to a tidy symmetry between men's and women's oppression was unconvincing to profeminist men of a more radical bent. It was, they maintained, rather like saying that slave owners in the pre-Civil War American South were as oppressed by the institution of slavery as slaves were. They did not

---

[6]Robert Bly, *Iron John: A Book About Men* (Reading, Mass.: Addison-Wesley, 1990).
[7]For example, Deborah S. David and Robert Brannon, *The Forty-nine Percent Majority: The Male Sex Role* (Reading, Mass.: Addison-Wesley, 1976), and Jospeh H. Pleck and Jack Sawyer, *Men and Masculinity* (Englewood Cliffs, N.J.: Prentice-Hall, 1974).
[8]Quoted in Pleck and Sawyer, *Men and Masculinity*, pp. 173-74.

deny that masculine privilege might lead to accompanying stresses such as those cited by liberal profeminist men. But they insisted that this analysis did not adequately acknowledge the power asymmetries—always to men's greater net benefit—that had plagued gender relations for centuries.

As with the question of how to deal with past racial privilege, radical profeminist men debated as to how much blame men should absorb for their own sins and those of their fathers. They agreed that "as men, we are all involved in the oppression women experience, and we benefit from it each day." But, continued a trio of writers in 1983, "this is no reason to fix blame on ourselves as 'the oppressor.' Blame and guilt don't help in understanding why people function as they do or in getting them to change."[9] If hegemonic masculinity was the result of larger social forces, they reasoned, then surely no individual male could be blamed for any of its nasty results. By contrast, an 1977 article titled "All Men Are Misogynists" stated that "we [men] are the ones who need the help; we are the ones who are the enemy; we are the ones who oppress and objectify women; and we are the incomplete, crippled human beings."[10]

To deal with this sense of self-condemnation, some of the more radical profeminists set up men's consciousness-raising groups, analogous to the unstructured groups early second-wave feminists created to examine the restrictions of stereotypical femininity. Though uncertain whether men could leave their competitive habits outside the confines of such meetings, they nonetheless embraced them "as flawed instruments by which to unlearn male power and privilege."[11] Others adopted a more focused, practical agenda—for example, setting up counseling centers to deal with male batterers and rapists, many of which continue to do valuable and effective work right up to the present.[12]

Debating Root Causes

In the liberal and radical men's groups described so far you can see that a crucial difference centers on the question of what or who is ultimately responsible for the supposedly more destructive features of masculinity. This is a sensible ques-

---

[9]Peter Blood, Alan Tuttle and George Lakey, "Understanding and Fighting Sexism: A Call to Men," in *Off Their Backs . . . and on Our Own Two Feet* (Philadelphia: New Society, 1983), pp. 9-23; quoted in Clatterbaugh, *Contemporary Perspectives on Masculinity*, p. 50.

[10]Leonard Schein, "All Men Are Misogynists," in *A Book of Readings for Men Against Sexism*, ed. Jon Snodgrass (Albion, Calif.: Times Change, 1977), pp. 69-74.

[11]Clatterbaugh, *Contemporary Perspectives on Masculinity*, p. 51.

[12]For example, the Boston-based group EMERGE and the St. Louis-based group RAVEN (Rape and Violence Ends Now), which has also produced *The Ending Men's Violence National Referral Directory*.

tion to ask, given that it's difficult to change something until you decide what causes it in the first place. Liberal profeminist men believe that socially construct-ed gender stereotypes are equally damaging to men and women and that gradu-ally shifting our culture's attitudes, laws and customs toward a more androgynous ideal will have a benign trickle-down effect on everyone's behavior. But radical profeminist men reject this view of symmetrical oppression as being too superfi-cial; they focus instead on what they see as the deeper problem of patriarchy. They insist that until men are willing to admit that they wield institutionalized and unjustified power over women and become willing to give up that "invisible knapsack of privilege,"[13] there will be no lasting peace in gender relations.

But what is the source of so-called patriarchal masculinity? And is there only one version of masculinity in Western society, or are there in fact various subcul-tural *masculinities,* hierarchically arranged with differential access to social power and hence different degrees of responsibility for unjust social relations? As the profeminist men's movement and its academic expression in men's studies con-tinued to develop in the 1980s, it increasingly leaned towards the latter position.[14]

Self-styled "socialist feminist" men point out that the "costs of masculinity" lamented by liberal profeminists apply mainly to a small percentage of men making up managerial and professional classes. Working-class men, who sell their labor by the hour, are vulnerable to forced overtime and layoffs, and have little chance of upward mobility, can hardly be said to suffer from the strain of being "wealthy," "successful" or "leaders of men." Yet they *have* traditionally been able to control the labor of women in their own class: in the waged work-place by denying them access to the shop floor, and at home by assigning eco-nomically dependent wives the domestic and childrearing labor that allows men to concentrate on jobs and bond with other men. Socialist feminists thus con-clude that class and patriarchy are *jointly* responsible for distorted gender rela-tions. Working-class men (and their academic supporters) must see the connection between sexism and working conditions, and strive with rather than against working-class women to restructure the relations of production if a truly just society is to emerge.[15]

---

[13]Peggy McIntosh, "White Privilege and Male Privilege: A Personal Account of Coming to See Correspondences Through Work in Women's Studies," in *Race, Class and Gender: An Anthol-ogy,* ed. Margaret L. Anderson and Patricia Hill Collins, 2nd ed. (Belmont, Calif.: Wadsworth, 1995), pp. 76-87 (see chap. 1).

[14]Some of the first expressions of this viewpoint are in Harry Brod, ed., *The Making of Mascu-linities: The New Men's Studies* (Boston: Allen & Unwin, 1987), and Michael Kaufman, ed., *Beyond Patriarchy: Essays by Men on Pleasure, Power and Change* (Toronto: Oxford Univer-sity Press, 1987).

[15]Clatterbaugh, *Contemporary Perspectives on Masculinity,* chap. 6; Messner, *Politics of Mascu-linities,* chap. 4.

Furthermore, many men's movement theorists argue, not just class but also race and sexual orientation interact with patriarchy. For example, since hegemonic white males have historically monopolized the best jobs and positions of influence for themselves, black men have been made to feel inadequately masculine because of their lesser success as breadwinners. And because aggressive heterosexuality and fear of seeming feminine have been such strong parts of the masculine script, gay men have been equally marginalized and mistreated. On this account there is not one universal standard of masculinity but a series of socially distinct, hierarchically arranged "masculinities" along with gate-keeping mechanisms restricting access to the hegemonic class of males who garner the most rewards economically, sexually and politically.[16]

Despite differing theories about origins and varieties of masculinity, most of the above-described strands of the men's movement—liberal, radical, socialist, antiracist and gay-affirming—converge in a North American umbrella organization (which has women members as well) known as the National Organization for Men Against Sexism, or NOMAS. Begun in 1982, it has academic connections to a Men's Studies Association and practical connections to counseling centers that specialize in dealing with men's violence. Though its membership has never exceeded a few thousand people, it includes ongoing task groups on issues as diverse as men and mental health (a liberal profeminist concern), sexual harassment (a radical profeminist concern), and eliminating racism and homophobia (concerns of marginalized groups such as black and gay men). In keeping with the postmodern emphasis on pluralism, NOMAS is a "big tent" organization, its members united by commitment to a progressive agenda for social justice as filtered through "a multi-dimensional, anti-sexist perspective about men and masculinity."[17]

But there are limits to the diversity of views that NOMAS tolerates. As convinced social constructionists, they do not welcome essentialist views of masculinity—ones that appeal to biology, religious texts or psychology to defend fixed masculine traits or a traditional division of labor and status between the sexes. Thus in spite of their concerns for the reempowerment of black men, NOMAS intellectuals did not enthusiastically endorse the 1995 Million Man March in Washington, D.C., organized by Nation of Islam leader Louis Farrakhan. This was partly due to Farrakhan's use of religious language to shore up traditional gender stereotypes and to reassert the headship of men over women, implying

---

[16]See in particular R. W. Connell, *Gender and Power* (Stanford, Calif.: Stanford University Press, 1987). See also Clatterbaugh, *Contemporary Perspectives on Masculinity,* chaps. 7-8, and Messner, *Politics of Masculinities,* chap. 5.

[17]NOMAS website <www.nomas.org>, August 2000.

(NOMAS leaders thought) that black men's main problem was that hegemonic white males had denied them their rightful share in the perks of patriarchy.

NOMAS has been even more critical of the mythopoetic men's movement. This is partly because of the latter's emphasis on men's personal development—"healing men's wounds"—and its apparent indifference to political activism. But it is mainly due to the mythopoetic movement's reliance on Carl Jung's psychology of male archetypes, which are seen as innate mental tendencies that can be recovered when men share old mythic tales and ritually participate in "deep masculine" activities such as hunting and drumming. NOMAS adherents believe that such solutions to male angst are empirically groundless and that they encourage, rather than eliminate, sexist attitudes toward women.[18] Nor are they sympathetic to the so-called men's rights movement, according to which it is men, not women, who bear the greatest costs of traditional gender socialization and who, in the wake of feminism, now suffer additional injustices in areas such as divorce, child custody, job access and false accusations of sexual abuse.[19] The problem with the men's rights movement, asserts profeminist philosopher Kenneth Clatterbaugh, "is that it is trying to make a case for male oppression in a social reality of male privilege."[20]

Patriarchy as Original Sin

This has been a very cursory tour of the varied landscape of secular men's movements in North America. But I trust it is detailed enough to inspire a certain respect for those of its members who sincerely want to reform masculinity at the personal or the societal level, and often both at once. Despite internal differences, males in profeminist men's movements are united by a conviction that something in gender relations needs to change and that they have a responsibility to help it happen. In an era too often characterized by narrow self-interest, such idealism and reforming activism are not to be written off lightly.

Why, then, have the numbers associated with these men's movements always been so much smaller than those in the various expressions of second-wave feminism? And why—as even movement spokespersons acknowledge—do

---

[18]See especially Kimmel, *Politics of Manhood*. For a somewhat more sympathetic approach see Michael Schwalbe, *Unlocking the Iron Cage: The Men's Movement, Gender Politics and American Culture* (Oxford: Oxford University Press, 1996). For responses to these criticisms from participants in the mythopoetic men's movement, see Kimmel, *Politics of Manhood*, sec. 5.

[19]See for example Warren Farrell, *The Myth of Male Power: Why Men Are the Disposable Sex* (New York: Simon & Schuster, 1993).

[20]Clatterbaugh, *Contemporary Perspectives on Masculinity*, p. 199.

their numbers continue to decline or at best hold steady? "In the 1990s," pro-feminist Clatterbaugh conceded, "the secular men's movement is on the wane. The circulation of major publications is down, and the number of men attending conferences is either stagnant [at a few hundred] or declining."[21] He cited several explanations that his NOMAS colleagues would probably affirm: suspicion about the purity of men's motives on the part of feminist groups they are trying to help; the movement's failure to attract grassroots members in addition to ac-ademics, students or professional-class psychologists; and hostility or indiffer-ence to socialist ideals in wake of the collapse of communism. Moreover, Clatterbaugh observed, "profeminists are inviting men to join a movement that promises to let women participate in society on an equal basis, thus producing more competition . . . [fewer] opportunities and more power sharing—this in a society where many men already feel relatively alienated and controlled."[22] They are, in effect, asking men to saw off the already shaky branch on which many feel they are sitting, but without supplying any discernible safety net to catch them.

These explanations all have merit, but I do not think they run deep enough to account for the patchy success of well-intentioned men's movements such as NOMAS. As noted earlier, in order to confront a problem effectively, you must accurately identify its root cause. So we need to ask if the diagnosis of distorted gender relations offered by the profeminist men's movement is actually radical enough to accomplish this. The NOMAS mission statement is very telling in this regard. It states:

> The simple truth is that the oppression of women, homophobia, . . . subtle or bla-tant racism, and numerous wounds and sex-role burdens placed on men in our so-ciety are all part of the institution of patriarchy. Each injustice associated with sex, gender or race contributes to all the others. All oppressions are linked, and con-sciousness of any oppression leads to awareness of them all. . . . The totality of our opposition to the consequences of patriarchy is our greatest strength.[23]

A more comprehensive look at NOMAS's mission and goals confirms that "patriarchy" is, in effect, being used as a synonym for any kind of oppression—whether by class, race, age, gender, disability or sexual orientation. Patriarchy is more precisely defined as a social arrangement in which men as a group re-ceive more power and privileges than women, in which male activities are more highly valued than female ones, and in which economic, legal and cultural

---

[21]Ibid., p. 195.
[22]Ibid., p. 198.
[23]NOMAS website (www.nomas.org), August 2000.

norms combine to keep this system going.[24] Using the term to cover *all* kinds of injustice not only dilutes its meaning; it places an impossible burden of responsibility on men—particularly men who are unlucky enough to be "privileged" by color, age, class and sexual orientation—for virtually all of humankind's social ills. If patriarchy—whether narrowly or broadly defined—is effectively defined as the original sin, especially where there is no apparent belief in grace, how many men can be expected to sit around and confess their sins to each other? For most, it's just too demoralizing.

The Real Root of Patriarchy

Is patriarchy the original sin of humankind—the root from which all other kinds of injustice have sprung in the course of history? Or is it, as the biblical drama indicates, one of many *consequences* of a deeper, more radical form of sin in which all humans are complicit? The biblical account of the human condition challenges both the materialist philosophy of secular socialism and the extreme social constructionism of much social science, both of which are strong currents in the men's movements I have just described. Although deeply embedded in their material and social environments, humans, on the biblical account, are at root made in the image of God and as such are responsible first and foremost to God.

The biblical drama also proclaims that it is first and foremost from God that we need forgiveness, both for the basic *sin* of trying to operate on our own human strength and for the resulting *sins* that include the all-too-easy habit of neglecting or misusing others. Without such biblical realism even the best-intentioned reform movements are likely to come up with only half-solutions. The biblical account affirms that for all human beings without exception, original sin is the stubborn determination to function apart from God. From this generic sin more specific sins flow, patriarchal attitudes and actions being among them.

To see patriarchy as the final answer to the question *What's wrong with our world?* is a little like treating the symptoms rather than the cause of a disease. Some good can be accomplished, and it's clear that many profeminist men work very hard to change practices in themselves and others that they see as being rooted in patriarchy. But their overall influence has been modest and continues to decline. As one of their numbers, journalist Don Shewy, put it in the mid-

---

[24]Pamela D. Couture, "Rethinking Private and Public Patriarchy," in *Religion, Feminism and the Family,* ed. Anne Carr and Mary Stewart Van Leeuwen (Louisville, Ky.: Westminster John Knox, 1993), p. 249.

1990s, "How come good men don't seem to get things done today?"[25]

Shewy's answer to that question was a highly unusual one in leftist-leaning men's circles. "One thing that can be said about right-wing conservatives," he conceded, "is that they're generally religious people, or at any rate church goers, meaning that they recognize some transpersonal commitment. Many Americans (including many on the left) have no such navigational system, no attachment to something beyond material reality. It's unfashionable even to talk about God."[26] In the absence of such navigational aids, he added, "we fall into generalizations about men and women that quickly take the form of polar opposites. If men are powerful, women are powerless. . . . If men are competitive, then women are not and cannot be. Or that if women feel pain, men don't."[27]

Promise Keepers: A Moving Target in an Evangelical Landscape

It is in light of such statements that we need to examine what became by far the largest men's movement of the late twentieth century: the Christian parachurch organization known as Promise Keepers. This self-styled "Christian men's movement" began in 1990 when two athletic coaches at the University of Colorado, Dave Wardell and Bill McCartney, discovered a shared desire to help men strengthen their ties to God and to their families. McCartney's vision was that by the year 2000 "every football stadium across America will be filled with men—across racial lines." Such a Christian outreach, gathering diverse men into sports settings where most already felt comfortable, might well "turn our nation around."[28]

With a group of seventy other men, McCartney crafted a statement of faith

---

[25]Don Shewy, "In Defense of the Men's Movements," in *Politics of Manhood,* ed. Kimmel, pp. 333-54, quotation from p. 334.

[26]Ibid., p. 334. Where there is talk of religion by NOMAS leaders, it is usually in terms of an ethical background that strengthens a humanist worldview and commitment to progressive politics, not a foundational commitment to which all other commitments are accountable. See for example Michael S. Kimmel, "Judaism, Masculinity and Feminism," in *Men's Lives,* ed. Michael S. Kimmel and Michael A. Messner, 3rd ed. (Boston: Allyn & Bacon, 1995), pp. 42-44.

[27]Shewy, "In Defense of the Men's Movements," p. 340.

[28]Quoted in William H. Lockhart, "Defining the New Christian Man: An Investigation into Books Related to the Promise Keepers Movement," *Priscilla Papers* 11, no. 2 (1997): 21-25, quotation on p. 21. See also Ken Abraham, *Who Are the Promise Keepers? Understanding the Christian Men's Movement* (New York: Doubleday, 1997); Messner, *Politics of Masculinities,* chap. 2; Clatterbaugh, *Contemporary Perspectives on Masculinity,* chap. 9; and Mary Stewart Van Leeuwen, "Servanthood or Soft Patriarchy? A Christian Feminist Looks at the Promise Keepers Movement," *Journal of Men's Studies* 5, no. 3 (1997): 233-61. My own direct contact with the Promise Keepers movement includes attending (on a press pass) two stadium events (Pittsburgh 1996 and Philadelphia 1998), attending PK's "Stand in the Gap" rally on the Mall in Washington, D.C., in September 1997, attending a PK Clergy Conference in Philadelphia (February 1998), and having continuing conversations with PK adherents and regional and national office staff.

for the prospective organization—one that was evangelical and trinitarian, affirming biblical revelation as the final authority for Christian faith and practice. They chose the name Promise Keepers (PK) for a ministry that would feature summer stadium gatherings for men throughout the United States. These stadium events were to begin with a Friday-evening evangelistic meeting of a sort that, aside from its all-male audience and speakers, was hardly new in America. It harked back to the eighteenth- and nineteenth-century camp meeting revivals of the First and Second Great Awakenings and borrowed many organizational features from the twentieth-century Billy Graham Crusades. These included the idea that it would be easier for Christians to invite unchurched friends to an arena or stadium than to the less familiar confines of a church service.[29]

What *was* unique was what took place the next day, after men had responded to the Friday-evening altar call for commitment or recommitment to Christ. As a new twist on the old tradition of following conversion with discipleship training, PK stadium speakers would spend an entire Saturday—punctuated by music and prayer—explaining "seven promises" that embodied "Godly masculinity." These included (1) Christian worship and obedience, (2) friendship with and accountability to other Christian men, (3) moral and sexual purity, (4) faithfulness in marriage and family life, (5) support of the church, (6) racial reconciliation and (7) evangelizing others.[30]

In 1991 PK's first stadium event drew forty-two hundred men to Boulder, Colorado, to hear its seven promises expounded under the theme "Where Are the Men?" In 1992 over twenty thousand came to the same site to be taught "What Makes a Man." To this PK added a leadership conference that drew an additional fifteen hundred men interested in promoting Christian men's ministries. In subsequent years both kinds of events flourished, and in 1996 twenty-two stadium rallies were held in spring and summer across all the major regions of the United States. That year—the peak of PK's success—the rallies attracted a combined attendance of around a million men from many denominational backgrounds at an admission fee of sixty dollars each.[31] In addition a 1996 PK conference for clergy in Atlanta drew some thirty-nine thousand men.

---

[29]See for example George Marsden, *Understanding Fundamentalism and Evangelicalism* (Grand Rapids, Mich.: Eerdmans, 1991), and Randall Balmer, *Mine Eyes Have Seen the Glory: A Journey into the Evangelical Subculture of North America* (New York: Oxford University Press, 1993).

[30]Bill Bright et al., *Seven Promises of a Promise Keeper* (Colorado Springs: Focus on the Family, 1994).

[31]There has been no systematic attempt to find out how many at PK events are repeat attendees. However, testimonies posted on the PK website (August 2000) feature men who enthusiastically report having been to as many as eight stadium events.

By this time the organization had an annual budget of over $100 million, not just from stadium admissions but from the sale of books, records, clothing featuring the PK logo, and the magazine *New Man*.[32] Leaders were now being trained to set up small, local "accountability groups" to assist men's continued growth throughout the year.[33] By 1996 fully half the organization's four-hundred-strong paid staff were people of color, as were about half the leaders giving lectures and sermons to stadium crowds. This was an indication of the seriousness of PK's sixth promise: "To reach out beyond any racial and denominational barriers to demonstrate the power of biblical unity." By this time U.S. media interest in the movement was substantial, and when PK organized a fall 1997 gathering of close to a million on the Mall in the middle of Washington, D.C., under the theme "Stand in the Gap," over a thousand journalists were assigned to cover it.[34]

Why did such a large religious men's movement arise in the last decade of the twentieth century? Promise Keepers, speaking through one of its staff in *New Man* magazine in 1995, credited a mighty moving of God's Spirit and hoped that history would see PK as a catalyst for and even broader evangelical revival.[35] But there were historical and sociological forces at work too. I believe that three such forces converged to help bring about this intriguing movement: men's sense of economic insecurity in the late twentieth century, the changes in gender relations initiated by the feminist movement and a growing sense of disillusionment with American individualism.[36]

The Postindustrial Revolution

Just as in the Industrial Revolution of the nineteenth century, seismic economic shifts took place at the end of the twentieth. That era saw the opening up of a global economy, the expansion of multinational corporations and the flight of

---

[32] *New Man* was begun by the Pentecostal/charismatic Strang Publications in 1994 as "The Official Magazine of Promise Keepers." In 1997, by mutual agreement, PK and Strang withdrew this official endorsement so that the magazine could cover a wider range of men's ministries while still maintaining friendly relationship with Promise Keepers.

[33] John P. Bartkowski, "Breaking Walls, Raising Fences: Masculinity, Intimacy and Accountability Among the Promise Keepers," *Sociology of Religion* 61, no. 1 (2000): 33-53.

[34] See Mary Stewart Van Leeuwen, "Mixed Messages on the Mall," *Christian Century* 114, no. 29 (1997): 932-34; Van Leeuwen, "Servanthood or Soft Patriarchy?" and also the PK-related theme issue of *Priscilla Papers,* 11, no. 2 (1997), published by the evangelical organization Christians for Biblical Equality.

[35] David Halbrook, "Is This Revival? How Does the Promise Keepers Movement Compare with the World's Historical Revivals?" *New Man* 2, no. 6 (1995): 20-26.

[36] See Van Leeuwen, "Servanthood or Soft Patriarchy?" and also the special issue on the Promise Keepers of *Sociology of Religion,* 61, no. 1 (2000).

North American capital to cheaper labor markets overseas. Added to this was a massive technological shift from an industrial to a postindustrial "information society," brought about by the computer revolution. These changes heightened the risk of unemployment for some and wage stagnation or even decline for others, a risk compounded by the decreased power of North American trade unions since the 1960s.[37]

These changes added to almost everyone's insecurity, but especially to men's in a society that for over a century had identified masculinity almost exclusively with earning money. Even middle-class, intact nuclear families now needed two adults in the waged workforce to survive economically; and although the wage gap between men and women was narrowing, in the United States close to half of that was due not to women's increased but to men's *decreased* earning power since the 1970s. So, as they did in wake of the Industrial Revolution, men began to ponder the meaning of masculinity and search for ways to recover or reshape its definition.[38]

The Feminist Factor

A second parallel with men's religious movements of a century ago was the presence of an organized feminist movement that prompted women to question the existing norms for gender relations. Almost nothing—either positive or negative—is said about feminism in the Promise Keepers' assorted literature.[39] Yet it is clear that as in the various secular expressions of the men's movement, feminism is in large part what these men are responding to. Many analysts noted specific parallels between PK and the mythopoetic men's movement. Both stressed that the Industrial Revolution was a significant turning point for men because it took husbands and fathers out of the home and into an amoral, competitive marketplace. Both agreed that one result of this was men's progressive loss of the ability and motivation to be involved in childrearing, except at one remove as breadwinners. Both affirmed that this

---

[37]For a more detailed theological analysis of these trends, see Max L. Stackhouse and Peter J. Paris, eds., *Religion and the Powers of the Common Life: God and Globalization,* vol. 1 (Harrisburg, Penn.: Trinity Press International, 2000).

[38]See Bartkowski, "Breaking Walls, Raising Fences," and especially his discussion of the contrasting themes of masculine "instrumentality" and masculine "expressiveness" in PK's literature and rhetoric.

[39]But for an interesting exception, see Michael G. Maudlin, "What Are the Feminists Trying to Tell Us?" *New Man* 4, no. 8 (1997): 34-38. In this article Maudlin defends the thesis that "feminism is fundamentally a Christian idea, one that is often ripped from its proper context" (p. 24).

resulted in an absence of positive male role models for boys and young men. And both movements—like the men's lodges of the nineteenth century—proposed to help remedy this by creating all-male gatherings in which men could grieve over the absence of past father figures and form mentoring relationships to compensate for this loss.

But here the parallels end, for PK differed in the way it related these historical and psychological factors to gender relations. The mythopoetic men's movement was criticized by feminists of both sexes for seeming to blame women for the current state of men's psyches. Having previously collaborated in maintaining a dichotomy between (feminine) domestic and (masculine) public life, mythopoetic men then blamed women for being overly salient in the lives of boys, robbing them of access to their fathers and turning them into "soft" overly feminized males.[40] Although contemporary feminism is in fact united in challenging this very dichotomy, some mythopoetic male leaders continued to blame feminist women for the feelings of masculine insecurity that resulted in large part from this gendered public-private split.

Promise Keepers departed from this rhetoric in three important ways. First, they sent a strongly evangelical message of personal repentance and conversion, empowered not by human effort or by a recovery of romantic masculine mythology but by faith in the trinitarian God of Christianity.

Second, they stressed men's responsibilities as much as they stressed men's wounds. PK leaders asserted that if divorce, domestic violence, sexual irresponsibility and father absence were running rampant in society, regardless of what historical forces contributed, individual men had to confess complicity and ask their own family members for forgiveness. And far from blaming women for men's current role confusion, PK leaders praised them for keeping important social institutions such as church and home functioning and called on men to help shoulder the load. "Let's face it," said PK board member Gary Oliver in 1995. "If it weren't for women, there would be no prayer in many churches, missionaries would not get ongoing support, and there would be a lot fewer Bible studies. There has definitely been a vacuum of men doing what God has called them to do in the church."[41]

Third, despite the use of sports stadiums for mass meetings and their not-infrequent appeal to athletic metaphors, PK leaders did not generally try to reinvent the muscular masculinity celebrated by both the mythopoetic men's

---

[40]For example, Bly, *Iron John,* and for feminist critiques of same, see Hagen, *Women Respond to the Men's Movement,* and Kimmel, *Politics of Manhood.*

[41]Quoted in Edward Gilbreath, "Manhood's Great Awakening," *Christianity Today* 39, no. 2 (1995): 20-28, quotation from p. 24.

movement and their own recent Christian forefathers.[42] As we saw in the last chapter, the Men and Religion Forward Movement of the early twentieth century avoided any connection between male religiosity and "feminine" traits and activities. Gail Bederman, a historian of the M&RFM Movement, has noted that its leaders "never, ever spoke about their wives."

> They never spoke about domesticity at all. . . . And they never, ever blamed men for failing with their families [or] concede[d] that masculinity was anything but masterful, powerful and in constant control. By contrast, the very name Promise Keepers refers to the idea that men have broken their promises to their wives and are treating them poorly. Indeed, a sense of husbandly failure is evidently the source of much of the emotion at Promise Keepers events. Nothing could be more unlike the Men and Religion Forward Movement.[43]

Thus PK appropriated the feminist critique of stereotypical masculinity and reclothed it in what they regarded as a biblical theology of true manhood. PK followers were enjoined to reject the portrait of the friendless American male—self-reliant, unfeeling, competitive, distant from women, children and other men—and instead to practice the biblical virtues of encouragement, forgiveness, mutual confession and mutual aid.[44] PK publications urged men to admit their shortcomings and fears to family members and, without abdicating appropriate parental authority, to express tenderness and accessibility to children of both sexes, rather than stereotypical male remoteness and severity.[45]

Individualism Reconsidered

A final reason for the rise of Promise Keepers has to do with a growing disenchantment in America with the cult of individualism. In addition to making men more family-friendly, PK tried to help them find some kind of personal moral compass in a sea of relativistic hedonism. For several decades a key assumption of North American individualism had been that focusing on personal needs and desires would not be incompatible with the well-being of society as a whole.

[42]My analysis here contrasts with that of Wheaton College sociologists of sport James Mathisen and Tony Ladd. See for example their "Old and New Muscular Christians: Moral Crusaders in Sport from Tom Brown to Bill MCartney and the Promise Keepers," paper delivered at the Comparative Literature Symposium of Sport, Texas Tech University, Lubbock, January 1996.

[43]Gail Bederman, "Response to Panel on Religion, Sports and Manhood," paper presented at the American Academy of Religion, New Orleans, November 1996, pp. 4-5.

[44]Jon P. Bloch, "The New and Improved Clint Eastwood: Change and Persistence in Promise Keepers Self-Help Literature," *Sociology of Religion* 61, no. 1 (2000): 11-31.

[45]See for example E. Glenn Wagner, "Strong Mentoring Relationships," in *The Seven Promises of a Promise Keeper,* pp. 57-66.

But some thirty years after the start of the sexual revolution, the no-fault divorce revolution and the destigmatization of nonmarital childbearing (topics to which later chapters will return), it was becoming more and more obvious that social stability could not coexist with unrestrained individual self-indulgence.

Moreover, men who had happily absorbed the creed of individualism as they grew up in the years after World War II gradually found it turning into ashes in their mouths. Far from being a source of personal liberation, many found that materialism, recreational drugs and the uncontrolled pursuit of eros—whether via pornography consumption or multiple sex partners—were traps from which they desperately needed deliverance. Such temptations are of course nothing new, as Wilbur Chapman realized when he preached about the sins of greed, intemperance and adultery to Boston men in 1909. But whereas Chapman and other revivalists of his time urged males, with the help of God, to exercise stoic, individual self-denial, PK leaders added processes such as psychological self-understanding and ongoing accountability to Christian male friends as ways of dealing with sexual, substance and interpersonal problems. Thus PK's leaders plundered what they believed to be useful from the therapeutic culture of the late twentieth century, even as they preached against its individualistic excesses.[46] Without taking a formal position on the relative responsibilities of individuals, voluntary organizations and governments in the promotion of a just and stable society, Promise Keepers chose in practice to emphasize the role of changed individuals working together in a voluntary movement as a vital component of social transformation.[47]

Mixed Messages About Gender

There were, however, aspects of the Promise Keepers movement that were legitimate targets of criticism from both secular and Christian feminists. Chief among these was the confusion of messages PK sent regarding gender roles and gender hierarchy. Christians with equally high views of Scripture have differed throughout history as to whether the thrust of biblical teaching is towards greater gender equality or the continuing requirement of male headship in family, church or society. Indeed in the last two decades of the twentieth century two evangelical organizations, Christians for Biblical Equality and the Council on

---

[46]See Abraham, *Who Are the Promise Keepers?* chap. 4 ("Promises to Each Other"), for detailed examples.
[47]See also Stephen D. Johnson, "Who Supports the Promise Keepers?" *Sociology of Religion* 61, no. 1 (2000): 93-104.

Biblical Manhood and Womanhood, sprang up to promote distinctly opposite views on this issue.[48] By contrast, Promise Keepers often projected inconsistent messages about gender relations.[49]

Thus in the 1994 volume *Seven Promises of a Promise Keeper* (which included pieces by eighteen contributors) men were urged in one chapter to "take back the reins of [family] leadership God intended them to hold"[50] and in another to recognize that "equality of leadership [between men and women] "is the way God intended the church to operate . . . male and female leaders sharing the burden for their families and their community."[51] This equivocation also appeared within individual articles, as when psychologist Gary Smalley told men on one page of a *New Man* article to view their wives as important players on a team where the husband was the head coach and on another to treat them "as your equal, your adult partner . . . equally capable of calling the plays."[52] And it appeared in the mix of regular speakers at PK's summer stadium events, one of whom copastored a Pentecostal church with his wife and another of whom did not permit adult women in his church to teach classes that included adult men.[53]

Such mixed messages provoked predictable challenges from Christian and secular feminists alike. The movement's seven principles of "Godly masculinity" were seen as suggesting that women are less capable than men of practicing what are really generic Christian virtues.[54] PK's habit of publicly honoring pastors during its all-male rallies seemed based on the assumption that all pastors were—or should be—male.[55] And more than one critic pointed out that although PK commendably challenged racist attitudes in its audiences by having

---

[48]Though considerably smaller in scope and number of adherents than PK, each of these organizations has ongoing publications and a dedicated core of members. Christians for Biblical Equality is headquartered at 122 West Franklin Avenue, Suite 218, Minneapolis, MN 55404-2451, and has a website at <www.cbeinternational.org>. (Full disclosure: I am a charter member of this organization and sit on its board of reference.) The Council on Biblical Manhood and Womanhood can be contacted at P.O. Box 1173, Wheaton, IL 60187, or at the website <www.cbmw.org>.

[49]See also William H. Lockhart, "'We Are One Life,' but Not of One Gender Ideology: Unity, Ambiguity and the Promise Keepers," *Sociology of Religion* 61, no. 1 (2000): 73-92.

[50]Tony Evans, "Spiritual Purity," in *Seven Promises of a Promise Keeper,* pp. 73-81, quotation from p. 75.

[51]H. B. London Jr., "The Man God Seeks," in *Seven Promises of a Promise Keeper,* pp. 141-50, quotation from p. 142.

[52]Gary Smalley, "Treat Her like a Queen," *New Man* 3, no. 1 (1996): 30-33, quotations from p. 33.

[53]Van Leeuwen, "Mixed Messages on the Mall," p. 933.

[54]Rebecca Merrill Groothuis and Douglas Groothuis, "Women Keep Promises Too: Or, The Christian Life Is for Both Men and Women," *Perspectives: A Journal of Reformed Thought* 10, no. 7 (1995): 19-23.

[55]For example, Rodolfo Carrasco, "One Small Step for Humankind: The Promise Keepers Do L.A.," *Prism* 2, no. 7 (1995): 16-17, 24.

a high percentage of men of color among its speakers and leaders, it seemed at the same time to think that gender relations could be reformed without any input from women.[56]

Revivalism Wins Out

In the mid-1990s, journalists and scholars began to challenge PK leaders about the fact that while most of their speakers and writers preached husbandly headship, some advocated full equality between marriage partners. Pressed to explain this inconsistency, the organization's representatives claimed that PK had no formal position regarding male headship. Like revivalist leaders of earlier times, they claimed it was an issue on which evangelicals with equally high views of the Bible could legitimately disagree, so they would not make their speakers or writers toe any party line.[57] This did not satisfy critics, who pointed out that PK's ambiguous messages about male headship functioned as a kind of projective test. Male listeners could hear in them whatever they wanted, then go home to wives and children who had not had the benefit of sifting through these mixed messages for themselves. And in the absence of any independent evaluation research (which PK could have undertaken, given the size of its annual budget) no one could say how PK wives were in fact reacting to this movement.[58]

Thus whether for principled or pragmatic reasons, PK's pronouncements on gender relations moved steadily away from the hierarchical model as the movement matured. At the highly visible Stand in the Gap rally on the Washington Mall in 1997, its leaders were careful to use inclusive language and not (as they had done in the past) to equate this massive male-centered gathering with the body of Christ. At one point during the day, men who held elected office at the national, state or local level were asked to stand for supportive prayer. However, the platform leader identified these as only "symbolic representatives of all the

---

[56]Groothuis and Groothuis, "Women Keep Promises Too!"; Van Leeuwen, "Servanthood or Soft Patriarchy?"; Faith Martin, "Promise Keepers: A Volunteer's Perspective," *Priscilla Papers* 11, no. 2 (1997): 15-18; Donna Minkowitz, "In the Name of the Father," *Ms.* 6, no. 3 (1995): 64-71; L. Dean Allen II, "Promise Keepers and Racism: Frame Resonance as an Indicator of Organizational Vitality," *Sociology of Religion* 61, no. 1 (2000): 55-72.

[57]Sociologist John P. Bartkowski has confirmed the existence of these two attitudes among evangelicals—patriarchal versus egalitarian—in his analysis of a large sample of popular evangelical marriage manuals. See his "Debating Patriarchy: Discursive Disputes over Spousal Authority Among Evangelical Family Commentators," *Journal for the Scientific Study of Religion* 36, no. 3 (1997): 393-410.

[58]Mary Stewart Van Leeuwen, "Men Behaving Not So Badly," *Theology, News and Notes* 45, no. 1 (1998): 8-10.

men *and women* not here who govern us."[59] PK president Randy Philips, in his opening remarks, stated that the purpose of the assembly was not "to exalt in our gender as males, but to exalt Jesus Christ who is savior and God." No woman should feel threatened by this, he continued, "because the ground is level before the cross." Citing New Testament passages much loved by biblical feminists, he affirmed that "in the kingdom there is no male or female. In God, men are empowered to act like Jesus, who came not to be served, but to serve."[60]

By 1998 Promise Keepers had adjusted publicity for its pastors' gatherings to make it clear that women clergy (and laity of both sexes) were welcome too. By the year 2000 the organization's website included "What does PK think the role of women should be?" among its "Frequently Asked Questions." Its official answer was as follows:

> The role of women is not a topic we address at our events; however we do believe husbands are called to love their wives just as Christ loved the church (Eph 5:25). PK believes that men and women are completely equal at the foot of the cross. Paul writes in Galatians 3:28, "There is neither Jew nor Greek, slave nor free, male nor female, for you are all one in Christ Jesus." As we continue to pursue reconciliation in the Body of Christ, we believe unity in Christ transcends ethnic, social, and gender distinctions.[61]

What Next?

Thus Promise Keepers, visibly the largest men's movement of the 1990s, has moved from an ambiguous position on gender equality to one that is at least implicitly friendly to the idea of mutual submission between the sexes rather than male headship. Some inconsistencies remain. The movement is still criticized for its focus on all-male gatherings—not just by liberal and other feminists but also by some conservative Christians involved in the growing marriage education movement (to which we will return in a later chapter). Journalist Michael McManus, who with his wife runs an organization known as Marriage Savers, has repeatedly faulted PK on this issue. "Marriage cannot be strengthened by simply having men talk to men, the current Promise Keepers pattern," he asserts. "Women must be involved with men in a marriage movement—husbands

---

[59]Quoted in Van Leeuwen, "Mixed Messages on the Mall" (my italics; based on field notes taken at the rally).
[60]Ibid. See also Galatians 3:28; Philippians 2:1-11.
[61]<www.promisekeepers.org> (August 2000).

and wives in strong marriages, reaching out to help other couples prepare for a lifelong marriage, strengthen existing marriages, and save troubled ones."[62]

In the mid-1990s men's movement theoretician Kenneth Clatterbaugh predicted that Promise Keepers' popularity would be short-lived. He noted that the men's revivals of a century earlier were "enormously successful" for a few years but quickly faded. "The issues changed with World War I, and men tended to lose interest in hearing the same message over and over. Today's Promise Keepers probably faces a similar fate."[63] And indeed the organization had trimmed its sails considerably by the turn of the millennium. Both its budget and its staff had shrunk to about a quarter of what they were at the organization's peak in the mid-1990s, and its enormous summer stadium rallies had been downsized to arena gatherings of under twenty thousand each.[64] Moreover, independent evaluation research had shown that from 1992 to 1996—PK's peak years— church attendance and involvement among American men actually *declined* by some 15 percent.[65]

Promise Keepers leaders have tried to put a positive spin on these developments: the men who *are* in church are much more serious about their faith, they believe. Furthermore, PK is now only one of over eighty denominational and parachurch men's ministries, informally linked by the National Coalition of Men's Ministries. Most of these were formed in the 1990s; their aim is to equip local church leaders for continuing education and support of their own members rather than focusing on sporadic mass meetings.[66]

The Promise Keepers movement may prove to have been a catalyst for men's deeper involvement in church life, on a more equal basis with women than has been the case for close to a century. But it could also prove to be a catalyst for marginalizing women further. Following the Men and Religion Forward Movement of 1911-1912, churches became so male-focused that women were pushed to the sidelines, and their previously independent (and highly successful) mission organizations were disbanded and absorbed into male-run church bureaucracies. "Nobody was bothering about the women and girls," a woman journalist wrote in the 1920s. "They were safely within the fold and there was no other

---

[62]Michael J. McManus, "The Role of Marriage in Strengthening Fatherhood," in *The Faith Factor in Fatherhood: Renewing the Sacred Vocation of Fatherhood,* ed. Don E. Eberly (Lanham, Md.: Lexington, 1999), pp. 145-78, quotation from p. 146.

[63]Clatterbaugh, *Contemporary Perspectives on Masculinity,* p. 192.

[64]<www.promisekeepers.org> (August 2000; link to "2000 Conference Schedule").

[65]George Barna, quoted in Morley, "The Next Christian Men's Movement," *Christianity Today* 44, no. 10 (2000): 86.

[66]Joe Maxwell, "Men Are Back," *New Man* 7, no. 5 (2000): 27-37; Patrick Morley, "The Next Christian Men's Movement," *Christianity Today* 44, no. 10 (2000): 84-87.

place for them to go. Anyway, there was more joy over one man who joined the church than over a dozen women. [The Men and Religion Forward Movement] is now bearing fruit."[67] Only time will tell whether either of these scenarios or some other will come to pass in wake of Promise Keepers' decade-long, highly visible outreach to men.

---

[67]Martha Bansley Bruere, "Are Women Losing Their Religion?" *Colliers*, February 7, 1925, pp. 17, 42, quoted by Gail Bederman, "'The Women Have Had Charge of the Church Work Long Enough': The Men and Religion Forward Movement of 1911-1912 and the Masculinization of Middle-Class Protestantism," *American Quarterly* 41, no. 3 (1989): 432-65, quotation from p. 457.

PART FOUR

CONTEMPORARY

APPLICATIONS

10

Men, Marriage
and Male Parenting

ONE OF THE MIXED BLESSINGS OF GROWING OLDER is the experience of watching a younger generation of family members grow from birth to adulthood. By "younger generation" I mean not just my own children but nieces, nephews, cousins and the children they bring into the world. After a recent extended-family gathering at a summer cottage, I began to think about generational differences in family crises. In my grandparents' and parents' generations, divorce was virtually unheard of, although family disruption and impoverishment due to the untimely death or illness of a spouse were not uncommon, and there is evidence that what used to be called "shotgun weddings" took place on both sides of my family. It was my own generation—the post-World War II baby boomers and their "proto-boomer" older siblings—that began to partake of the divorce culture with a vengeance. As a result, over the years my husband and I have watched with distress as the marriages of various relatives in both our families have disintegrated.

The divorces took place at progressively earlier stages from the 1960s to the 1980s. Divorcing couples closer to my parents' generation tended to separate when their children were almost grown; but younger relatives and in-laws have divorced—sometimes more than once—at the stage when they had young children or none at all. In a couple of cases the complications of child custody caused a niece or nephew to drop almost completely off the family radar screen. Children whom I met in their infancy, and whose baby pictures still sit in photo albums with those of my sons, went with their separated mothers—and sometimes a new stepfather—never to be seen (or in one case, heard from) again. Now, at the turn of the millennium, we watch as another generation grows to adulthood. The cycle of divorce continues, particularly among the children of couples who themselves divorced when their children were still of school age. And among Generation X relatives, cohabitation and out-of-wedlock births have occurred not infrequently.

There were sober reasons for many of the divorces in both my husband's family and my own: abuse, adultery, addiction, abandonment, chronic financial irresponsibility. In such cases divorce is often the lesser of two evils. I should perhaps add that both my husband and I come from fairly large extended families in which stable marriages are still more common than the patterns I have just described. But even if that were not the case, would it matter? Can I offer good reasons, as a Christian social scientist, to privilege stable marriages over the contemporary plurality of household forms to which our own families bear witness? In particular, why is marriage important for men, and why are men important for marriages and families?

Earlier chapters examined men's relationship to marriage and family in historical and crosscultural perspectives. Now it is time to return to these questions within our own Western societal context. I begin with some summary statistics about the current state of marriage and family life. Next I summarize empirical evidence, accumulated over several decades, for the positive effects of marriage in men's lives and the negative effects of various forms of singleness. Then I grapple with the question whether the benefits of marriage and family life to men inevitably come at the expense of greater stress and unhappiness for the women who are their wives. Finally, I return to a topic begun in previous chapters—why (other things being equal) it is better for children of both sexes to have married fathers present rather than absent from their lives.

█ Some Millennial
█ Demographics

Actress Mae West once quipped in the 1940s that while marriage was a great institution, she wasn't fond of living in institutions. She was apparently ahead of her time in making this assertion, because over the last four decades of the twentieth century the proportion of people in the United States who marry steadily declined, while the rate of nonmarital cohabitation, divorce and children living in single-parent households increased dramatically.[1] In 1960 almost 70 percent of Americans over the age of fifteen were married; by 1998 it was closer to 55 percent. Although couples are now more likely to wed in their mid

---

[1]Unless otherwise indicated, the U.S. statistics in this section are taken from *The State of Our Unions 2000: The Social Health of Marriage in America* (New Brunswick, N.J: National Marriage Project, Rutgers University, 2000), pp. 21-36.

to late twenties (as compared to their early twenties in 1960), this tendency to delay marriage has not noticeably strengthened the institution. While divorce rates have declined somewhat since the 1980s, they are still much higher than in 1960, when there were nine divorces per thousand married women; in 1980 there were twenty-three per thousand, and by 1998 that proportion had dropped only slightly, to twenty. At the start of the third millennium first marriages in the United States have a 33 percent risk of dissolving within ten years and a 43 percent risk within fifteen years. Second marriages fare even worse, with almost a 40 percent chance of dissolution within ten years.[2]

The decline of marriage since 1960 has been paralleled by an almost 1,000 percent increase in cohabitation—that is, the sharing of a household by unmarried sexual partners. In 1998 it was estimated that a quarter of U.S. single women aged twenty-five to twenty-nine were living with a boyfriend and that an additional quarter had done so at some point in their lives. Indeed by the time of the 2000 U.S. Census, nearly 72 percent more people lived as unmarried partners than a decade earlier—an increase from 3.2 to 5.5 million individuals—and some 40 percent of cohabitants have had children outside of marriage.[3]

Not surprisingly, marriage, divorce and cohabitation trends have also affected childrearing patterns. In 1960, 49 percent of all U.S. households included at least one child under eighteen, a figure that fell to 34 percent by 1998. The shape of those households also changed: whereas 88 percent of children lived with two parents in 1960, only 68 percent did so in 1998—and of the latter total 13 percent lived in a stepparent household rather than with both their biological parents. In addition, some twenty million U.S. children were living in single-parent households at the turn of the millennium. In fact, the U.S. Census of 2000 showed that during the 1990s the number of families with children headed by women grew nearly five times as fast as ones headed by married couples.

These trends are not unique to the United States. Asked in the fall of 2000 to name the biggest change he had seen in his forty-year political career, U.S. Senator Daniel Patrick Moynihan replied: "The biggest change, in my judgment, is that family structure has come apart all over the North Atlantic world." Using unwed births as a summary statistic for this phenomenon, Moynihan pointed out that in 1960 unwed births accounted for about 6 percent of the total in the United States, 5 percent in Canada, 7 percent in Britain

---

[2]Data are from a 1995 study by the Centers for Disease Control (Atlanta), as reported in *USA Today*, May 25, 2001, and archived in <http://archives.his.com/smartmarriages/index.html#start>.

[3]Thomas Ginsberg, "The Number of Unmarried Partners, Census Shows, Is on the Rise," *New York Times*, May 20, 2001, p. E3.

and 4 percent in France. Forty years later the respective percentages for these countries were 32, 33, 36 and 37.[4] The demographic changes detailed above for the United States are closely paralleled in other Western industrialized democracies.

Christian
Complicity

However, the United States is unique among Western democracies in its high levels of religious observance. In the late 1990s 77 percent of Americans saw religion as being an important part of their lives, and close to 40 percent of their charitable giving went to religious institutions. Some 34 percent described themselves as evangelical Protestants, a significantly larger group than those claiming mainline Protestant, Catholic, Jewish or no religious affiliation.[5] Furthermore, mainline Protestant denominations have declined in membership as evangelical churches have expanded: almost 60 percent of U.S. church congregations established in the last two decades of the twentieth century were evangelical in their theological stance.[6] And of course the statistics for divorce, cohabitation and out-of-wedlock childbearing are substantially lower in such churches than in the population at large, right? Well, not exactly.

In fact, the divorce rate in many parts of the U.S. "Bible Belt," including four states dominated by the Southern Baptist Church, is about 50 percent higher than the national average. Moreover, while the U.S. 2000 census found an overall increase in cohabitation of 72 percent in the 1990s, the rate of increase in the "buckle" of the Bible belt—states such as Oklahoma, Arkansas and Tennessee—was between 97 and 125 percent. These figures do not take into account the actual religious sentiments of those southerners who have divorced, but other nationally based studies have tried to do so. For example, in the mid-1990s, when the overall U.S. divorce rate was twenty-three per thousand adult women, pollster George Barna's national study showed that the rate among self-identified "born-again" Christians was twenty-seven, and among fundamentalist Christians thirty per thousand. Was this because people in the latter categories were drawn to faith as a result of disastrous break-ups—that is, many of their divorces took place *before* they became Christians?

---

[4]"Moynihan on the Family," *Smart Marriages* e-Newsletter, September 26, 2000, which can be accessed at <http://archives.his.com/smartmarriages/index.html#start>.

[5]National Election Studies, Center for Policy Studies, University of Michigan <www.umich.edu/~nes>. The other percentages were mainline Protestant 22 percent; Catholic 26 percent; Jewish 2 percent; none 13 percent.

[6]Hartford Institute Survey, 2001 <www.hirr.hartsem.edu>.

Apparently not, since Barna's data indicated that 87 percent had divorced *after* their conversion experience.[7] By the turn of the millennium, things had changed little: Barna found that 33 percent of "born-again" Christians who had ever been married had experienced divorce, compared to 34 percent of adults who rejected the label "born-again."[8]

Conservative U.S. Christians are thus deeply complicit in the trend toward the destabilization of marriage. Gradual adoption of changing cultural norms obviously accounts for part of this trend. Like most other Americans, Christian young people are "intoxicated by love and cosseted by a culture that delights in weddings but tolerates divorce."[9] However, this does not explain why their divorce rates are even *higher* than in the population at large. One possible answer comes from Les and Leslie Parrott, who are marriage and family therapists and educators with a long history of working with evangelical groups. "Young people tell us that if they are in love and God is with them, then that's all they need. Later, if they are not happy, they say 'God wants me to get a divorce.'" Young Christians thus often use God in a fatalistic way to rubber-stamp their immediate feelings, both when entering and when exiting relationships; consequently, Leslie Parrott notes, "there is very little appreciation that marriage requires hard work and communication skills."[10]

Charles Colson suggests a further reason for these trends: the absence of a Christian worldview, even among many who read the Bible and claim to respect its authority as the Word of God. "It's not enough to know our Bibles, to cite chapter and verse," Colson points out. "We also need a broader framework connecting our spiritual beliefs to our overall vision of reality."

> For example, a Christian world-view perspective on divorce asks what God's purpose was in creating marriage. Marriage is not primarily a means of meeting emotional needs. It is fundamentally a social institution, providing structure for spouses to take care of each other and their children. It draws isolated individuals into a wider network of relatives and kin. It nurtures concern for the future. This world-view understanding of marriage provides the plausibility structure for specific scriptural commands regard-

---

[7] Barna's findings are taken from Charles Colson, "Any Ol' World View Won't Do," *Jubilee Extra*, May 1998, p. 4.

[8] "Briefly Noted," *Christian Century* 118, no. 23 (2001): 15.

[9] Blaine Harden, "Bible Belt Couples 'Put Asunder' More, Despite New Efforts," *New York Times*, May 21, 2001, pp. A1, A14, quotation from p. A14. Similar contradictions can be seen in other Western industrialized nations. For example, in France a poll released in December 2000 showed that although almost a quarter of respondents no longer saw marriage as a lifelong commitment, almost half of those anticipating matrimony planned to spend an average of forty thousand dollars on their wedding. "Marriage Is Back in Fashion," *Smart Marriages e-Newsletter*, December 4, 2000 <http://archives.his.com/smartmarriages/index.html#start>.

[10] Quoted in Harden, "Bible Belt Couples," p. A14.

ing sexual morality. Without it, biblical sexual morality may appear arbitrary and negative, and even Christians begin quietly ignoring it in their daily lives.[11]

Alternately, instead of "quietly ignoring" biblical sexual morality, many Christians have become selective literalists in their interpretation of it. In recent years there has been an outpouring of literature from both liberal and conservative Christians on the subject of homosexuality, which is often romanticized by the former and demonized by the latter.[12] By contrast the erosion of marriage, reflected in high rates of divorce, cohabitation and unwed childbearing, has become an accepted feature of church life across the theological spectrum. Yet the Bible speaks much more frequently and clearly about marriage than it does about homosexuality. And large, random-sample studies of sexuality in several Western nations consistently show that the percentage of self-identified homosexuals is approximately 3 percent among men and about half that among women, so whatever they are contributing to the decline of marriage is dwarfed by the behavior of "normal" heterosexuals.[13] Duke University chaplain William H. Willimon, though not endorsing same-sex unions, writes that he can "feel the anger of those homosexual and lesbian Christians who wonder how in the world they got blamed for the failure of heterosexuals to keep their promises and for the breakdown of the American family."[14]

Colson is right to note that marriage is not simply a means to realize each partner's individual needs—material or emotional—though that is the dominant rhetoric not only in the culture at large but also among family therapists and marriage educators.[15] Marriage is a social *institution*—a whole more than the sum of its parts, and a sexual community in which the nurture of children, by procreation or adoption, is a central function. It is part of a created order that has lawfulness and purpose, socially as well as physically. In the language of Reformed theology, marriage is a "sovereign sphere" with its own rights and duties, intended to work together with other institutions—such as commerce, science, education, the arts and religion—to form a just and healthy society.[16] The

[11]Colson, "Any Ol' World View," p. 4.

[12]For a further critique of both extremes, see Mary Stewart Van Leeuwen, "To Ask a Better Question: The Heterosexuality/Homosexuality Debate Revisited," *Interpretation* 51, no. 2 (1997): 143-58.

[13]Robert T. Michael, John H. Gagnon, Edward O. Laumann and Gina Kolata, *Sex in America: A Definitive Survey* (Boston: Little, Brown, 1994), chap. 9.

[14]William H. Willimon, "Under Fire: A Surfeit of Sexual Politics," *Christian Century* 118, no. 14 (2001): 6-7, quotation from p. 7.

[15]For a balanced critique of such practices, see John Wall and Bonnie Miller-McLemore, "Health, Christian Marriage Traditions and the Ethics of Marital Therapy," in John Wall et al., eds., *Marriage, Health and the Professions* (Grand Rapids, Mich: Eerdmans, 2002). See also William J. Doherty, *Soul Searching: Why Psychotherapy Must Promote Moral Responsibility* (New York: BasicBooks, 1995).

[16]For a further discussion of the concept of sphere sovereignty, see Luis Lugo, ed., *Religion, Pluralism and Public Life: Abraham Kuyper's Legacy for the Twenty-first Century* (Grand Rapids, Mich.: Eerdmans, 2000).

language of personal development is not wrong or irrelevant to the task of marriage: because each person is created with a variety of gifts, no one's calling can be reduced to their function in a single sphere of life, whether marriage or any other. But as ethicists John Wall and Bonnie Miller-McLemore point out, such language "needs to be brought into a richer conversation with other languages like commitment, covenant, mutual responsibility, and social goods, as these have been well understood in various Christian traditions."[17]

Marriage is neither an essential nor a superior state for the realization of Christian maturity and service. Yet because there is much misunderstanding about the benefits of marriage in men's lives, I need to take time to document these, even while noting that in a fallen world marriage will also require sacrifice and endurance—"for better or for worse"—and that we cannot strengthen the institution merely by appealing to its instrumental benefits. In this respect marriage is like religion, which a large body of research has shown is good for people's mental and physical health.[18] But as Swarthmore College psychologist Barry Schwartz rightly notes, religion and spirituality are not like jogging: "If people start being spiritual simply because it's good for them, then it won't be. The beneficial effects of spirituality may derive from the genuineness with which people attach themselves to spiritual communities and practices."[19] These call for learning, discipline and self-sacrifice, and any personal benefits are unlikely to accrue to people who try to sidestep such requirements. The same is true of marriage.

Marriage and Men's Physical Health

Even so, the benefits of marriage for men—physical, psychological and economic —are real. They are, of course, *average* benefits, which means that any particular married man may or may not display them all, but they are measurable and statistically significant. Demographer Linda Waite and coauthor Maggie Gallagher note that much of the physical health advantage of marriage for men "can be summed up in a single phrase: fewer stupid bachelor tricks."[20] On a host of health-related

---

[17]Wall and Miller-McLemore, "Health, Christian Marriage Traditions."

[18]See Gregg Easterbrook, "Faith Healers: Is Religion Good for Your Health?" *New Republic,* nos. 4409/4410 (July 19 and 26, 1999): 20-23. See also David Larson, "Does Religion or Spirituality Contribute to Individual and Marital Health?" in *Marriage, Health and the Professions,* ed. Wall et al., pp. 283-304.

[19]Barry Schwartz, "Prescribing God," *New Republic,* no. 4415 (August 30, 1999): 4-5.

[20]Linda J. Waite and Maggie Gallagher, *The Case for Marriage: Why Married People Are Happier, Healthier and Better Off Financially* (New York: Doubleday, 2000), p. 53. Unless otherwise indicated, data cited in this section are from Waite and Gallagher's very thorough review of the literature.

variables, single men—whether never-married, divorced or widowed—take many more risks than their married peers: they are more likely to smoke, drink, drive too fast, get into fights and take various other risks that result in injuries. Married men engage in dramatically lower rates of such behaviors.

One might reasonably wonder whether these differences are due to a selection effect—that is, more sober-minded men are more likely to marry in the first place, while the wild-oats-sowing type are more likely to remain unmarried or to have short-lived, unsuccessful marriages. But longitudinal studies tracking men from adolescence through their thirties have challenged this: it is more the case that marriage actually *changes* self-destructive patterns—a change that begins as early as a year before the actual wedding date. The same is true for women, but since unmarried women generally engage in fewer "stupid bachelor tricks" to begin with, their net gain in health and longevity as they sober up prior to and during marriage will obviously be less.

Waite and Gallagher note that "men also benefit from what social scientists call social support and husbands call nagging."[21] Most single men are notoriously bad at taking preventive and corrective health measures, but once married, they are apt to report that there is someone in their life who monitors their health, and that person is almost always a wife. Here there is another asymmetry: wives get far less monitoring of their health by husbands than vice versa—but again, even when single, women are likely to monitor their own health more carefully. And whether single or married, women on average seek and get a lot of social support from friends, whereas men are more likely to depend exclusively on their wives for emotional intimacy as well as "health nagging."

The emotional intimacy of a good marriage even improves the immune system of both spouses, whereas chronic conflict produces poorer immune function and in turn more illness. In addition, divorced persons of both sexes show poorer immune-system functioning than matched samples of married people—a difference that persists for many years after divorce occurs. The net result of all this is that men, on average, add years to their lives by being married. One American longitudinal study involving more than six thousand households found that even after controlling for factors such as education, class and ethnicity, almost 90 percent of married men alive at age forty-eight would still be alive at age sixty-five. For never-married, widowed or divorced men, it was closer to 60 percent.[22]

---

[21]Ibid., p. 55.
[22]Lee A. Lillard and Linda J. Waite, "'Till Death Do Us Part: Marital Disruption and Mortality," *American Journal of Sociology* 100 (1995): 1131-56.

Marriage and
Men's Mental Health

Almost four decades of accumulated data show that the advantage of marriage to men's physical health is matched by positive gains in mental health
and happiness as well.[23] As early as 1966, research demonstrated that unmarried American men scored worse than their married counterparts on measures
of depression, neurosis and phobic disorders. As with physical health, such
differences are not simply the result of selection effects—that is, the possibility that more emotionally healthy men are more likely to get married in the
first place. Several nationally representative longitudinal studies, some with
sample sizes of more than thirteen thousand people, have shown that on a
variety of measures of emotional well-being—depression, self-acceptance,
hostility, subjective happiness, sense of purpose and environmental
mastery—men make steadily positive gains after marrying, while all types of
singles (never-married, widowed, separated and divorced) experience accumulating declines over time.

The positive effects of marriage on men's mental health persist even after
data are controlled for differences in ethnicity, education and income. In
1965 Daniel Patrick Moynihan brought attention to the decline of marriage
and the rise of unwed childbearing among African Americans, whose rate at
that time was around 25 percent, compared to only a tenth that much among
whites.[24] While Moynihan was criticized for supposedly implying some
unique cultural defect among African Americans, his concern turned out to
be prophetic: thirty years later the figures among whites were what they had
been among blacks in the 1960s, with comparable social and psychological
results. The positive effects of marriage are thus not artifacts of ethnicity or
class within the United States, and many of them have been replicated in
other nations.[25] Nor are these effects canceled out by the presence of children. Raising children is often stressful, but even with children present, married couples in every ethnic, educational and class category are, on average,

---

[23]See Waite and Gallagher, *Case for Marriage,* especially chaps. 5 and 12.

[24]Daniel Patrick Moynihan, "The Negro Family: A Case for National Action," in Lee Rain-
water and William L. Yancey, *The Moynihan Report and the Politics of Controversy* (Cambridge, Mass.: M.I.T. Press, 1967). For an updated assessment that includes practical
theological nuances, see Don S. Browning, Bonnie J. Miller-McLemore, Pamela D. Couture, K. Brynolf Lyon and Rombert M. Franklin, *From Culture Wars to Common Ground:
Religion and the American Family Debate* (Louisville, Ky.: Westminster John Knox, 1997),
chap. 8.

[25]For example, Steven Stack and J. Ross Eshleman, "Marital Status and Happiness: A Seventeen-
Nation Study," *Journal of Marriage and the Family* 560 (1998): 527-36.

less depressed and more emotionally healthy than comparable singles of all types.[26]

Men, Marriage, Money and Sex

Marriage also increases both men's earnings and their wealth (assets such as savings and property). Economists call this the "marriage premium" and have found it in virtually every country they have studied. Furthermore, the income difference between married men and their single counterparts increases over time. As with men's health habits, earnings begin to improve even in the year before marriage, continue to rise more steeply (than those of single men) during a stable marriage and start to erode if the marriage breaks down. Thus, Waite and Gallagher note, "the same man who begins to earn more when he moves toward marriage earns less as he moves away from it. This pattern strongly suggests that something about the working partnership with a wife, rather than selection or discrimination [in favor of married men by employers] is responsible for a husband's higher earning capacity."[27]

Economists are right to conclude that something about marriage per se accounts for most of the improvement in men's earnings and wealth: less than half of the "marriage premium" can be attributed to the fact that men who have more money to begin with are more likely to get married.[28] And this too has implications that cut across class and ethnic lines. For example, a standard theory has been that if you want inner-city men to be responsible husbands and fathers, you must first find them jobs. While the availability of jobs is clearly crucial, the efforts of social worker Charles Ballard among inner-city African American men in Cleveland have shown, over almost twenty years, that if you can first convince young men of their importance as husbands and fathers, they will then be motivated to finish school, find jobs and stay working.[29] For men, marriage motivates earning at least as much as earning motivates marriage.

---

[26]Linda J. Waite and Mary Elizabeth Hughes, "At Risk on the Cusp of Old Age: Living Arrangements and Functional Status Among Black, White and Hispanic Adults," *Journal of Gerontology: Social Sciences* 543 (1999): S136-44.

[27]Waite and Gallagher, *Case for Marriage,* p. 100.

[28]Ibid., pp. 100-101.

[29]David Popenoe, *Life Without Father: Compelling New Evidence That Fatherhood and Marriage Are Indispensable for the Good of Children and Society* (New York: Free Press, 1996), pp. 74-76. It should be noted that in Ballard's samples few men married the mothers of their children, even after they had become more attached and responsible as fathers. Though for most men marriage and childrearing seem to constitute a seamless garment, it is possible for fatherhood alone to increase men's financial achievements, at least in the kinds of communities Ballard has worked in.

Finally, something needs to be said about men's sexual lives, in light of the longstanding myth that single men have both more—and better—sex than men who are chained to one woman through marriage. The durability of this myth is partly due to the fact that until the 1990s no truly random-sample studies of sexual behavior (as opposed to ones using unrepresentative "samples of convenience") had been done, in part because conservatives blocked government funding for such studies, fearing what they might reveal. Ironically, when random-sample studies were finally conducted in the United States with support from private foundations, such fears proved to be largely groundless. Married men both have sex more often and report it to be more satisfying—physically and emotionally—than single men, and while cohabiters match married men in quantity of sex, they reported less satisfaction with it.[30] Furthermore, sexual satisfaction is positively correlated with the degree of commitment men feel to their marriages. The most counter-stereotypic finding of all, however, is that married men who attend church weekly *and* believe strongly that sex should be limited to marriage report higher sexual satisfaction than those with more liberal views.[31] So the complementary myths of the swinging bachelor and the sexually deprived, religiously stuffy husband are largely just that—myths.

His and Her Marriage: How Different Are They?

This brief survey of the marriage literature is meant to challenge the age-old legend that wedlock is a "ball and chain" for men while remaining a lucrative deal for women. But in recent decades the opposite picture has begun to take hold in many social scientific and feminist circles—that "his" and "her" marriages are asymmetrical to the detriment of women. On this view the average marriage yields good health, power and satisfaction for men, while for women it brings stress, depression and the progressive loss of self. How did this reversal of stereotypes on marriage come about, and is it any more accurate than its predecessor?

The body of American research that gave rise to this bleak picture was gathered mainly between the end of World War II and the beginning of the second wave of feminism in the early 1960s. That was a period in which the doctrine of separate spheres for women and men flourished to an unusual degree. After

---

[30]Edward O. Laumann, John H. Gagnon, Robert T. Michael and Stuart Michaels, *The Social Organization of Sexuality: Sexual Practices in the United States* (Chicago: University of Chicago Press, 1994).

[31]William R. Mattox Jr., "What's Marriage Got to Do with It: Good Sex Comes to Those Who Wait," *Family Policy,* February 1994, pp. 1-7. See also Laumann et al., *Sex in America.*

years of wartime restrictions, family separations and widespread postponement of childbearing, many people were ready for what was to become a typically suburban lifestyle. Low-interest loans enabled veterans to finance houses in new subdivisions. Many wives were ready to embrace domesticity and motherhood as their husbands commuted to jobs in offices and factories. The birth rate shot up and produced the notorious baby boom, whose offspring are now about to strain the resources of the social security system as they move toward retirement.

In the late 1960s sociologist Jessie Bernard began to review the literature on marriage and mental health that had accumulated over the two decades since the end of the war, eventually publishing her findings in a 1972 book, *The Future of Marriage*.[32] Her conclusion was that marriage had an adverse effect on women's mental health even as it was apparently beneficial to men's. For example, she reported research from the 1960s showing that on measures such as depression, neurosis, phobic tendencies and passivity, married women scored worse than single women, while married men scored better than single men. In addition, other research showed that while singles of both sexes had similar rates of mental illness, married women showed higher rates than married men. Bernard and other social scientists inferred that it must be something about marriage in particular that made women more vulnerable.

This picture, however, does not square with more recent studies conducted with more methodological sophistication. These later studies indicate that the physical health advantages of marriage for women, while not as great as for men, are still substantial. The residual difference, as I noted earlier, is in large part due to the fact that single women take fewer risks than married men to begin with and thus have comparatively less to gain when they enter marriage. Thus while men's physical health indices take a large positive jump at the beginning of marriage and then improve at a more moderate rate thereafter, married women's health improves at a more consistent pace.[33] Much the same is true of mental health and happiness. Longitudinal studies completed in the 1980s and 1990s (and controlling for initial health as well as for ethnicity, class and education) have routinely showed that married

---

[32]Jessie Bernard, *The Future of Marriage* (New York: Bantam, 1972). Full disclosure note: I myself endorsed some of Bernard's conclusions in my 1990 book *Gender and Grace*, unaware (like most social scientists at the time) of their methodological flaws and the fact that, to the extent that they were true, they were becoming rapidly dated by feminism's successful expansion of role choices for women. A detailed history and methodological critique of this particular controversy can be found in Waite and Gallagher, *Case for Marriage*, chap. 12.
[33]Waite and Gallagher, *Case for Marriage*, chap. 4.

women, with or without children, are on average less depressed and psychologically healthier than their single counterparts.[34]

There is indeed a difference in the *overall* rates of depression suffered by adult women and men—one that shows up in both modern and preindustrial societies, suggesting that a biological component may be involved.[35] But marriage itself, at least in North American samples, accounts for almost none of this gap. Whatever their level of depression when entering marriage, both women and men on average improve, and improve about equally, as the marriage proceeds.

Finally, although marriage improves men's physical health somewhat more than women's, women gain relatively more financially from getting married. By choosing to marry, women share the advantages of husbands' usually higher earnings, as well as getting a "marriage premium" on their own earnings, as long as they stay in the waged workforce, and prior to having children. In the last chapter I will discuss the complications of children and the need, especially in the United States, for policies that reduce women's financial and other vulnerabilities during childrearing years, after divorce and in old age. But for the moment my point is simply that overall the benefits of marriage to men and women are both large and pretty much equal, despite differences on certain individual measures.

Resolving the Two Tales of Marriage

What accounts for the discrepancies between the two quite opposite readings of women's fate in marriage? For one thing, to the extent that Bernard's conclusion was accurate up to the early 1960s, it is now dated. One of the chief complaints of the women who started the second wave of feminism at that time was that men by and large were able to engage in multiple roles, both domestically and publicly; by contrast, most women were confined to the role of homemaker, which, however much they valued it, was often isolating and stressful and put them in a steadily more dependent position economically. All that has changed dramatically. The doctrine of rigidly separate spheres for men and women has

---

[34]For example, Waite and Hughes, "At the Cusp of Old Age"; Allan V. Horowitz, Helene Raskin White and Sandra Howell-White, "Becoming Married and Mental Health: A Longitudinal Study of a Cohort of Young Adults," *Journal of Marriage and the Family* 58 (1996): 895-907; Nadine F. Marks and James David Lambert, "Marital Status Continuity and Change Among Young and Midlife Adults: Longitudinal Effects of Psychological Well-Being," *Journal of Family Issues* 19 (1998): 652-86.

[35]In the United States, for example, rates of depression for men and women in the 1990s are around 5 percent and 10 percent of each population respectively.

been steadily dismantled, bringing the range of women's choices closer to that traditionally enjoyed by men. And another body of research has shown that having a variety of roles (waged work, family, hobbies, service opportunities) is good for the mental health of both men and women, provided that their number and demands do not become so great as to produce what is known as "role strain"—about which I will also have more to say in the final chapter.[36]

In addition, it is likely that Bernard overstated her case for married women's depression even when relying on data collected in the decades just after World War II. For example, she was quite aware of the fact that women and men operate in rather different marriage markets. As I noted in the first chapter of this book, the cultural norm has long been for women to marry up and men to marry down in terms of age, income and education. Bernard herself coined the term "marriage gradient" to describe this phenomenon—yet she and most of her contemporaries ignored it when comparing the well-being of married and single people. The post-World War II unmarried women whom she studied were "the cream of the crop" in socioeconomic terms, with more education, better salaries and higher occupational status than women in general, and all of these factors help to protect against depression regardless of sex or marital status. Thus "Bernard simply failed to distinguish between the effects of marriage and the effects of high social status on women's depression."[37] When later studies did control for social status, the advantages of marriage for women became clear.

In sum, it is now evident that the positive effects of marriage are not greatly skewed toward men *or* women, nor are they due to advantages individuals bring with them to marriage, but to certain qualities of marriage itself when it is "good enough," even if not perfect. What might these qualities be?

First, the "till death do us part" aspect of marriage helps partners to trust each other, to learn about and accommodate each other's tastes (sexual and otherwise) and to develop some skills while downplaying others that the spouse has in his or her repertoire. Second, marriage involves a pooling not just of skills but of economic and social resources. In Linda Waite's words, this provides for spouses "a sort of small insurance pool against life's uncertainties, reducing their need to protect themselves—by themselves—from unexpected events."[38] Third, married couples benefit from economies of scale—the "two can live about as

---

[36]For a review of this literature, see Hilary M. Lips, *Sex and Gender: An Introduction*, 3rd ed. (Mountain View, Calif.: Mayfield, 1997), chap. 9.

[37]Waite and Gallagher, *Case for Marriage*, p. 165.

[38]Linda J. Waite, "Social Science Finds: Marriage Matters," *The Responsive Community* 6, no. 3 (1996): 26-35, quotation from p. 33.

cheaply as one" effect. Finally, marriage connects people to other family members, social groups and institutions, including churches, which provide further support and—just as important—opportunities for service that help to give life purpose and meaning.

Obviously, cohabiting men and women can also benefit from things like economies of scale and pooling of skills. But cohabitation by its very nature does not imply a lifetime commitment—indeed half of such relationships in the United States end within two years, and almost all within five years. Moreover, cohabiting couples often have quite discrepant views about the future of their relationship, with men usually less committed than their partners.[39] Consequently, cohabitation is a particularly poor bargain for women, who are the ones apt to be left holding the baby if they happen to get pregnant. Cohabiting couples are also much less likely than married persons to pool economic resources; in many respects they live as roommates who just happen to sleep together. And while marriage connects couples to others, cohabitation tends to do the opposite: it isolates couples from family and from other supportive and service-promoting groups.[40] Again, there is something about the permanence of marriage that makes a difference to the well-being of the adults involved. And as we shall see shortly, the same is true for children.

Children of Divorce

Over the past several decades social scientists have collected a lot of data on the fallout of divorce for children, using the same mixture of longitudinal studies and statistical controls for other factors that characterize the research literature on marriage. And amazing as it might seem in a culture still so divorce-prone, regardless of their place on the ideological spectrum, most social scientists now agree that divorce is anything but a minor blip on children's developmental landscape. Children of divorce on average show more antisocial behavior toward peers and adults, more depression and more learning problems than children from intact homes with their two original parents. They are almost twice as likely to drop out of school, to become teenage parents and to be neither in school nor in the workforce as young adults. As older adults they tend to have less sense of psychological well-

---

[39]For a further discussion of trends related to nonmarital cohabitation, see David G. Myers, *The American Paradox: Spiritual Hunger in an Age of Plenty* (New Haven, Conn.: Yale University Press, 2000), chap. 3.

[40]Steven L. Nock, *Marriage in Men's Lives* (New York: Oxford University Press, 1998).

being, less marital satisfaction, a heightened risk of divorce and even a short-er average life span.[41]

Is there really a causal connection between divorce and these negative out-comes? It has been argued, for example, that it is not the absence of a parent but simply postdivorce economic strain on single-parent families that accounts for these results. But the negative effects have been shown to persist even when income is controlled for—for example, when generous alimony is paid or when children's economic status is raised by the custodial parent's remarriage. At best only half the variance associated with these problems is attributable to the eco-nomic stresses that accompany single parenthood, important and troubling though these are.[42]

Others suggest that studies have failed to compare conflict-ridden families that have undergone divorce with similar families that have stayed together. Surely, they argue, children in the latter families would show the same range and quantity of problems, thus proving that the operant factor is not divorce per se but the miserable homes children lived in *prior* to divorce. But this is again too simple, as shown by a mammoth, thirty-three-year longitudinal study involv-ing virtually all the British children born during the first week of March 1958. Through the years, interviews were conducted at various times with their moth-ers, fathers and teachers, and (as time progressed) with the children themselves, of whom over two-thirds of the original sample were still available at age thirty-three. During that time, of course, some of their parents had divorced and others had not, allowing the researchers to examine ongoing conflict differences (and similarities) across both groups. The result: only about half the problems suf-fered by children of divorce could be attributed to predivorce levels of conflict in the home. Indeed in America only about a third of divorces occur in what are defined as high-conflict marriages, and it is only such divorces that leave chil-dren, on the whole, better off than they would be in an intact family.[43] By thrust-ing children into a series of negative life experiences, divorce almost always

---

[41]For a review of this literature, see Sara McLanahan and Gary D. Sandefur, *Growing Up with a Single Parent: What Hurts, What Helps* (Cambridge, Mass.: Harvard University Press, 1994). For a detailed account of one longitudinal study, see Judith S. Wallerstein, Julia M. Lewis and Sandra Blakeslee, *The Unexpected Legacy of Divorce: A Twenty-five-Year Landmark Study* (New York: Hyperion, 2000). For an in-depth (and more qualitative) account developed by adults who themselves went through divorce as children, see Stephanie Staal, *The Love They Lost: Living With the Legacy of Our Parents' Divorce* (New York: Delacorte, 2000), and for a more optimistic view of children's postdivorce resilience, see E. Mavis Hetherington and John Kelly, *For Better or for Worse: Divorce Reconsidered* (New York: W. W. Norton, 2002).

[42]See David Blankenhorn, *Fatherless America: Confronting Our Most Urgent Social Problem* (New York: BasicBooks, 1995), especially chap. 10, for a review of the pertinent literature.

[43]Paul R. Amato and Alan Booth, *A Generation at Risk: Growing Up in an Era of Family Up-heaval* (Cambridge, Mass.: Harvard University Press, 1997).

multiplies social problems and the welfare resources needed to cope with them.[44]

Perhaps most significant, another body of research shows that the effects of divorce are also common in children of single parents who never married and thus have no history of marital conflict.[45] So clearly there is something about *intact, two-parent* families that matters. Reasonably harmonious and mature parents support and spell each other in childcare. They are a constant presence in the child's life and can thus adjust to developmental changes and supply consistent moral guidance. They provide a backdrop of day-to-day predictability that allows children to concentrate on age-appropriate tasks. Divorce changes all this, usually for the worse.

Why Do
Fathers Matter?

But does it matter that the two consistent adults in a child's life are a mother *and* a father? This is a pertinent question, given that in the United States almost six times more children of divorce live with their mothers than with their fathers, and that only one in five will see their fathers as often as every week thereafter. Indeed it is a pertinent question for *intact* families in which fathers are often absent, as has been the norm in Western society since the Industrial Revolution. In previous chapters I noted that boys growing up in the context of such asymmetrical parenting must develop their sense of gender identity in the frequent or almost total absence of fathers. Thus they are apt to conclude that becoming a man means becoming as unlike women as possible. As they grow older, some men escalate this exercise in compensatory masculinity. At worst, they may scorn and abuse women while engaging in other antisocial acts, singly or with other males. At best, they may avoid what they perceive to be women's work, including hands-on caretaking of their own children. In this way they help to reproduce a cycle of overly feminized parenting and misogyny in the following generations.

We saw in the chapter on masculinity across cultures that antifemale and hypermasculine behaviors and attitudes are indeed strongest in cultures where the caretaking of young children is most strongly avoided by men. Oppositely, low levels of misogyny and compensatory masculinity are likeliest in families and

---

[44]Andrew J. Cherlin et al., "Longitudinal Studies of Effects of Divorce on Children in Great Britain and the United States, *Science* 252 (1991): 1386-89.
[45]McLanahan and Sandefur, *Growing Up with a Single Parent*.

cultures where there is active, nurturant fathering in children's lives. But the effects of father presence extend to daughters as well. "Fathers in general," writes psychiatrist Anthony Clare, "promote their daughters' developing autonomy by inviting them to participate in non-traditional areas of mastery."[46] In one study of high-achieving women students at Massachusetts Institute of Technology, fathers were typically described by science-oriented daughters as encouraging, intellectually stimulating, proud of their daughters' growing abilities and involved in joint activities with them throughout their growing-up years.[47] Mothers, of course, are also vitally important as role models for their daughters' desire to achieve professionally and intellectually. But fathers' encouragement additionally signals to young women that they are interesting persons in their own right and that their status as successful women does not depend simply on their sexual and reproductive value to men.

Other research confirms the importance of nurturant fathering in helping daughters to resist the temptations of what might be called lowest-common-denominator femininity—that is, early sexual activity and unwed childbearing. Mavis Hetherington's work comparing the social behavior of adolescent girls from intact, divorced and mother-widowed homes is quite telling. In her studies, girls from intact homes related naturally and confidently to their male peers and to adult males, while girls whose fathers had died tended to be shy and inhibited. But girls from divorced families were much more likely to seek out males and act seductively toward them. They engaged in earlier and more sex than the other two groups, and a follow-up study showed that they were more likely to marry early, inappropriately and with a greater risk of divorce.[48]

Informal investigations among African Americans by journalist Jonetta Rose Barras show that adult women from fatherless homes (whether due to divorce, desertion or never having been in the home to begin with) are more apt to regard themselves as unworthy and unlovable, to fear rejection, abandonment and commitment and to be susceptible to rage, anger and depression. "Too often," Barras observes, "women who are wounded by the loss of their fathers go from man to man, from bed to bed, calling sex 'love' and hoping to be healed by the physical closeness." She adds, "Sometimes sex is not enough. Fatherless girls develop an obsession with having a baby [as] a defense against loneliness,

---

[46]Anthony Clare, On Men: Masculinity in Crisis (London: Arrow, 2000), p. 177.

[47]Leonard Tessman, "A Note on Father's Contribution to His Daughter's Way of Loving and Working," in Father and Child: Development and Clinical Perspectives, ed. Stanley H. Cath, Alan R. Gurwitt and John Munder Ross (New York: Wiley, 1982), pp. 219-38.

[48]E. Mavis Hetherington, "Effects of Father Absence on Personality Development of Adolescent Daughters," Developmental Psychology 7, no. 3 (1972): 313-26.

against abandonment. . . . At least when he leaves we will have someone—we won't be alone. In fact, we'll still have him, because we have his baby. It is ludicrous, but nevertheless we cling to this reasoning."[49] Reviewers of the relevant social science literature agree that such vulnerability is common to underfathered women regardless of class or ethnic background. As one scholar summarizes it, "Deprived of a stable relationship with a nonexploitative adult male who loves them, these girls can remain developmentally 'stuck,' struggling with issues of security and trust that well-fathered girls have already successfully resolved."[50]

If involved fathering lessens the risk of inappropriately expressed femininity in daughters, what is it about nurturant fathering that lowers the risk of hypermasculine behavior in sons? Negatively, involved fatherly presence acts as a check on boys' aggressiveness as they grow up, something that mothers cannot do quite as easily. Knowing the hazards and temptations of growing up male, adult men can contribute to the socialization of young boys simply by seeing through them more readily and by being willing to confront and redirect hypermasculine "acting out" before it reaches epidemic proportions. Criminologist James Q. Wilson points out that "neighborhood standards may be set by mothers, but they are enforced by fathers, or at least by adult males. Neighborhoods without fathers are neighborhoods without men able and willing to confront errant youth, chase threatening gangs, and reproach delinquent fathers."[51]

But just as important are the positive effects that involved fathers can have. By reassuring their sons that they are valued and loved as unique beings, fathers can implicitly certify them "masculine enough" to get on with the more important business of being human. In other words, nurturant fathers can relieve sons of the anxiety of "proving themselves" adequately masculine by engaging in truculent and misogynist activities, and can thus help free them to acquire more adaptive—and less rigidly gender-stereotyped—relational and work skills. Psychologist Frank Pittman has been especially perceptive about this second positive aspect of fathering. Drawing on three decades as a counselor to men struggling with identity issues, he writes:

> Most boys nowadays are growing up with fathers who spend little, if any, time with them. Ironically, when the boy most needs to practice being a man, his father is

---

[49]Jonetta Rose Barras, *Whatever Happened to Daddy's Little Girl? The Impact of Fatherlessness on Black Women* (New York: Ballantine, 2000), p. 70.

[50]Blankenhorn, *Fatherless America*, p. 47.

[51]James Q. Wilson, "Culture, Incentives and the Underclass," in *Values and Public Policy*, ed. Henry J. Aaron, Thomas E. Mann, and Timothy Taylor (Washington, D.C: Brookings Institution, 1994), pp. 70-71.

off somewhere playing at being a boy. . . . Instead of real-life fathers, boys grow up with myths of fathers, while mothers, whatever their significance out there in the world, reign supreme at home in the life of the boy. If fathers have run out on mothers, in any of the many ways men use to escape women, then boys can't imagine that their masculinity is sufficient until they too run away from women and join the world of men. . . . Fathers have the authority to let boys relax the requirements of the masculine model. If our fathers accept us, then that declares us masculine enough to join the company of men. In effect, boys then have their diplomas in masculinity and can go on to develop other skills. . . . A boy may spend his entire life seeking that acceptance, and with it a reprieve from masculine striving. If boys can't get acceptance from their fathers, then they are dependent on the company of other men to overwhelm the fathers' rejecting voices or the echoing sound of paternal silence.[52]

The Radical Conclusion

So the bottom line appears to be this: children of both sexes need to grow up with stable, nurturant adult role models of both sexes to better develop a secure gender identity that then—paradoxically—allows them to relate to each other primarily as human beings, rather than as gender-role caricatures. This does not require that such role models always and only be the child's biological parents. But it strongly suggests that there are limits to the diversity of family forms that we should encourage around the core norm of heterosexual, role-flexible coparenting.

As our culture has rushed to embrace an increasing plurality of household forms, we are learning some lessons the hard way. In a sense, stable marriages and families are like the vitamins and minerals in healthy food. It is easy, for example, to take Vitamin C for granted and not notice its benefits until you are citrus-deprived and come down with a case of scurvy. To expand the metaphor, we could say that our culture has been eating relational junk food for the past thirty years and is only now noticing the accumulating effects. Having begun to do so, the next challenge is to provide the resources for the strengthening of marriage, family and other gendered relationships in a way that is just and fair to everyone involved. Here we have yet another emerging body of research to help us, as well as a number of grassroots movements involving Christians and other concerned men and women. These will be examined in the final chapter of this volume.

---

[52]Frank Pittman, "Beyond the B.S. and the Drum-Beating: Staggering Through Life as a Man," *Psychology Today* 25, no. 1 (1992): 78-83, quotation from pp. 82-83. See also his volume *Man Enough: Fathers, Sons and the Search for Masculinity* (New York: Putnam, 1993).

11

Men, Masculinity and Nonrelational Sexuality

MORE THAN TWO DECADES AGO I spent several months in the Central African rain forest with my husband, our infant son and some social science colleagues, doing comparative research on the cognitive and childrearing patterns of the Mbeka pygmy and their taller African neighbors, the Bagandou. At one point in this process we had to stop collecting data for about a week. The reason: it was flying termite season, and most of the locals—young, old and in between—had left the villages for what turned out to be an extended campout and termite feast. Sautéed over a fire in a bit of oil, these insects taste like roasted peanuts, and it was a much-anticipated annual excursion for the Bagandou to follow and catch them by the hundreds and feast on them for several days running. They are nourishing as well as tasty, providing an excellent source of protein during the dry season when game meat is hard to come by. And just as we tell stories and teach our children songs while popping corn or toasting marshmallows on camping trips, so do the Bagandou while frying their annually captured termites in and around the rain forest.

However, I know about the virtues of termite cuisine only by hearsay. Despite having an adventurous palate that has willingly sampled monkey, warthog and a host of other exotic dishes, I draw the line at eating insects. My Christian concern for global justice has done nothing to alter my policy, though I have great admiration for one of my colleagues, a physiological psychologist, whose research involves finding ways for North Americans to overcome their aversion toward bugs as part of their diet. If we in the West could learn to eat lower on the food chain, she points out, we could go some way toward solving the world's food crisis and still stay well nourished. She's right, but she'll never persuade me to take part in any of her experiments.

Insects are too firmly embedded in my mind as invasive, disease-carrying pests.

Beyond Biology

Contrast this dietary anecdote with a quite different one, based on a more recent occurrence. The occasion was a potluck luncheon for a staff member at my university who was about to retire. After filling my plate from a table spread with food, I took a bite from a small triangular sandwich and was instantly transported back to my Ontario childhood. You see, the sandwich filling was flaked, tinned salmon mixed with mayonnaise and vinegar, something I had rarely tasted since the days when my father took my brother and me back to his own childhood one-room schoolhouse to attend community square dances. Flaked salmon sandwiches cut in small triangles were a regular offering at those gatherings, about which a host of fond memories were now suddenly revived in me after almost half a century.

I was so taken with the experience that the next day I rummaged in the cupboard for a long-forgotten tin of salmon and, under my husband's amused gaze, made myself another salmon sandwich. My husband is indifferent to salmon sandwiches, but he has his own childhood memories of Dutch immigrant birthday parties where *slagroomgebakjes* (whipped-cream pastries) were the order of the day. These he eats with great reverence and nostalgia whenever he happens to stumble across a Dutch bakery, which fortunately is not too often.

It is obvious that for human beings food is never just food. Throughout our lives as individuals and communities we invest food with tremendous symbolic meaning, both negative and positive, regardless of its actual nutritional value. And the same is true of sex, despite the efforts of some evolutionary psychologists to reduce it to a set of one-directional, gene-perpetuating strategies. Indeed the meaning we assign to sex-related events and images regularly alters our most basic physiological processes. If you are still inclined to doubt this, you might try a simple test: sit down one day and start leafing through your old high school yearbook with an adolescent by your side. I can almost guarantee that the teenager—even if he or she is just a few years younger than you—will take one at look at the photo of the prom queen or football player for whom you or your peers once burned with lust and be totally turned off. The hairstyles will be pronounced weird, the clothing dorky and the people sporting them completely unsexy. Far from being a mere reflex, sexual arousal interacts with our deepest anxieties and hopes and is awash with culturally constructed meaning.

A Brief Apologia

My aim in this chapter is to examine what sex often means to men in our culture and to point to some reasons for the troubling behaviors that can result. However, I am well aware that, of all the topics in this book, my attempt as a woman to deal with male sexuality may be considered the most presumptuous. Is this not the one area of life in which the phrase "opposite sexes" continues to resonate? Do not men's and women's differing anatomy, reproductive roles and sex hormone ratios dictate that this is the one sphere in which women and men must treat each other as eternal mysteries? If Sigmund Freud, as an early and famous student of sexual behavior, finally had to concede that he could not figure out what women want, by what authority can one of his female academic descendants be any less reticent in her claims about men?

These are fair questions, but there are good reasons for me to have written this chapter anyway. For one thing sexual activity, like gender, is a relational term. It is like an ongoing dance that men and women mutually (though not always symmetrically) negotiate on the platform of their biological complementarity and—more often than is realized—according to implicit and explicit rules that family and culture have taught them regarding acceptable parameters of sexual expression. Even (or perhaps especially) when we rebel against those rules, we are still profoundly affected by them as we make sexual choices. As the dance takes shape, each sex may indeed feel mystified by the other, but in the process we also learn something about each other.

More important, what women and men share in terms of their creation in God's image, their solidarity in sin and their call to redemption and sanctification is more basic than the physical or social differences that separate them. Throughout the biblical drama in which all humans are witting or unwitting players, sexuality is portrayed a God-given good that, like any other aspect of creation, is vulnerable to distortion and idolatry. Men and women may misuse sexuality in what seem to be very different ways, but the underlying impulses and temptations—to treat sex as a bargaining chip or a power trip; to invest it with an inflated, almost magical significance; to isolate it from God's call to develop as whole persons living in covenantal community—afflict women and men alike and thus make empathy possible despite the different bodies and subcultures we inhabit.[1]

---

[1]Lewis Smedes elaborates these themes in his *Sex for Christians* (Grand Rapids, Mich.: Eerdmans, 1976).

Finally, what I say about male sexuality in this chapter converges in many ways with the thinking of contemporary scholars and therapists of both sexes, working together and separately in various parts of the Western world. The scholars include social psychologists who have focused attention on the ways visual media in particular shape the sexual responses of men.[2] The therapists are both clinical psychologists and medically trained psychiatrists working in the tradition of depth psychology, which focuses on the unconscious and often symbolic meanings that sex acquires as a result of emotion-laden family and other relational dynamics. They include Liam Hudson and Bernadine Jacot at London's Tavistock clinic,[3] Ronald Levant, William Pollack and Samuel Osherson at Harvard University,[4] New York City therapist Alon Gratch,[5] and psychiatrist Anthony Clare at Trinity College Dublin.[6] There is also a French voice in philosopher Elisabeth Badinter of the École Polytechnique in Paris, whose 1995 book on masculine identity became a bestseller in France among readers of both sexes.[7]

The real challenge, as in other chapters, is not so much being a woman interpreting male experience as being a Christian social scientist trying to discern what resonates with biblical truth and what does not, regardless of its origin or the sex of its writers.

Some Sobering Statistics

Ronald Levant, a clinical psychologist who specializes in male identity issues, has noted that many midlife men make two quite opposite assertions when they first come to him: first, that sex is among the most important aspects of their life, if not *the* most important, and second, that they are disappointed in their sex life.[8] So it seems that male sexuality is a source of ambivalence and confusion even to men themselves. And its ambiguous place in individual men's lives is certainly reflected

---

[2]This work and its primary sources are readably summarized in David G. Myers, *The American Paradox: Spiritual Hunger in an Age of Plenty* (New Haven, Conn.: Yale University Press, 2000), especially chap. 8.

[3]Liam Hudson and Bernadine Jacot, *The Way Men Think: Intellect, Intimacy and the Erotic Imagination* (New Haven, Conn.: Yale University Press, 1991).

[4]Ronald F. Levant and William Pollack, eds., *A New Psychology of Men* (New York: BasicBooks, 1995); Samuel Osherson, *Finding Our Fathers: How Man's Life Is Shaped by His Relationship with His Father* (New York: Fawcett Columbine, 1986), and *Wrestling with Love: How Men Struggle with Intimacy* (New York: Fawcett Columbine, 1992).

[5]Alon Gratch, *If Men Could Talk . . . Here's What They'd Say* (Boston: Little, Brown, 2001).

[6]Anthony Clare, *On Men: Masculinity in Crisis* (London: Arrow, 2000).

[7]Elisabeth Badinter, *XY: On Masculine Identity,* trans. Lydia Davis (New York: Columbia University Press, 1995).

[8]Ronald F. Levant, "Non-relational Sexuality in Men," in *Men and Sex: New Psychological Perspectives,* ed. Ronald F. Levant and Gary R. Brooks (New York: Wiley, 1997), pp. 9-27.

in sex-related statistics for several areas of behavior. For example, sexual harassment in the workplace—legally defined as pressure to render sexual favors as a condition of employment or advancement, or the creation of a hostile work environment by the use of sexual advances, language or other displays—is an overwhelmingly male activity. A 1993 review of eighteen North American studies indicated that about 42 percent of women and 15 percent of men had experienced sexual harassment. Of those totals, 95 percent of the women and a fifth of the men reported being harassed by males only.[9] Throughout the 1990s, the vast majority of sexual harassment charges lodged with the U.S. Equal Employment Opportunity Commission (EEOC) came from women, although complaints from men had also risen as high as 14 percent by 1999, and those accused of harassment were almost always men.[10] Christian work environments are not always free of this problem: for example, a 1990 American survey of United Methodist clergywomen showed that 77 percent had experienced sexual harassment—41 percent from male denominational colleagues or other male pastors.[11]

When it comes to serious cases of sexual assault, men are also deeply implicated. In prevalence studies conducted in Western nations, an average of one in seven women reports having experienced rape or attempted rape, and experts agree that a further, large percentage of such assaults is unreported.[12] In the late 1990s two U.S. surveys of male prisoners found that just over 20 percent had experienced coercive sexual behavior at the hands of other male inmates.[13] In 1997 men victimized by other men while serving in the armed forces accounted for 22 percent of those who sought treatment for sexual trauma in veterans' hospitals.[14] In the United States just over 60 percent of female sexual assault victims are below age sixteen, and almost a third under age eleven.[15]

However, regardless of sex, most children are not victimized by their biological fathers but by male acquaintances and other relatives. In fact, U.S. preschoolers living with one biological parent and one stepparent have been found to be forty

---

[9]L. F. Fitzgerald and S. L. Shullman, "Sexual Harassment: A Research Analysis and Agenda for the 1990s," *Journal of Vocational Behavior* 42 (1993): 5-27.

[10]Reed Abelson, "Men, Increasingly, Are the Ones Claiming Sex Harassment by Men," *New York Times,* June 10, 2001, pp. A1, A41.

[11]"Women Clerics Find Sexual Harassment," *Washington Post,* December 1, 1990, p. C12.

[12]Linda J. Waite and Maggie Gallagher, *The Case for Marriage: Why Married People Are Happier, Healthier and Better Off Financially* (New York: Doubleday, 2000), chap. 11.

[13]Shankar Vedantam, "Focus Urged on Sex Abuse of Boys," *Philadelphia Inquirer,* December 2, 1998, p. A3.

[14]David Moniz, "More Male Veterans Reporting That They Were Sexually Assaulted," *Philadelphia Inquirer,* September 22, 1997, p. A8.

[15]A helpful compendium of relevant statistics, and of sources where others can be obtained, has been assembled in Catherine Clark Kroeger and Nancy Nason-Clark, *No Place for Abuse: Biblical and Practical Resources to Counteract Domestic Violence* (Downers Grove, Ill.: InterVarsity Press, 2001), chap. 1.

times more likely to be sexually abused than children living with two natural parents. One study has found that unmarried mothers' boyfriends commit almost half of all reported child sexual abuse by nonparents, even though they contribute less than 2 percent of nonparental childcare.[16] Here too the church is not immune, as can be seen in the thousands of lawsuits recently brought against four denominations by native Canadians claiming systematic physical and sexual abuse at the hands of residential school staff during the years that such schools were operated by churches on behalf of the Canadian government.[17]

Finally, there is the escalating availability of visual pornography, almost 90 percent of whose consumers are male.[18] With the advent of the Internet, as many as twenty million U.S. adults per month were visiting cybersex websites by the year 2000. Online sex is by far the most profitable business on the Internet, with revenues increasing from $52 million in 1996 to $2 billion in 1999.[19] Peddling pornography is, of course, not a new activity, but it has reached new levels of accessibility, anonymity and affordability on the Internet. "The temptation may be old," writes Christine Gardner, "but the technology is new. With an increasing number of computers and Internet access in each home, pornography is just a click away, as convenient as ordering flowers or sending e-mail."[20] Yet again Christians are not immune. When *Christianity Today* polled its readership in 2000 on pornography use, over a third of both clergy and laity admitted to having visited a sexually explicit website, and almost 20 percent of clergy said they visited such sites from a couple of times a month to more than once a week. Under 8 percent of all respondents had sought professional help for this habit, and close to a third of the clergy users had told no one—including their spouse—about it.[21]

▎ *Harmless Entertainment?*

Does any of this matter from a purely practical point of view? Does pornography consumption have a role-modeling effect that shapes behavior toward others in

---

[16]Leslie Margolin, "Child Abuse by Mothers' Boyfriends: Why the Overrepresentation?" *Child Abuse and Neglect* 16 (1992): 541-51.

[17]Ferdy Baglo, "Canadian Churches Seek to Resolve Abuse Cases," *Christianity Today* 45, no. 9 (2001): 21.

[18]For a collection of essays from a profeminist men's movement perspective (but one that predates the advent of the Internet), see Michael S. Kimmel, ed., *Men Confront Pornography* (New York: Crown, 1990).

[19]Frederick S. Lane, *Obscene Profits: The Entrepreneurs of Pornography in the Cyber Age* (New York: Routledge, 2000).

[20]Christine J. Gardner, "Tangled in the Worst of the Web," *Christianity Today* 45, no. 5 (March 5, 2001): 42-49, quotation from p. 44.

[21]Ibid., pp. 44-45.

damaging ways? Or is the truth quite opposite: like pounding nails when you're angry, viewing pornography is cathartic, draining off sexual tension and making it *less* likely to be directed toward unwilling others?

Although the catharsis theory has many adherents—from free speech defenders to corporate media moguls—it is the role-modeling explanation that is overwhelmingly supported by well-designed social psychological research. The basic paradigm for such research is to randomly assign participants—usually male—to one of two experimental conditions: viewing various kinds of video pornography (soft and/or violent erotica) or viewing a like amount of nonpornographic material—a political debate, for example—under similar conditions. Prior to viewing, all participants are premeasured for certain attitudes, and then they are remeasured at the end of the experiment. Such studies consistently show that viewing aggressive pornography significantly lowers threshold tendencies toward violent behavior.[22]

Pornography that portrays women as welcoming sexual assault despite preliminary protestations to the contrary—like Scarlet O'Hara in the famous marital rape scene in *Gone with the Wind*—increases male viewers' acceptance of coercion in their own sexual relations.[23] Viewing sexually explicit films makes research participants, on average, more tolerant of short-term prison sentences for convicted rapists, more accepting of extramarital sex and more tolerant of male seduction of underage girls.[24] The most potent mix in such studies appears to be a combination of erotic and violent imagery—but even without violence, viewing so-called soft porn has other questionable consequences. It makes real-life partners and potential partners seem less adequate.[25] It increases men's tendency to view women in purely sexual terms, and inclines them to misinterpret merely friendly behavior from a woman as a sexual come-on.[26] It also provides

---

[22]Like many others, I am not completely comfortable with this research paradigm because of its potential effect on participants' future behavior. However, in keeping with the ethics guidelines of the American Psychological Association, most pornography researchers are careful to debrief their subjects thoroughly—that is, fully explain the aims of the research and negate any impression that the viewed behavior is to be taken as neutral or morally positive. Participants are often followed up for varying periods of time to confirm that no negative long-term effects have occurred.

[23]Neil M. Malamuth and James B. Check, "The Effects of Media Exposure on Acceptance of Violence Against Women: A Field Experiment," *Journal of Applied Social Psychology* 15 (1981): 436-46.

[24]Dolf Zillmann and J. B. Weaver, "Pornography and Men's Sexual Callousness Toward Women," in *Pornography: Research Advances and Policy Considerations,* ed. Dolf Zillmann and Jennings J. Bryant (Hillsdale, N.J.: Erlbaum, 1989), pp. 95-125.

[25]Douglas T. Kendrick and Sara E. Gutierres, "Contrast Effects and Judgments of Physical Attractiveness: When Beauty Becomes a Social Problem," *Journal of Personality and Social Psychology* 38 (1980): 131-40.

[26]Douglas McKenzie-Mohr and Mark P. Zanna, "Treating Women as Sexual Objects: Look to the (Gender Schematic) Male Who Has Viewed Pornography," *Personality and Social Psychology Bulletin* 16 (1990): 296-308.

a skewed image of sexual reality. As social psychologist David Myers points out, in the fourteen-thousand-odd televised sex acts annually seen by the average viewer, almost no one "gets herpes or AIDS. No one gets pregnant. No one has to change diapers, get up in the middle of the night, or heroically struggle to socialize a fatherless child. . . . More than two-thirds of the time the activity is portrayed as desirable, less than 10 percent of the time undesirable."[27]

The research outlined above is part of a body of well-designed studies with largely similar outcomes. But we might well ask whether such studies can be generalized to real-world situations. After all, their experimental effects, though statistically significant, tend to be of short duration (otherwise it would be clearly unethical to involve people in studies exposing them to pornography, especially of the violent variety). Furthermore, participants in such studies are almost always traditional undergraduates, and it might be argued that young male adults, near the peak of their testosterone-producing abilities, are disproportionately vulnerable to such messages. However, research with broader samples and a wider time horizon undercuts this benign interpretation. For example, in Hawaii reported rape cases rose almost 100 percent between 1960, when restraints on pornography sales were loosened, and 1974 when restraints were temporarily reimposed. After that rape rates fell, only to rise again when restraints were once more lifted.[28] And across all the United States, sales of sexually explicit magazines correlate positively with rape rates, even after researchers have statistically controlled for the percentage of young men in each state.[29] Such findings also belie the catharsis theory of pornography, which would predict a lower—not a higher—rate of rape in states with a high consumption of sex magazines.

What psychological dynamic lies behind both the consumption of pornography and the impulse to engage in depersonalized, even violent sexual behavior? Social psychologist Neil Malamuth cites two main ingredients, which he calls "promiscuous-impersonal sex" and "hostile masculinity"—that is, a pattern of unrestricted sex with many different partners combined with a defensive, hostile attitude toward women.[30] We have already seen how the first of these is rein-

---

[27]Myers, *American Paradox*, p. 234.

[28]John H. Court, "Sex and Violence: A Ripple Effect," in *Pornography and Sexual Aggression,* ed. Neil M. Malamuth and Edward Donnerstein (New York: Academic, 1985).

[29]Larry Baron and Murray A. Straus, "Sexual Stratification, Pornography and Rape in the United States," in *Pornography and Sexual Aggression,* ed. Neil M. Malamuth and Edward Donnerstein (New York: Academic, 1985).

[30]Neil M. Malamuth, Christopher L. Heavey, Gordon Barnes and Michele Acker, "Using the Confluence Model of Sexual Aggression to Predict Men's Conflict with Women: A Ten-Year Follow-Up Study," *Journal of Personality and Social Psychology* 69 (1995): 353-69. See also Myers, *American Paradox*, chap. 8.

forced by popular culture, ranging from soft to hardcore pornographic images and activities. "We decry impersonal or exploitative sex, unprotected sex, and teen pregnancy and its associated social pathologies," observes Myers. "Yet these are exactly what our current media fare gives us. . . . The repeated, vivid, consistent portrayal of casual sexuality, uncontested by equally potent alternative sources of sexual information, makes television an ideal medium for scripting children's future sexual behaviors."[31] But while children and adults of both sexes are regularly exposed to such media images, hostile masculinity is a peculiarly male attitudinal syndrome with roots running even deeper than the social learning that comes from media consumption. To understand these, we need to supplement social psychology with some physiological observations and some clinically based depth psychology.

Nonrelational Sexuality in Males

It is an ongoing controversy among psychologists as to whether self-generated behaviors like pornography viewing—in contrast to substances like drugs and alcohol that are ingested or injected—can be labeled "addictive." But if addiction is defined as loss of control, continuation of the behavior despite significant adverse consequences, and preoccupation or obsession with obtaining a substance or pursuing a behavior, then the term rightly applies to the approximately 200,000 Americans—the vast majority of them men—who have spent so much time consuming Internet pornography that they have lost or seriously jeopardized jobs, family relationships and financial security. Although such behavioral compulsion does not involve putting external drugs into the body, preliminary research suggests that it can affect levels of internal brain chemicals such as dopamine and endorphins. The release of these mood-enhancing chemicals keeps the behavior going, and like addictive drugs they are vulnerable to adaptation, so that progressively more extreme sexual scenarios are needed to generate the sought-after sensations.[32] As with testosterone, this is a case where behavioral choices may create an escalating feedback cycle with physiological processes. This has led Al Cooper, a staff psychologist at Stanford University who has conducted detailed research into

---

[31]Myers, *American Paradox*, p. 218.
[32]Jennifer Schneider, *Cybersex Exposed: Recognizing the Obsession* (Minneapolis: Hazelden, 2001); Patrick Carnes, *Don't Call It Love: Recovery from Sexual Addiction* (New York: Bantam, 1991); Jane E. Brody, "Cybersex Gives Birth to a Psychological Disorder," *New York Times,* May 16, 2000, pp. F7, F12.

online sex, to call it "the crack cocaine of sexual compulsivity."[33]

Feminist scholars and activists have written much about the way pornography production and consumption exploit women and children.[34] But as feminist critic Deirdre English notes, men too are victimized by the pornography industry. "The overwhelming feeling," she writes, "is one of the commercial exploitation of male sexual desire. There it is, embarrassingly desperate, tormented, demeaning itself, begging for relief, taking any substitute and *paying* for it. Men who live for this are suckers, and their uncomfortable demeanor shows they know it. If as a woman you can detach yourself . . . you see how totally tragic they appear."[35] Some forty years earlier C. S. Lewis made similar observations in *Mere Christianity*. He invited readers to imagine what they would think of a prosperous culture whose inhabitants regularly went to theaters where they could view covered silver platters paraded across a stage and, just as the lights dimmed, the cover removed for a momentary display of a juicy lamb chop or a bit of bacon.[36] Yet we too often assume that this is just how men are destined to be with regard to women's bodies. The fuller explanation, as Lewis recognized, lies at least partly in economics: "A man with an obsession is a man who has very little sales resistance."[37]

However, the compulsive consumption of pornography is only an extreme expression of a more general male cultural syndrome that psychologist Ronald Levant calls "nonrelational sexuality." Seen by many evolutionary psychologists and libertarians as natural, morally neutral or at least inevitable, this syndrome can be summarized in terms of several supposedly fixed male tendencies. For instance, men are said to regard sex more as an end in itself and less as a means to other ends such as sharing intimacy and building a life with another. They are said to be reflexively aroused by the sight of female anatomy and as a result to quickly and helplessly sexualize all sorts of social situations, whether or not such assumptions are warranted. For men sexual arousal is supposed to be like a runaway train; once in motion, it cannot be deflected until it reaches its orgasmic destination. Men are assumed to get aroused quickly, to proceed to orgasm easily and frequently, to be chronically concerned with their own sexual performance, to be interested in a variety of sexual partners for the sheer sake of variety and

[33]Quoted in Brody, "Cybersex," p. F7.

[34]For example, Catherine A. MacKinnon, *Feminism Unmodified: Disclosures on Life and Law* (Cambridge, Mass.: Harvard University Press, 1986).

[35]Deirdre English, "The Politics of Porn: Can Feminists Walk the Line?" in *The Best of Mother Jones,* ed. Robert Reynolds (San Francisco: Foundation for National Progress, 1985), pp. 47-48; quoted in Clare, *On Men,* p. 210.

[36]C. S. Lewis, *Mere Christianity* (London: Collins Fontana, 1952), chap. 5.

[37]Ibid., p. 99 (HarperSanFrancisco ed., 2001).

to resist emotional or physical closeness once orgasm has been achieved.[38]

Levant is careful to acknowledge that nonrelational sexuality exists on a continuum from low to high, with most men somewhere in the middle range. Nonetheless, he shares with other depth psychologists the conviction that this is a pervasive syndrome with strongly cultural roots. Many evolutionary psychologists, by contrast, assume that a nonrelational orientation to sex is biologically hard-wired into men. If so, they conclude, we must simply accommodate to the fact that boys will be boys.[39] Alternately, some suggest that we find purely biological remedies. At one extreme men's concerns about erectile dysfunction are to be overcome with anti-impotence drugs like Viagra—for which almost two million prescriptions were dispensed in the first three months after its approval in the United States in 1998.[40] At the other extreme, drugs like Depo-Provera (a synthetic progesterone) are supposed to lower the testosterone level—and hopefully the sexual acting out—of chronically or dangerously promiscuous men.[41]

The Roots of Nonrelational Sexuality

But this biologically reductionist approach to male sexuality assumes that the direction of causality is only from biology to behavior; it ignores the substantial body of research that demonstrates the impact of behavior on biology.[42] Levant and other depth psychologists believe that many of the roots of men's nonrelational approach to sex lie in early childhood attachment experiences and the way boys are socialized to become masculine. We have already seen how asymmetrical childrearing patterns increase the risk of boys' becoming misogynist men. To the extent that childcare is culturally defined as women's domain, boys must experience an early and sharp emotional separation from their mothers in order to develop a clear sense of male gender identity. Girls, by contrast, can

---

[38]Levant, "Nonrelational Sexuality in Men," p. 12. See also Bernie Zilbergeld, *The New Male Sexuality* (New York: Bantam, 1992).

[39]For example, Zilbergeld, *New Male Sexuality*.

[40]Clare, *On Men*, p. 123.

[41]For example, physiological psychologist James M. Dabbs cites the example of a gay male couple who requested Depo-Provera to lower their testosterone levels so they would be less tempted to have sex with other men. Their endocrinologist agreed to the request, and "the men are now happy and content in their monogamous gay relationship." See James McBride Dabbs and Mary Goodwin Dabbs, *Heroes, Rogues and Lovers: Testosterone and Behavior* (New York: McGraw-Hill, 2000), p. 101.

[42]For a further discussion of this "interactive" model, see Judith K. Balswick and Jack O. Balswick, *Authentic Human Sexuality: An Integrated Christian Approach* (Downers Grove, Ill.: InterVarsity, 2001).

normally prolong their attachment to their mothers, knowing that they will become certifiably female simply by identifying with and imitating their primary caretaker. As psychiatrist Samuel Osherson puts it, "A girl can look at her mother and see herself and her future; but when a boy looks at his mother, he sees 'the other.' So feelings may come to be seen as the province of women, while self-control or distance may seem more manly."[43]

Too often this process for boys is complicated by the absence—physical, psychological or both—of fathers and other adult males who can show boys that while achievement and self-discipline are worthy masculine goals, so too are desires for connection, comfort and affirmation amid the pain and fear of failure that life inevitably deals out to all of us. William Pollack in the United States and William Hudson and Bernadine Jacot in the United Kingdom have described how boys' early separation experiences create an unease and emotional dislocation that almost always goes underground. Pollack refers to it as "the traumatic abrogation of the early holding environment"; Hudson and Jacot speak, more graphically, of "the male wound."[44] But all agree that cutting short boys' early attachment needs raises the risk that as men they will develop attitudes of "defensive autonomy" and/or "destructive entitlement."[45] Defensive autonomy leads many men to find distance more comfortable than closeness in their relationships with women—and, by extension, their children, acquaintances and coworkers of both sexes. Destructive entitlement, often reinforced by cultural norms of male privilege and superiority, leads many men tacitly to expect that women will give them constant physical and emotional affirmation to make up for their early deprivations, with little or no requirement of reciprocity.

In the realm of adult sexuality, the fear of closeness that flows from these male wounds clashes with a strong desire for sexual union and can result in more or less problematic defense mechanisms. In an earlier chapter I noted how traditional gender socialization teaches boys to use anger as the almost exclusive emotional channel for feelings of fear and sadness. In parallel fashion, boys' early emotional separation from mothers and frequent failure to get compensatory affirmation from fathers and other males inclines them as adolescents and adults to use sex as the all-purpose narcotic for coping with supposedly unmanly emotions such as loneliness, shame and self-doubt. A history of asymmetrical parenting combined with our cultural patterns of male socialization thus makes it difficult

---

[43]Osherson, *Wrestling with Love*, p. 62.

[44]William S. Pollack, "No Man Is an Island: Towards a New Psychoanalytic Psychology of Men," in *A New Psychology of Men*, ed. Ronald F. Levant and William S. Pollack (New York: Basic-Books, 1995), pp. 33-67; Hudson and Jacot, *Way Men Think*, chap. 3.

[45]See also Levant, "Nonrelational Sexuality in Men," pp. 20-22.

for men to identify and be comfortable with a full range of emotional expression in themselves and others and more inclined to sexual activity that, in Ronald Levant's words, is "detached, objectified, and agentic—in short, nonrelational."[46]

In its extreme forms this nonrelational orientation sets the stage for compulsive and even violent forms of sexuality—for example, sexual fixation on separate female body parts in preference to an ongoing relationship with a whole, complex person (a constant theme in visual pornography). And for males who have been not only emotionally impoverished in childhood but actually abused physically, emotionally or sexually, the fear of seeming feminine (read *vulnerable*) may lead to more extreme reactions. In Hudson and Jacot's words, such a man may "infuse his behavior with misogynous resentment or hatred. He may resort inappropriately to violence or become promiscuous. He may also become a pervert—that is, direct his sexuality away from adult women to less-threatening children of either sex, towards material objects such as women's clothing, or towards nonrelational sexual behaviors like exhibitionism, voyeurism, or pornography-aided masturbation.[47] Irish psychiatrist Anthony Clare very trenchantly summarizes the connection between boys' typical gender socialization and men's risk for developing a deeply nonrelational sexual style:

> From very early on [a boy] is encouraged to deny, certainly downplay, a whole aspect of his self which embodies feelings of helplessness, frailty, impotence, a sense of uncertainty and ambiguity. Little boys don't cry, yet want to. Grown men do feel, but have learned well to disguise their feelings. . . . [Thus] while men have so often defined women in terms of sexuality, erotic desire and reproduction and so often defined themselves as multifaceted beings, ironically it is men who operate in the shadow of their own sexuality, fearing it, proving it, forcing it. . . . Women threaten such single-mindedness. Their very rootedness in the realities of life, its biology, its relentless practicality, serves to cast doubt on the validity, the worth, the ultimate purpose of masculine desires and ambitions. All that woman represents—birth, life, domesticity, intimacy, dependence—has to be destroyed. . . . That which is desired is detested, for that which is desired exercises a terrible, nagging, irresistible temptation and poses an immense challenge to the male sense of control.[48]

Does Biology Matter at All?

So far I have laid out three reasons behind men's propensity for nonrelational

---

[46]Ibid., p. 22.
[47]Hudson and Jacot, *Way Men Think,* p. 118.
[48]Clare, *On Men,* pp. 56-57, 200-201.

sex. First, our culturally accepted way of organizing family life and boys' socialization for independence raises the risk that they will become fearful of display-
ing so-called feminine vulnerability in any of their relationships. As a result, in
adulthood many men develop more or less detached forms of sexual expression
as a routine way of dealing with feelings of stress and weakness. Second, profit-
driven media reinforce these tendencies by modeling and glamorizing promiscuous-impersonal sexuality and hostile male attitudes toward women. Far from
draining off surplus sexual energy, the consumption of such images tends to
heighten exploitative sexual attitudes and behaviors. Finally, men's own choices
may have actual biological consequences: for example, viewing pornography in
its ever more anonymous, accessible and affordable forms can create a physiological need for more and more extreme scenarios, sometimes even resulting in
financial and relationship ruin for men caught in its web.

Does this mean that raw biology, in the form of genes, sexual anatomy and
hormones, plays no role in men's sexual struggles? This is a difficult question to
answer. Any theory that suggests a simple relationship between human biology
and certain behaviors at least has to show that such behaviors occur with great
consistency across time and cultures. Yet the chief defenders of such theories
have very little systematic historical and crosscultural data about men's sexuality
to draw on. In addition, they typically appeal heavily to the results of experimental research done with animals, in whom the connection among genes, hormones and behavior—unmediated by a large and flexible cerebral cortex—is
much more direct than in humans.[49] The crosscultural data that do exist certainly
support the thesis that social learning plays a large role in shaping men's sexual
behavior and attitudes. For example, anthropologist Peggy Reeves Sanday's survey of rape prevalence in 156 cultures, both modern and preindustrial, found
that in close to 50 percent of these rape was an almost nonexistent practice,
while only 18 percent (including, regrettably, the United States) could be classified as highly rape-prone, in the sense of frequently allowing, trivializing or
overlooking rape.[50]

On the other hand a review of research on the strength of the human sex
drive, covering hundreds of studies by many investigators using different methods and measures (though mostly with Western, usually American samples), has
shown that on average men outscore women regardless of what indicators are

---

[49]See for example Robert M. Sapolsky, *The Trouble with Testosterone, and Other Essays on the
Biology of the Human Predicament* (New York: Simon & Schuster, 1997), and Natalie Angier,
Woman: An Intimate Geography (Boston: Houghton Mifflin, 1997) for a further discussion of
these methodological issues.

[50]Peggy Reeves Sanday, *Female Power and Male Dominance* (New York: Cambridge University
Press, 1981).

used. These include desired frequency of sex, desired variety in sexual activities, frequency of sexual fantasy and masturbation, number of sexual partners, and willingness to make financial and other sacrifices to obtain sexual gratification. In addition, there is clinical evidence to suggest that for both men and women androgens—and particularly testosterone—are one (though by no means the only) factor in producing sexual desire. For example, women who have surgically lost ovaries (their main source of testosterone) may suffer from a decline in sexual desire, arousability or orgasmic capacity that can sometimes be rectified by taking testosterone via a skin patch. Some female-to-male transsexuals report heightened sexual interest and arousability as they take testosterone to adjust their secondary sex characteristics, whereas male-to-female transsexuals report a decline after testicular castration and the administration of estrogen to produce female secondary sex characteristics. And in men and women generally, although sex drive goes down as testosterone production decreases with age, across all age groups (and whether self-identified as gay or straight) men on average continue to show higher interest in sex than women on a variety of measures.[51]

As with all attempts to settle the nature-nurture controversy, such studies are suggestive, not definitive, for they lack the controls that would allow us unequivocally to conclude that men "naturally" exceed women in strength of sex drive. We cannot randomly assign people to be male or female at birth while controlling for other traits, nor can we randomly assign them to grow up in different cultures with varying rules for male and female sexual activity. The only way to completely disentangle the effects of biology from those of environment would be to hold one constant while allowing the other to vary, as happens in the case of identical twins who are raised in separate families. Such "natural experiments" have shed much light on the biological heritability of traits as diverse as cancer proneness, musical ability, alcoholism and depression.[52] But they can tell us nothing about the degree to which behavioral differences between the sexes originate in nature or nurture, simply because identical twins are always of the same sex.

---

[51]Roy F. Baumeister, "Gender Differences in Erotic Plasticity: The Female Sex Drive as Socially Flexible and Responsive," *Psychological Bulletin* 126, no. 3 (2000): 347-74, and Roy F. Baumeister, Kathleen R. Catanese and K. D. Vohs, "Is There a Gender Difference in Strength of Sex Drive? Theoretical Views, Conceptual Distinctions and a Review of Relevant Evidence," *Personality and Social Psychology Review,* in press. See also Dabbs and Dabbs, *Heroes, Rogues and Lovers.*

[52]For example, Thomas J. Bouchard Jr., "Longitudinal Studies of Personality and Intelligence: A Behavior Genetic and Evolutionary Psychology Perspective," in *International Handbook of Personality and Intelligence,* ed. Donald H. Saklofske and Moshe Zeidner (New York: Plenum, 1995).

In addition all behavioral sex differences fall into overlapping distributions, most of which show only a small average difference *between* the sexes, in contrast to a much greater range of scores *within* each sex sampled. (Recall the more prosaic example of men's and women's overlapping height distributions to picture how this works.) Indeed for some measures of sex drive even the average difference is deceptive. For example, when young men and women are asked how many sex partners they aspire to have over a lifetime, men's *average* response (depending on the study) is a number anywhere from three to twenty (!) times higher than women's. Yet these differences often turn out to be due to extreme responses on the part of a minority of men; the most common number of desired partners cited by respondents of both sexes is *one!* Thus, concludes the group of scholars reviewing the research on sex drive, "large numbers of young men and women aspire to having only one sex partner across a lifetime, but there is a minority of promiscuously inclined men that is much larger than the minority of promiscuously inclined women."[53] Even the role of testosterone on sex drive is ambiguous, they acknowledge, since in their literature review they found as many studies showing *no* significant relationship between the two as there were studies showing a positive correlation.

Does Religion Matter at All?

In spite of the above qualifiers I agree with the conclusion of these reviewers that gender differences in sex drive probably stem from a combination of natural and cultural influences. "The best bet," they write, "is that society's influence may have at various times tried to increase or reduce the gender difference in sex drive, but it did not likely reverse the natural order of things, nor did it create the difference out of nothing."[54] Men's vulnerability to a nonrelational sexual style is thus, in the jargon of social science, *overdetermined:* it is the result of several factors—biology, early family dynamics, social learning and patterns of individual choice—working in a reciprocal, interactive way. But because it is so easily underestimated, especially in a culture that is prone to biological reductionism, I have highlighted the depth psychological aspect: the way that asymmetrical parenting combined with traditional masculine socialization puts men at risk of using sex to deal with issues that are not primarily about sex at all. Therapist Alon Gratch notes that for most of his male clients "everything is about

---

[53]Baumeister et al., "Is There a Gender Difference?"
[54]Ibid.

sex, except sex, which often enough is about shame, emotional absence, masculine insecurity, self-involvement, aggression, and self-destructiveness. . . . The sexual arena is where men naturally play out emotional conflicts which, ultimately, are not about sex after all."[55]

However, as Roy Baumeister and his colleagues rightly conclude, whatever their origins and variability, such differences cannot be used by *either* sex to justify coercive or exploitative behavior. For a variety of reasons, they note, "men may not be able to prevent themselves from desiring sex under many circumstances, but they can prevent themselves from acting on those desires. By the same token, women may not want sex as much as men, but they can refrain from exploiting males' dependency that arises from the difference in sex drive."[56] This brings us to the role of religious and more specifically Christian commitment in the development of sexual values and behavior. On the one hand, we have seen that Christians are little, if any, less likely than the population at large to be involved in premarital sex, sexual harassment and various forms of sexual abuse. On the other hand, social scientists of every ideological stripe agree that one of the best ways to predict whether adolescents will postpone sexual activity in order to focus on other aspects of their development is to find out if they are active in a church youth group![57] How are we to understand such contradictory findings?

Here it may help to return to some points made in the early chapters of this book. There we learned that according to commonly held gender stereotypes, "real men" are—and should be—less interested in religion than women. This should come as no surprise, since the Christian gospel strongly challenged the competitive, self-aggrandizing male culture of honor in the time and place where it was first proclaimed. The writers of the Gospels and epistles, building on the foundation of the Hebrew Scriptures, announced a human—not just a female—ideal of cooperation, servanthood and humility. The cultural barriers between "feminine" private and "masculine" public life were to a large extent broken down, and even slavery was subverted in principle if not in practice. The apostle Paul summarized this vision in his letter to the Galatian church: "As many of you as were baptized into Christ have clothed yourselves with Christ. There is no longer Jew or Greek, there is no longer slave or free, there is no longer male and female; for all of you are one in Christ Jesus" (Gal 3:27-28). More globally, Paul wrote to the Corinthians, "if anyone is in Christ, there is a

---

[55]Gratch, *If Men Could Talk*, p. 18.
[56]Baumeister et al., "Is There a Gender Difference?"
[57]David B. Larson, James P. Swyers and Michael E. McCullough, *Scientific Research on Spirituality and Mental Health* (Rockville, Md.: National Institute for Healthcare Research, 1997).

new creation . . . from God, who reconciled us to himself through Christ, and has given us the ministry of reconciliation." Christians were to pursue that vision "in honor and dishonor, in ill repute and good repute . . . as poor, yet making many rich; as having nothing, and yet possessing everything" (2 Cor 5:17-20; 6:8-10).

Churches and Christian families that are confident enough to pursue this countercultural ideal have potentially rich resources for recapturing the intent of the cultural mandate given to all humans at creation—that is, for helping boys and men to develop their relational and emotional skills while at the same time affirming girls' and women's capacity to achieve. I strongly suspect that it is just such churches and families that account for many of the statistics on successful teenage sexual abstinence. At the same time, there are still many Christian men who feel conflicted about appearing culturally "feminized" by virtue of their faith. Such men may be tempted to compensate for this perceived loss of status not by rejecting the modern version of the male culture of honor but in effect by re-creating it in their own churches and families, sometimes with women's complicity.[58]

Irish psychiatrist Anthony Clare points out that a parallel process regularly occurs in previously colonized nations. He notes that it is often the men who feel most resentful about being disempowered by past colonial overlords (as the Irish have felt about the British) who are likely to marginalize and disempower the women of their own country and not even recognize their inconsistency in doing so.[59]

Thus churches and related agencies may be turned into thoroughly hierarchical institutions, with women (to the extent that they are allowed to participate) kept at the very lowest levels. In so distancing themselves from the women who are their fellow believers, men may feel correspondingly less "feminized" themselves. Others may cope with the cultural stereotype of the emasculated Christian by becoming authoritarian husbands and fathers. Although compared to the culture at large such men may feel like low-status, nonhegemonic males, they can still participate indirectly in the male culture of honor by constructing highly patriarchal subcultures in homes and churches.

The material reviewed in this chapter suggests that it is just such men who risk getting caught up in one or other form of compulsive sexuality as a way of coping with the self-imposed strain of meeting masculine norms for control,

---

[58]See also Mary Stewart Van Leeuwen, *Gender and Grace: Love, Work and Parenting in a Changing World* (Downers Grove, Ill.: InterVarsity Press, 1990), chap. 5.
[59]Clare, *On Men*, p. 206.

competition and separation from all things womanly. That this dichotomy is often defended as a biblical ideal, rather than seen as a tragic distortion of the cultural mandate and of the image of God in both sexes, simply adds to its problematic character.[60] But in light of what we have learned about masculinity in this and previous chapters, there is reason to believe that a more balanced and creation-affirming way of life is possible both for men and women. Implementing such a vision will require change at many levels—individual, familial, legal and economic—and will not come easily. But the results will be well worth the effort, and in the following chapter I will propose what I think are some essential aspects of that vision.

---

[60]See for example John Piper and Wayne A. Grudem, eds., *Recovering Biblical Manhood and Womanhood* (Wheaton, Ill.: Crossway, 1991).

12

An Agenda for Gender Reconciliation

In the mid-1990s a Midwestern U.S. couple named Charles and Joy Blanchard explained to a public television interviewer how they had organized their waged work and family life. Charles worked a six-hour shift from 6:00 p.m. to midnight at a local factory, and Joy worked a 6:00 a.m. to noon shift at the same factory. This meant that Charles was the primary parent in the morning, dressing, feeding and caring for their two sons when they were preschoolers, as well as doing household chores. Once their boys reached school age, he not only got them off to school but participated regularly in their class life as a room parent and a member of the PTA. Arriving home at noon, Joy became the primary parent and homemaker, giving Charles a chance to rest or take part in other activities such as gardening, amateur team sports, home improvement projects and spending time with friends before heading off to his next six-hour shift at the factory.

The fact that each parent worked a thirty-hour week made it possible for them not only to coparent their children and share the running of their household but also to develop as individuals and contribute to their community in ways not dominated by their waged work. There was time for canning, quilting, reading, hunting, visiting with family and doing volunteer work at the local library. Joy and Charles were equally close to their sons and equally involved in their school and extracurricular lives. Both contributed to the family economy as members of the waged workforce, each taking a somewhat reduced load as compared to the national norm of "full-time work." This enabled both to be competent, knowledgeable parents and householders, active in community life and bringing home roughly equal pay packets.

Ahead of
Their Time

You probably assumed that Charles and Joy Blanchard came of age in the late 1970s or early 1980s, inspired by the second wave of American feminism to be mavericks who would break down the dichotomy between the "feminine" sphere of domestic life and the "masculine" sphere of public and economic achievement. But in their television interview this *retired* couple, now with grown-up sons and almost-grown grandchildren, were speaking about a work pattern that was common in the 1950s among employees at the Kellogg's cereal factory in Battle Creek, Michigan. In the immediate post-World War II era, just when the doctrine of separate spheres for men and women was at its moral and legal zenith in North America, Kellogg's management and labor unions routinely provided for both men and women to work five-day, six-hour shifts. This was an organizational pattern begun in 1930 and phased out only as recently as 1985. Described in detail by social historian Benjamin Hunnicutt, Kellogg's half-century-long experiment with the six-hour workday serves as a crucible to distill many of the issues about masculinity dealt with in previous chapters. It also provides a backdrop for strategizing about ways to improve gender relations in the future.[1]

Throughout this book we have seen that the lives of men, women and children have been artificially separated by forces ranging from the religious and the psychological to the economic and cultural. Women still struggle to develop their public selves even as they work to maintain the ties that bind families and communities together, often experiencing a famine of time as they do so.[2] Many men struggle to achieve a similar balance, but usually from a rather different history. Having been raised to correlate masculinity mainly with public and economic achievement, and having as children seen few males living any other lifestyle, adult men are often afraid that they will somehow be emasculated if they share control of the public arena with women and participate more fully in family life themselves. Children, for their part, are at high risk of losing a parent (almost always their father) due to divorce or separation, and even those from intact families are vulnerable to unintended neglect by parents struggling to meet the demands of a workaholic, materialistic society. It is estimated that five to seven million U.S. children are left unattended at home each day, in large

---

[1]Benjamin Kline Hunnicutt, *Kellogg's Six-Hour Day* (Philadelphia: Temple University Press, 1996). The interview with Joy and Charles Blanchard was conducted by Hunnicutt in 1993 for PBS station KCTS in Seattle, Washington.

[2]Arlie Russell Hochschild, *The Second Shift* (New York: Avon Books, 1989), and *The Time Bind: When Work Becomes Home and Home Becomes Work* (New York: Metropolitan, 1997).

part because parents are unable to get their waged workday to coincide with the schoolday. And at the prosperous turn of the third millennium, Americans were spending more—not less—time doing waged work, an average of 350 hours (the equivalent of nine forty-hour weeks) more than Europeans, to the added detriment of marital and family stability.[3]

In light of all this, I believe the most pressing question for gender relations at the turn of the third millennium is this: How can we put children first without putting women last and without putting men on the sidelines of family life? In other words, how can we honor children's need for stable, nurturant families without reembracing the doctrine of separate spheres for men and women? This is a fundamentally religious question, because any answer to it will reflect what we most deeply believe humans are made for. For Christians committed to the authority of Scripture, it is a matter of our response to the creation story found in the first chapters of Genesis. Do we indeed affirm that both aspects of the cultural mandate—sociability and dominion—are addressed to both sexes? And do we have a high enough view of marital faithfulness and our responsibility to children to affirm that mandate while embracing—individually and institution-ally—the kinds of changes that may be needed for the sake of the next generation? I will consider possible answers to these questions later in this chapter. But to set the stage for them, let us look at the Kellogg's experiment in more detail.

▌A Vision ▌ for Balance

W. K. Kellogg and his brother John Harvey Kellogg were born in the mid-nine-teenth century to a Seventh-day Adventist family living in Battle Creek, the home of that denomination's publishing and administrative offices. In keeping with the Adventist emphasis on the body as God's temple, John Harvey set up a sanitarium that eventually became a world-famous retreat for people suffering from what was then called "neurasthenia"—that is, overwork and nervous ex-haustion associated with the increasing pace of modern life. Business magnates like John D. Rockefeller, Henry Ford and Harvey Firestone were among the Bat-tle Creek Sanitarium's clients, as were writers Lowell Thomas and Will Durant, polar explorers Roald Amundsen and Richard Byrd, and evangelist Billy Sunday. The sanitarium regimen included rest, physical and occupational therapy, bland

---

[3]Ann Crittenden, *The Price of Motherhood: Why the Most Important Job in the World Is Still the Least Valued* (New York: Metropolitan, 2001), p. 260.

diet and "water cures," in line with the theory that "vigorous exercise of parts of the body and mind neglected in ordinary life and occupations could provide a kind of release and restoration that simple immobility could not."[4]

In pursuit of the Adventist ideal of a simple diet low in caffeine, alcohol and meat, W. K. Kellogg developed several kinds of flaked cereal, first for the sanitarium's clients and eventually for commercial manufacture. By 1920 Kellogg's was a household name for ready-to-eat cereals, and the company's commercial success made small Battle Creek as well known as any major U.S. city. Both the Kellogg brothers were renowned workaholics—W. K. wrote with regret in later life that he had "never learned to play"[5]—an irony in light of their promotion of the ideal of a balanced lifestyle. But in spite (or perhaps because) of this inconsistency, W. K. had a lifelong interest in public health, education, recreation and child development. To this end he gave substantial sums of money for parks, camps, nature preserves, recreational and sports facilities (some right in his own factories) and in 1930 established the still-active Kellogg Foundation. As one of his own managers put it in an interview with historian Hunnicutt, W. K. Kellogg "felt a responsibility to be a good steward of what the Lord gave him."[6] Part of that stewardship, he believed, was to develop a form of "welfare capitalism" that would enable workers to lead balanced lives in the context of humanely structured employment.

Kellogg instituted the six-hour workday during the Great Depression, in part as a way to create jobs in a time of desperately high unemployment.[7] With four six-hour (as opposed to three eight-hour) factory shifts, the company payroll could be increased by 25 percent. Although this also meant a 25 percent reduction in each employee's workweek, the company gradually raised the hourly wage to compensate for much of this, confident that it would continue to make a profit because employees would work more effectively and take fewer breaks on the shortened shift. The company also eliminated overtime work and the extra overhead that this involved, though an employee bonus was added for extra productivity during the six-hour time frame.

And indeed the change proved to be an asset to management and workers alike. Productivity and profits stayed high, and employees of both sexes lauded

---

[4]Hunnicutt, *Kellogg's Six-Hour Day,* p. 40.
[5]Ibid., p. 41.
[6]Ibid., p. 211.
[7]Hunnicutt also speculates (ibid.) that Kellogg's Adventist theology contributed to the experiment: "Like American Jews, the Adventists faced the problem of keeping their Sabbath on Saturday in a nation where Sunday religious observance was the rule. Blue laws complicated the work week for the Adventists, who like Jews were often forced to work on Saturday to make up for Sunday closings. Kellogg's concerns about the management of work hours may have this indirect link with the Adventists' struggles."

the reduction in their workweek and the extra time it gave them for family, recreational, civic and church activities. In fact, when Kellogg factory workers were
unionized in 1937 by the National Council of Grain Producers, the "uniform six-
hour day" was their first contract demand. Even the males in the few remaining
eight-hour factory departments (e.g., machine maintenance) voted three to one
for uniform six-hour shifts, despite the commonly held stereotype that these
men had gravitated to eight-hour departments precisely because they wanted
bigger paychecks.[8]

Although this experiment may seem radical to us today, we need to recall
that as recently as 1900 the standard workweek was six ten-hour days. As mech-
anization expanded and living standards rose, this was reduced to five nine-
hour and eventually to five eight-hour days. There was much talk in the early
decades of the twentieth century about a further shortening of the workweek
and the need to distribute jobs equitably in light of redundancies created by increasingly sophisticated machinery. But when the Great Depression hit the United States in 1929, the fair distribution of shrinking employment opportunities
became an even more salient issue. It was also an issue that, at least in Battle
Creek, was seen as a local civic responsibility, not to be resolved solely by fed-
eral initiatives such as Franklin Roosevelt's New Deal. Even less was it to be
dealt with by still-employed people's becoming "work hogs"—grabbing up as
many paid hours as possible while others teetered on the brink of starvation.[9]
On the contrary, as long as workers earned enough to support themselves and
their families, most regarded the decreased workweek as a tangible asset that
kept waged work from becoming the sphere of life around which everything
else was forced to revolve.

The Triumph of Consumerism

If Kellogg's six-hour shift scheme had such positive outcomes for both workers
and owners, why did it begin to erode within a decade of its birth, even while
continuing as a popular option for over half a century? Surprisingly, given the
frequency of adversarial relations between unions and management, it was a coalition between these two that led to its demise, especially after Kellogg himself
retired from direct managerial involvement in the late 1930s. In addition, the
class and gender solidarity that had led to sharing of employment during the

[8]Ibid., pp. 75-76.
[9]Ibid., chap. 3.

Depression began to break down, and the steady rise of consumerism and mass culture replaced the idea of free time as a personal and social asset with the notion that over and above the minimum needed to refuel for paid work, structured leisure was only for "sissies" and "loafers."[10]

How did the union-management coalition undermine the six-hour work day? Rather than continuing to see a tradeoff between shorter hours with a production bonus and longer hours without one, a minority of older male union members began to agitate for both expanded hours *and* bonus possibilities, in order to produce the largest possible paycheck for themselves. They argued that the shortened workweek was in effect a form of worker exploitation because it limited their earnings. Hunnicutt observes that this was "a change in organized labor's [longstanding] shorter-hours policies and philosophy. . . . According to the new rhetoric, a shorter work day with the same weekly pay was no longer a step forward; nothing substituted for more money."[11] In addition, those favoring longer hours successfully lobbied for a policy of laying off employees with fewer years of service before reducing the hours of older workers. "Influential union members, especially men from the Mechanical and Container departments, had given up on work sharing . . . [and the] union was beginning to tilt toward the wage interests of established, senior workers over the employment needs of younger workers in danger of being laid off."[12]

This by itself would not have killed the six-hour day, which continued to remain popular with most workers. Indeed although longer shifts and overtime were temporarily necessary during World War II (and correspondingly lucrative for workers), 87 percent of female and 71 percent of male workers voted to return to the uniform six-hour shift afterward.[13] But by this time Kellogg's managers had lost the vision for welfare capitalism embraced by their company's founder. They resisted hiring more workers and supervisors for an additional shift because of the increased cost in benefits that would result, preferring instead to have fewer workers doing longer hours at higher pay. They also resisted the original strategy of raising hourly wages to compensate for reduced time and giving bonuses for greater efficiency, saying instead that those who wanted more pay should simply sign up for a standard eight-hour day, as employees of rival companies did.

Despite pressures from union and management alike, Kellogg's "six-hour mavericks" were able to hold their ground until well into the 1980s. They re-

---

[10]Ibid., pp. 142-46.
[11]Ibid., p. 94.
[12]Ibid., p. 95.
[13]Ibid., p. 100.

mained stubbornly convinced that shorter hours were in the best interests of
themselves, their families and their community. But they were fighting a losing
battle, not only against would-be "work hogs" and cost-conscious management
but also against the gradual reemergence of gender stereotypes. By 1947,
though most of the workers were still on six-hour shifts, over half of *male* workers were on eight hours. This made it easy for both union and management to
begin identifying the shorter shift with "women's work" or "girls' departments"
and to use this as both a justification for poorer wages and a way of shaming
men (unless they were old or disabled) away from it. The male code of honor
had been revived, its behavioral content adjusted for modernity: long hours of
work at the highest possible pay became the distinguishing mark of masculinity.

Not only was the six-hour shift "feminized," so were activities that took place
outside of it. Church work, fishing and hunting, service clubs, the PTA, family
gatherings—all these began to be seen as "wasted time" or "silly," only for those
insufficiently dedicated to paid work and "getting ahead." The language of separate spheres crept back as men began talking about "having" to be sole providers for families and feeling uncomfortable and out of place when "forced" to
hang around home if they had only six-hour contracts.

In addition, an ethos of consumerism began to eclipse the earlier ideals of
work sharing and a modest lifestyle, based on what Christian economists Bob
Goudzwaard and Harry de Lange have called "the growth premise." According
to this premise, "More consumption means more investment, and more investment means more production."[14] To create jobs and keep the economy robust,
new "needs" had to be identified that could be filled only if people worked
harder and made more money. For the new—almost invariably male[15]—economists such growth was equated with progress, despite its inexorable tendency
to enlarge the gap between rich and poor and despite its long-term impact on
family, community, the environment, and quantity and quality of jobs.

The subjective threshold for what was "enough" to live comfortably thus kept
steadily rising. And the harder people worked to attain a dubious range of ever-
expanding consumer goods, the more stress they experienced and the more
likely they were to fill what free time they did have with spectator, rather than

---

[14]Bob Goudzwaard and Harry de Lange, *Beyond Poverty and Affluence: Toward an Economy
of Care,* trans. Mark VanderVennen (Grand Rapids, Mich.: Eerdmans, 1995), p. 65.

[15]It is surely significant that economics is the one area in which there has never been a female
Nobel Prize winner, but this is not because women have not written about alternative eco-
nomic paradigms. See for example Marilyn Waring, *If Women Counted* (San Francisco: Harper
& Row, 1988); Marianne A. Ferber and Julie A. Nelson, eds., *Beyond Economic Man: Feminist
Theory and Economics* (Chicago: University of Chicago Press, 1993); and Shirley P. Burggraf,
The Feminine Economy and Economic Man (Boston: Addison-Wesley, 1997).

participatory, activities. Television and spectator sports increasingly eclipsed reading and amateur athletic participation, and volunteer work was left to "the girls" or, increasingly, to emerging cadres of professionals. In a host of ways Kellogg's workers in general and men in particular began to shed the civic and other activities—as well as the related skills—that a shorter workweek and a more modest lifestyle had made room for.[16]

The Price of Motherhood

In the mid-1970s, when most of the six-hour mavericks had been confined to lower-paying "female" departments, some Kellogg's women joined forces with local feminists to condemn six-hour shifts "as a sexist ploy to subjugate women . . . [and to press] management to abolish all hours-based 'gender distinctions' between departments."[17] Rather than reembracing a vision in which women and men could divide waged work, domestic and civic responsibilities in a more equal and humane way, they adopted the liberal feminist goal of making it possible for women to work as hard, as long and for as much pay as their male colleagues, even if this meant more stress for themselves and fewer jobs for others. Benjamin Hunnicutt notes that they "accept[ed] management's rhetorical forms and symbols [and] argued that women were just as needful and physically fit as the men, and had just as much to gain from their work—meaning, fulfillment, status, power, and similar benefits."[18] Like Professor Higgins in *My Fair Lady,* they in effect asked, "Why can't a woman be more like a man?"

At the start of the new millennium, American economic journalist Ann Crittenden revisited this query in wake of three decades of feminist activism and concluded that it was the wrong question to ask. The liberal feminist goal had been for women to become like the men whom in an earlier generation they would have aspired to marry—that is, to achieve for themselves the professional and economic status that they previously relied on husbands to supply vicariously. But Crittenden's research showed that in America such success is still generally possible only for women who do not have children. For despite the fact that almost half of U.S. women with children under eighteen were in full-time waged work by the year 2000 (and another 30 percent working part time), much of that work was still poorly paid in comparison to similar work done by men or by nonparenting women.

---

[16]Hunnicutt, *Kellogg's Six-Hour Day,* chaps. 6-7.
[17]Ibid., p. 138.
[18]Ibid.

Moreover, mothers with waged jobs put in longer hours of total work—paid plus unpaid—than almost anyone else in the U.S. economy.[19] A common stereotype exists that women are participating more in the public sphere at the expense of their children's physical and emotional needs. But time-use surveys have shown that most mothers do *not* spend less time with their children as they enter the waged workforce; they simply cut back on housework, sleep and other activities, including the "quality time" with their spouse that is vital to the health of marriages.[20] And while men are indeed doing more housework and childcare than their fathers did—especially on weekends—their own time-use reports show that even when spouses contribute equally to household income, fathers on average contribute no more than 30 percent of childcare and housework. Even when women earn more than their spouses—or when husbands have no paid job at all—fathers do not raise their contribution to household labor. The upshot is that at the turn of the millennium, fully employed mothers of children spend an average of thirteen hours a week more on household responsibilities than their husbands do.

As one economist summarized it to Crittenden, "Our data shows that there is not a true gift exchange in marriage. Although there is a lot of variation, between most spouses there is not complete reciprocity." Another scholar from Harvard noted that, in microeconomic terms, "this does not jibe with any rational theory of economic behavior. [For example,] if her hourly earnings are higher than his, she should be the one who works more hours outside the home, and he should do more of the work in the home. And that isn't happening"— although exactly the same "rational economics" has long been invoked as a way of justifying the opposite division of labor: men taking higher-paying jobs while women, unable to command similar wages, specialized in domesticity.[21]

Such nonreciprocity is irrational not just economically but psychologically. For as we have seen in previous chapters, the withdrawal of fathers from home life—whether due to divorce, death or an exaggerated division of labor—reduces men's own well-being and puts their children at risk for a range of social and emotional difficulties. Moreover, as Crittenden notes, "women are protecting their children from a parental 'time famine' by subjecting themselves to a 'time crunch.' Their grueling schedules explain why so many eventually decide to give up their paychecks, if they can afford to. It may be the only way they can get a good night's sleep."[22] And if the time crunch and father absence are prob-

---

[19]Crittenden, *Price of Motherhood,* chap. 1.
[20]See for example William J. Doherty, *Take Back Your Marriage: Sticking Together in a World That Pulls Us Apart* (New York: Guilford, 2001).
[21]Crittenden, *Price of Motherhood,* p. 24.
[22]Ibid., p. 22.

lematic for intact families, how much more so are they for single parents, the majority of whom are also women? "Children report that the parent who is in truly short supply is the father, whether their parents are married or single, whether their mothers work or not." Most report that mothers almost never miss events important to them as children, whereas fathers frequently do.[23]

An Alternative Scenario

For those convinced that such practices are anything but "normal" in the creational sense of that term, the alternative should be obvious. Christians need to adopt and encourage a more countercultural pattern of living, one that resists both the doctrine of separate spheres for men and women and a workaholic, excessively materialistic lifestyle. To promote the first, theologian Don Browning, who is director of the Religion, Culture and Family Project at the University of Chicago, proposes that churches endorse an "ethic of equal regard" in gender relations. This would mean that "husband and wife should each in principle have equal access to the privileges *and* responsibilities of both public and private worlds, although this may be realized differently in specific households depending on individual interests and talents."[24]

But an ethic of equal regard does not by itself address the temptations of materialism and workaholism so often embraced both by more traditional males and their liberal feminist imitators. Parents need adequate time to interact with their children, because it is human (not material) capital in the form of knowledge, skills, character formation and creativity and social capital in the form of supportive and healthy relationships that really account for most of the well-being of communities and nations.[25] To give parents the needed space to help children establish social and cognitive skills and to guide them into healthy relationships with family, community and faith traditions, members of the Religion, Culture and Family Project (of whom I am one) have taken a leaf from the Kellogg's archives. They have proposed that churches support a waged work-

---

[23]Ibid., p. 23.

[24]Don S. Browning, "The Task of Religious Institutions in Strengthening Families," Joint Declaration of the Religion, Culture and Family Project (University of Chicago Divinity School) and the Communitarian Network (George Washington University), August 1998, p. 2 (www2.uchicago.edu.divinity.family).

[25]Crittenden, *Price of Motherhood,* chap. 4. See also the *Human Development Report, 1995* of the UN Development Program (New York: Oxford University Press, 1995), and Mary Stewart Van Leeuwen, "Faith, Feminism and the Family in an Age of Globalization," in *Religion and the Powers of the Common Life,* ed. Max L. Stackhouse and Peter J. Paris (Harrisburg, Penn.: Trinity Press International, 2000), pp. 184-230.

week for single parents of no more than thirty hours and a combined waged workweek for a father and mother with young children of no more than sixty hours. This might be divided less equally at some points of the family life cycle (e.g., thirty-five to forty hours for one parent versus twenty to twenty-five hours for the other) and more equally at others, but in any event the goal is to allow both parents the possibility of continuing involvement in the arena of waged work, without creating a time crunch for either of them or a parenting deficit for their children.[26]

But neither of these principles—the ethic of equal regard and the shorter joint waged workweek for parents of young children—will produce positive changes in gender and family relations if marriages continue to deteriorate at the rate they have been doing over the past several decades. And Protestant churches have been deeply implicated in the trend toward the deinstitutionalization of marriage, especially in the United States. Not only are the highest rates of divorce and cohabitation present in some of the most professedly Christian groups and regions, but churches to a great degree have turned into "marriage mills." Too many pastors are ready to marry almost anyone wanting to rent their church's space, with virtually no requirement for marriage preparation or even more than the most nominal evidence of Christian belief and practice. As a result, far more time is spent on the immediate details of wedding planning than on long-term marriage preparation. Churches too often yield to "the individualism and impatience of couples and parents who expect ministers to perform marriages on demand without careful preparation,"[27] knowing that they can always find a more accommodating church nearby if a given pastor insists on being anything more than a genial master of ceremonies.

Thankfully, there is now an organized effort in many places to reverse such practices. For example, the city of Modesto, California, has lowered its divorce rate by almost 50 percent in the ten years since it instituted what has come to be known as a Community Marriage Policy. First advocated and publicized by evangelical journalist Michael McManus, it calls for all church ministers in a given urban area to agree that none of them will perform any marriage without the couple's having undergone a several-month preparation period.[28] In this period, engaged couples must take a minimum number of marriage instruction classes,

---

[26]Browning, "Task of Religious Institutions," p. 11. See also Don S. Browning, Bonnie J. Miller-McLemore, Pamela D. Couture, K. Brynolf Lyon and Rombert M. Franklin, *From Culture Wars to Common Ground: Religion and the American Family Debate* (Louisville, Ky.: Westminster John Knox, 1997), chap. 11.

[27]Browning, "Task of Religious Institutions," p. 8.

[28]Michael McManus, *Marriage Savers: Helping Your Friends and Family Stay Married* (Grand Rapids, Mich.: Zondervan, 1993).

presided over by trained leaders. In conjunction with these classes, they fill out one of several research-based premarital inventories that can predict which marriages are likely to end in divorce. (After taking such an inventory some 10 percent of couples decide either to postpone or to cancel their wedding.) They are also connected to older laypersons who serve as trained mentoring couples to the engaged and newly married.[29]

I myself recently gave a weekend of such church-based marriage preparation to one of my nieces and her fiancé, convinced that it would serve them better in the long run than a more standard wedding gift. They came back from the weekend reporting that they had increased their repertoire of communication and conflict-resolution skills and gained a better understanding of their differences and similarities.

Back to the Future

So far I have listed three elements of a new paradigm for gender relations: an ethic of equal regard, a reduction in the joint workweek for parents of young children and a more serious approach to marriage preparation. Many people have found ways to implement such a paradigm shift and create lasting and balanced marriages in spite of the social and economic forces that continue to make it difficult. As college professors my husband and I were the first of several couples teaching at the same institution who were able to share about a job and a half between us when our children were growing up, and to do so in a flexible way that did not greatly compromise fringe benefits (such as pensions and healthcare) or professional growth for either of us. Some pastoral couples have been able to arrange joint calls to churches on a similar basis.[30]

One proactive example of equal-regard life planning that I know concerns a Christian couple who have run a family business for over two decades. When they were about to marry, they discussed long-term work possibilities that would optimize the time both could spend with their children, supply both with opportunities for intellectual development and provide a reasonable but not luxurious living. They chose to open a bookstore in a small town in western Pennsylvania, which has since become a valuable source for conference, mail-order and Inter-

---

[29]Information on well-attested pre- and postmarital inventories (such as PREP, PREPARE, FOCCUS and ENRICH) as well as on church-based and other premarital preparation courses can be obtained from the website of the "Smart Marriages" movement, <www.smartmarriages.com>, or from the Religion, Culture and Family Project at <www.uchicago.edu/divinity/family>.

[30]See for example Sue Poss, "Couples Multiply Their Gifts by Serving as Co-pastors," *Mutuality,* Fall 2001, pp. 6-7.

net-advertised books of particular interest to Christians involved in social justice projects.[31] There are also examples of firms run by Christians that make such a balanced lifestyle easier. One such law firm in western Michigan both allows and encourages its lawyers of both sexes to reduce their required number of billable hours during the years when they have preschool children. Although this somewhat slows down their progress to partner status, it does not jeopardize it.

I began this book with a series of metaphors comparing gender relations to the activity of paddling a canoe. With regard to the above examples, we might now invoke the metaphor of road travel. The families described above reject the skewed practice of having the husband travel in the fast lane career-wise while the wife follows bumpily along on the shoulder, getting farther and farther behind. They have also rejected the liberal feminist solution of having both members of the couple travel full-tilt in the fast lane, for they know that this course of action creates chronic stress for spouses and children alike. It also forces all other life activities—art, worship, physical recreation, social and civic obligations—to bow to the tyranny of the waged workplace. Instead they have jointly chosen to do their career traveling in the middle lane, making compromises that allow for the physical, intellectual and emotional development of all family members, in the context of an adequate but not materially lavish lifestyle.

Is this new paradigm a radical departure from the past? Yes and no. Although Christians have often identified the "traditional family" with the doctrine of separate spheres for men and women, in fact the truly traditional family throughout most of history has been one in which workplace, dwelling space and childrearing space overlapped almost completely for both women and men. Think of your ancestors who worked family farms or ran small shops with family dwelling spaces above or behind, and highly permeable boundaries between the two. And home-based employment in the United States is certainly on the rise among both men and women (along with home-based schooling for a dedicated minority).[32] This unity of work and family life may never completely regain the normative status it had before the Industrial Revolution; nevertheless, as sociologist Steven Nock observes,

> married couples are defining marriage as an arrangement that depends on the combined resources generated by both partners. For the vast majority of people, neither husband nor wife alone is able to afford any other arrangement. In this sense,

---

[31]Hearts and Minds Bookstore, 234 East Main St., Dallastown, PA 17313 <read@heartsandmindsbooks.com>.

[32]For a balanced account of this movement in the United States since its origins in the 1970s, see Mitchell L. Stevens, *Kingdom of Children: Culture and Controversy in the Homeschooling Movement* (Princeton, N.J.: Princeton University Press, 2001).

Americans are returning to a *more traditional* form of marriage. The typical marriage in the first half of the twentieth century was an unusual one. The arrangement in which husbands were responsible for the entire family [cash] economy was an historical aberration that lasted only about half a century. Until the turn of [the twentieth] century, and since about 1970, most married couples relied on a combination of economic efforts by both spouses to keep the household going. Contemporary marriages will more closely resemble earlier arrangements than those of the early twentieth century. Such marriages will still require that husbands provide for wives and children. But they also will require that wives provide for husbands and children.[33]

Contempt for Caretaking

Nock's idea of "provision" is obviously connected to the idea of both spouses bringing home a wage packet. But it would be wrong to assume that the invisible work of unpaid caretaking and homemaking (until now done mostly by women) is not in itself a form of provision. Such work is rendered invisible by the fact that it has not been acknowledged as part of the "wealth of nations" and included in the Gross Domestic Product (GDP). Using the GDP to measure national productivity means that unless money is exchanged for goods and services, the latter do not count as part of the economy. Thus being a paid caregiver or a short-order cook counts as productive work; caring and cooking for one's own family or others (without cash remuneration) does not. Indeed people—again, mostly women—whose main work is caretaking have been regarded as "unproductive" economic dependents ever since the GDP was instituted in the twentieth century as the sole measure of national wealth.[34]

By the early 1990s the United Nations recognized the distortions of this approach and urged its member nations to develop satellite GDP accounts estimating the value of unpaid work.[35] Since then the national statisticians of Canada, Australia, Israel and several European countries, as well as tiny Burkina Faso in Africa, have begun collecting the relevant information for such a measure. (The United States remains a stubborn holdout against such a practice.) Preliminary studies have shown that the value of nonmarket production adds as much as 56 percent to the GDP in Australia, 55 percent in Germany, 46 percent in Finland

---

[33]Steven L. Nock, *Marriage in Men's Lives* (New York: Oxford University Press, 1998), p. 10 (his emphases).

[34]Crittenden, *Price of Motherhood,* chaps. 4-5.

[35]See the UN's *Human Development Report, 1995,* chap. 4, for details as to how these accounts are set up.

and 40 percent in Canada.[36] Yet in the United States this unpaid work—which is largely domestic labor and the work of caring for younger and older human beings—counts for *nothing* in terms of the accumulation of social security pension credits. In America, as an old saying affirms, apparently no good deed goes unpunished.

Nor in the United States does the work of caring count toward eligibility for health insurance, except via a connection to a waged spouse fortunate enough to have health benefits. In addition, there is no legal requirement that a wage-earning spouse must share his or her income with a more economically vulnerable homemaker. Although property (such as housing) acquired during a marriage is considered jointly owned, and therefore to be divided in the event of divorce, wages and pensions are deemed to belong solely to the person who has "earned" them. The unremunerated domestic labor—whether done by women or men—that produces most of our human and social capital and enables others to concentrate on waged work is simply not on our national radar screen. In a nation where marriages still have a 33 percent risk of dissolving within ten years and 43 percent within fifteen years, this undervaluing of the work of caring currently contributes much to the impoverishment of women and children after divorce. It also makes it difficult for anyone to leave the "fast lane," even temporarily, in order to engage in the work of care. In a highly divorce-prone society, few people are likely to trust their economic well-being to a spouse who can dispose of his or her earnings completely at will and who can unilaterally walk away from the marriage at any time.[37]

Given the pervasive contempt for caretaking that characterizes U.S. economic policy, it is no wonder that American men still avoid it. Not only must they contend with the psychological residue of their own history of underfathering, which tends to make them fearful of being "feminized" if they do "women's work." They must also face the fact that embracing domesticity, even temporarily or part time, is a sure recipe for escalating financial vulnerability. Consequently, in a culture that has long identified masculinity primarily with making money, reducing one's commitment to the all-consuming god of Mammon is a scary prospect that can seem to threaten the very foundations of male identity. And much of that fear is well-founded. In a country where health benefits are largely tied to full-time employment, and where even *unpaid* maternity leave was legally mandated only in 1993, it would be an irresponsible male who did not stay on the job treadmill when his wife became pregnant, unless she hap-

---

[36]Crittenden, *Price of Motherhood,* chap. 4.
[37]Ibid., chap. 7.

pened to be part of the fortunate minority whose waged-work benefits included paid maternity leave.

Despite the pervasive American rhetoric about the importance of "family values," childrearing is not regarded as a vital source of human and social capital but as an idiosyncratic hobby on a par with raising dogs or horses. (Indeed tax deductions in the United States for housing and feeding racehorses are more generous than those for parents raising children.[38])

A More Just Gender and Family Order

My point in highlighting the above statistics should now be obvious. If Christians are to be serious about putting children first without putting women last and without putting men on the sidelines of family life, then they need to work for structural as well as personal change. Otherwise the benefits of the more creationally balanced lifestyle that I have been advocating will be available only to those who have the resources to achieve them privately. In addition, men who are sincerely motivated to change will lack visible and tangible public support for doing so. Thus Christian individuals, churches and other agencies need to support the institutional changes that can provide the infrastructure for more just family and gender relations. The following are some of the most needed reforms, many of which are already in place or in progress in countries other than the United States.[39] It is worth noting that many of these reforms have their basis in Catholic social teaching that began with Pope Leo XIII's late-nineteenth-century encyclical *Rerum Novarum* and in parallel Protestant movements that resulted in the emergence of Christian Democratic parties in various European states.[40]

First, the shorter workweek has become a standard offering in several European countries. In Sweden parents are legally entitled to work a six-hour day until their children are eight, without jeopardizing their job security. (By contrast, in the United States only eight states have laws prohibiting discrimination against parents who decline to work overtime because of family responsibili-

---

[38]Ibid., chap. 4.

[39]See also Browning, "Task of Religious Institutions," and Crittenden, *Price of Motherhood,* pp. 256-74.

[40]See Christine F. Hinze and Mary Stewart Van Leeuwen, "Whose Health? Whose Marriage? A Reformed-Catholic Dialogue," in *Marriage, Health and the Professions: The Implications of the Health Benefits of Marriage for the Practice of Law, Medicine, Therapy and Business,* ed. John Wall, Don Browning, William J. Doherty and Steven Post (Grand Rapids, Mich.: Eerdmans, 2002), pp. 145-66.

ties.) In France the official workweek is now thirty-five hours; in the Nether-lands it is thirty-six hours, and workers have the legal right to condense this into four days if they wish. My husband's cousin Henk, an Amsterdam banker, takes advantage of this option even though his children are now grown. He uses the extra day (among other things) to cultivate a garden, to fulfill his calling as an elder in his church and to do day-trading with his stock portfolio. Although American companies have opposed shorter workweeks on financial grounds, they might find (as Kellogg's did and as some French companies now do) that if it were implemented, stress-related disorders, absenteeism and turnover might be reduced and productivity actually enhanced.

Second, we need to make it easier for fathers as well as mothers to take pa-rental leave after the birth of a child. At this point American women are legally entitled to only three months of unpaid maternity leave, which almost no hourly wage worker can afford the luxury of taking. This means that paid maternity leave of any sort is in effect restricted only to professional-class women whose jobs include it as a benefit. And paid paternity leave is virtually unheard of—as of 1997 only thirty-two American companies offered *any* leave specifically for fathers.[41] By contrast, when my Canadian niece got married in the summer of 2001, her pregnant matron of honor was preparing to take a full year's job-pro-tected leave from teaching at 55 percent of her current salary. Since the 1970s Sweden has mandated ten days of paid leave specifically for new fathers, in ad-dition to twelve months of leave (at 80 percent of current salary) that can be divided between parents. As of 1994 at least one of those months must be spe-cifically taken by the father (either in a block or spread out as desired), or else it will be lost to the family completely. It would be hard to imagine a stronger cultural statement about the importance of fathering.

American critics often assert that the public cost of such benefits almost guarantees that they will soon be dropped. But in fact they are so popular with both sexes that politicians in other nations compete to keep them funded, even as they may trim other aspects of the welfare safety net. Businesses do not have to foot the entire bill: some countries finance parental leaves by a combination of employer and employee contributions to the national pension fund, while others pay for them from payroll or other tax revenues or private company insurance schemes. The point is that generous, paid parental leaves are a basic right in every economically advanced nation except that most Christian of nations, the United States of America. Surely Americans can do better, for the sake of men, women and children alike.

---

[41]Crittenden, *Price of Motherhood,* p. 243.

Third, if parents (and others) are to benefit from a shorter workweek, then companies should be required to pay part-time workers the same hourly wages as full-time workers doing the same job and to provide proportional fringe benefits such as health insurance, sick leave, vacations and pension contributions. In the United States at the turn of the millennium, barely a quarter of part-time workers had either health insurance or private pensions as part of their job package. As Crittenden notes, "These inequities give employers a huge incentive to hire nonstandard workers—most of them mothers—on cheap, exploitative terms."[42] By contrast, the Canadian province of Saskatchewan recently rewrote its labor laws to require the provision of such benefits to part-time workers, and the Netherlands did the same several years earlier, with the result that a third of all jobs are now part time (in a country, recall, where the full-time workweek is thirty-six hours). In such an environment, adults of both sexes feel much more secure about committing time to the work of care, both in the home and elsewhere.

Finally, if it is the case that nonwaged caregiving contributes so much to the wealth of nations in the form of human and social capital, then it should be eligible for public pension credits. The current U.S. social security system penalizes anyone who takes time out to do unpaid caregiving; those years show up as zeros in terms of accumulated pension account contributions. Many other industrialized nations, by contrast, offer public pension credits covering years spent at home caring for either younger or older family members. Austria, Britain, France and Hungary all have such policies, varying in the amount of pension credited and the eligibility of persons by sex.

In addition, both public and private pension accounts should be legally "credit-shared" between spouses. That is, pension contributions, whatever their source, should go into one account over which husband and wife have joint title. Such a practice may make little functional difference in marriages that last a lifetime and in which financial sharing is taken for granted. But it constitutes an important safety net in cases of divorce where one spouse has less earning capacity due to having been out of the waged workforce doing family work. These spouses, usually women, risk being impoverished after divorce if access to some proportion of their partner's pension assets is not protected. Thus far both Canada and Germany have national legislation requiring spousal credit sharing of public pensions, and Germany extends this requirement to all private pensions funds as well.

---

[42]Ibid., p. 261.

Recovering
Biblical Manhood

The message of this final chapter is thus that both personal and structural
change are needed if we are to achieve a more just and creationally healthy
model for gender and family relations. The societal assumption over the last several decades has been that it is women who must make adjustments to enable
them to combine marriage, childrearing and waged work. But the message of
this book has been that both elementary justice and the health and happiness
of everyone will be well-served only when men, individually and corporately,
are prepared to risk attitudinal and behavioral change as well. In particular,
Christian men must be ready to substitute biblical notions of responsibility and
service for the dubious ideals of the male code of honor that keeps reinventing
itself, Hydra-like, in every generation.

"Real men in America are not supposed to accept limits," observed journalist
Andrew Schmookler in the early 1990s. "The American dream and the ideal of
progress in the U.S. economy express the idea that 'the sky is the limit.' Real
men are always headed onward and upward. So when some people began to
speak a few years back of 'limits to growth,' they were derided as defeatists by
the manly defenders of American dynamism."[43] This is classic male honor code
rhetoric, repackaged for an industrial era and buttressed by the older language
of male aggression. "Our image of manhood [has been] inseparable from the
role of the warrior," Schmookler continues.

> It is one thing for a man to *guard* what is his own—that is the work of a warrior.
> It is another for a man to take care of what has been entrusted to him—that sounds
> a lot like women's work. Thus the hero in the old Western movie *Shane* is not the
> farmer who grows crops and children but the gunman who protects him. . . . [We]
> have made warriors [our] heroes and made the virtues of the man of power [our]
> ideal of manhood.[44]

He reminds us that there is another ancient image of what a real man might
be, "the image of the good steward, the man to whom the care of things can be
entrusted."[45] It is time for us to recover that biblical image and to regard the
good steward as being—in the long run—even more manly than the vigilant
warrior. The good steward is one who promotes the biblical state of *shalom*,
whose literal meaning is that everything is in its rightful place. This means that

---

[43]Andrew Schmookler, "Manliness and Mother Earth," *Christian Science Monitor*, October 3,
1991, p. 8.
[44]Ibid., p. 8.
[45]Ibid., p. 8.

each sphere of life is given its proper due: science, art, worship, government, commerce and family life are kept in proper balance, each to fulfill its rightful calling, with none being allowed—in either personal or corporate existence—to swallow up or marginalize the others. Nor are these creational spheres of life to be divided by sex, for the cultural mandate is a human, not a gendered, mandate. This does not mean that men and women must become undifferentiated clones of one another. A genuine social partnership between men and women will allow for specialization by gender and by life-cycle stage for those who mutually wish it and agree to it. But such specialization should not result in either sex's becoming materially or psychologically vulnerable, socially isolated or permanently closed off from other avenues for growth and service.[46] Such distortions do not reflect what it means to be created in the image of God.

The final goal, to which God calls men and women alike, is the cultivation of the fruit of the Spirit—love, joy, peace, patience, kindness, generosity, faithfulness, gentleness and self-control—even as they put on the whole armor of God: the belt of truth, the breastplate of righteousness, the gospel of peace, the shield of faith "and the sword of the Spirit, which is the word of God" (see Eph 6:10-17). It is in living out such a calling that men will both lose and find themselves. I believe that this is an adventure like no other, and one well worthy of dedicated pursuit.

---

[46]For more on the social partnership model, see Neil Gilbert, "Working Families: Hearth to Market," in *All Our Families: New Policies for a New Century,* ed. Mary Ann Mason, Arlene Skolnick and Stephen D. Sugarman (New York: Oxford University Press, 1998), pp. 193-216.

Names Index